DEREK JARMAN AND LYRIC FILM

Derek

Jarman

and

Lyric

Film

THE MIRROR AND THE SEA

*Steven
Dillon*

University of Texas Press
AUSTIN

Quotations from *Up in the Air: Collected Film Scripts* by Derek Jarman (Vintage) are reprinted by permission of the Random House Group Ltd. and the estate of Derek Jarman. Quotations from *A Finger in the Fishes Mouth* are reprinted by permission of the estate of Derek Jarman. Quotations from Derek Jarman's *Dancing Ledge*, *Kicking the Pricks*, *Modern Nature*, *At Your Own Risk*, *Chroma*, and *Blue* are reprinted by permission of The Overlook Press, Random House Group Ltd., and the estate of Derek Jarman.

Figures 4.1, 4.2, 4.3, 5.1, and 5.2 are reproduced courtesy of the British Film Institute. Figures 6.1 and 6.2 are reproduced courtesy of Mike Laye. Figures 6.3, 6.4, and 6.5 are reproduced courtesy of Basilisk Communications. All photo stills were obtained from the British Film Institute. Every effort has been made to contact copyright holders of photo stills reproduced in this book.

First edition, 2004

Requests for permission to reproduce material from this work should be sent to Permissions, University of Texas Press, Box 7819, Austin, TX 78713-7819.

∞ The paper used in this book meets the minimum requirements of ANSI/NISO Z39.48-1992 (R1997) (Permanence of Paper).

LIBRARY OF CONGRESS CATALOGING-IN-PUBLICATION DATA

Dillon, Steven, 1960–
    Derek Jarman and lyric film : the mirror and the sea / Steven Dillon.
— 1st ed.
        p.   cm.
Includes bibliographical references and index.
ISBN 0-292-70223-X (alk. paper) — ISBN 0-292-70224-8 (pbk. : alk. paper)
    1. Jarman, Derek, 1942—Criticism and interpretation. I. Title.
PN1998.3.J3D55   2004
791.4302'33'092—dc22   2003018566

To Kathy and John

Contents

Acknowledgments

Thanks to the outside readers for the press, Chris Lippard and James Morrison. At the University of Texas Press, many thanks to Jim Burr and his colleagues Lynne Chapman and Kip Keller. Bates colleagues Charles Nero, Jane Costlow, and Rob Farnsworth read portions of the manuscript and provided excellent suggestions. Pierre Hecker shared a great deal of expertise about both film and Renaissance theater. I am grateful to Sanford Freedman for suggesting that we co-teach a film course some ten years ago. Students in my Lyric Film seminar, especially Nick Christie, Rob Andrews, Julie Hammond, and Sze Wei Ang, provided many good ideas. Katharine Oakes of the BFI stills department was very helpful with the pictures. Information of various kinds was provided by Tony Peake, Howard Malin, James Mackay, and Michael O'Pray. Marshall Brown has encouraged my scholarship for many years, as have my parents.

DEREK JARMAN AND LYRIC FILM

Derek Jarman and the History of Lyric Film

Deep red sun climbing from a still sea, the wet shingle ablaze with reflections. Walked into the garden floating on a sea of pearls. The garden casts mysterious shadows. Not a breath of wind.[1]

In Derek Jarman's *The Garden* (1990) two nearby but apparently unrelated images help indicate the genre of this film. Jarman has a name for these images, which were improvised on the first day of shooting: "emblemata."[2] These are pictures that invite you to read, to interpret. First image: a man in kingly costume looks directly into the camera; he returns in a few moments to the center of the screen and bites deliberately into an apple. We note that the king holds a long feather instead of a mace. A minute later in the montage, a second image: three boys pillow-fighting on a bed, the feathers flying up in the air. By rhyming twice on feathers, these images lead us toward the "tar and feathering" scene, in which the gay couple at the center of the film is tormented and mocked in a restaurant. These feathers, of the king and of the pillows, aim us toward that scene by preparing us with images rather than verbal logic. So much is perfectly clear. But these sets of images, although brief, contain more than little bridges of cinematic continuity, are more than a mere motif or riff on feathers. These images make pointed allusions to a particular history of film, a history that we need to notice and take seriously. Until now, however, this history has not been written in any very deliberate manner. It will be a main goal of this book to elucidate that history—the history of what I call lyric film.

To what, then, do the images allude? The king, frontally posed and later biting into a fruit, is strongly reminiscent of the poet-troubadour in Sergei Paradjanov's *The Color of Pomegranates*. The pillow-fighting recalls "lyric" moments in great French impressionist cinema, namely scenes in Abel Gance's *Napoleon* (1927) and Jean Vigo's *Zero de conduite* (1933). In other words, Jarman self-consciously aligns himself with a tradition of lyric film. The video box of *The Garden*, produced by Fox Lorber, is full of critical quotations that recognize the film's generic provenance: "A lavish film-poem about the mortification of the flesh!" (*Village Voice*). These video box quotations—"Derek Jarman's lyrical and visionary movie" (*Chicago Reader*)—serve not only to celebrate and to entice, but also to warn the prospective video audience that something rather nonnarrative awaits them. Although Jarman's lyricism in film after film is, undoubtedly, quite evident, we also realize that the word "lyrical" is a loosely and commonly used term of critical approbation. We might well say "poetic" when we mean no more than "beautiful"; such a comment may have nothing to do with poetry or genre or structure. But Jarman's films need to be understood in a much more specific and concrete way, insofar as they are related to poetry and poetic films.

Jarman's antipathy toward narrative and narrative cinema is repeatedly expressed with great clarity in his published journals and scripts. As he writes in the *War Requiem* text, "I've had to move carefully, given my reputation as an enemy of narrative film, since the recording company obviously wants a conventional narrative."[3] On the last page of his script for *Caravaggio*, he maintains that the structure of that film is, for him, unique: "This film is the first in which I have developed acting parts and bowed to narrative."[4] Jarman's films are intentionally set down against narrative,

2

therefore, but in that intention he is by no means alone. Both European and non-Western cinema are usually less narrative than Hollywood film—the Hollywood of "classical Hollywood narrative."[5] And avant-garde cinema is, broadly speaking, less narrative still.[6]

What is individual about Jarman's conception of film, and central to the tradition to which he belongs, is the degree to which he thinks of this contrast to narrative as *poetry*. The word "poetry," out of any context, is a remarkably vague and loaded term, but it is used by workers in the field of poetic cinema, I would argue, with alert knowingness and a sharp sense of history. Directors such as Jarman, Andrei Tarkovsky, and Pier Paolo Pasolini, as we shall see, do not just talk about poetry in their polemical tracts and journal entries—and they talk about poetry constantly—they include recognizable poems and poet-figures in their films. These directors repeatedly encourage us to read and interpret their films not as we would read a novel, but as we would read a poem.

Ludwig Wittgenstein—and Jarman's Wittgenstein as well—speaks of "language games": we need to identify what language game we are playing in order to communicate. "Do not forget that a poem," writes Wittgenstein, "although it is composed in the language of information, is not used in the language game of giving information."[7] If cinema is a kind of language, then we need to identify the kind of language that Jarman uses; we need to identify the kind of language game that we find ourselves in when we find ourselves next to words like "poetry." By itself, "poetry" has little meaning. Even as a contrast to "narrative," it is still rather empty, too abstract. But when used by a community of artists, the word begins to take hold, and we can come to grasp it in its relation to other expressive practices and discourses.

Not that all artists, of course, will understand the same thing by "poetry"! Artists do not all speak the same language, any more so than film critics or talking heads on television. In 1953, for instance, there was a famous roundtable discussion on "Poetry and the Film" in which Maya Deren described the contrast between poetic film and conventional film as the contrast between vertical and horizontal, but fellow symposium participants Arthur Miller and Dylan Thomas refused to understand her distinction. Deren felt severely put upon: "I mainly wish to say that I'm a little flabbergasted at the fact that people who have handled words with such dexterity as Mr. Thomas and Mr. Miller and Mr. [Parker] Tyler, should have difficulty with such a simple idea as the 'vertical' and the 'horizontal.'"[8] Deren is one of many film artists to have spoken of poetry and poetic structure in cinema less rigorously, perhaps, than literary theorists, yet more self-consciously and deliberately than other artists. Whereas Miller and Thomas claimed not to know quite what she was talking about, directors like Tarkovsky and Jarman surely would have; they would have been able to play her language game.

Like Tarkovsky, indeed, Jarman not only writes extensively and self-consciously about his cinema, he also writes often of poetry. In the context of his films, what does Jarman mean by poetry? In addition to his films, Jarman was well known for his painting, and sometimes regarded himself, indeed, primarily as a painter. Yet he also published a book of poems early in his career, which we shall study in the next chapter; and all of his journals and books contain numerous poems by himself and others. So poetry in part means poetry in lines, poetry recognizable as such. As we shall see, Jarman's interest in Benjamin Britten's *War Requiem* was due more to the poems by Wilfred Owen than to the music by Britten. Poetry for Jarman is certainly related to a literary sense of the term, the sense in which William Blake (quoted in *Imagining October*) and John Keats (whose collected works we see next to Owen's body in *War Requiem*) are poets.

Poetry for Jarman also does imply a contrast to narrative, similar to Deren's neoformalist contrast of "vertical" poetry to "horizontal" narrative.[9] Jarman's poetic impulses in this regard are manifest and intentional, as noted above, and are well attended to by critical audiences of Jarman's films; see, for example, Tracy Biga's essay "The Principle of Non-Narration in the Films of Derek Jarman."[10] When Jarman says that "*The Last of England* works with image and sound, a language which is nearer to poetry than to prose,"[11] he means that the film's images speak figuratively rather than declaratively and that the film proceeds by association rather than through cause and effect. Jarman uses "poetry" as an oppositional term to contrast the structure and shape of his films with that of linear, more regularly narrative kinds of cinema.

Yet this contrast of poetry to narrative may well seem tenuous, not just to disruption-prone poets like Dylan Thomas, but to more philosophically minded literary theorists as well. In one of the most searching critiques of Jarman's work, Leo Bersani and Ulysse Dutoit ask "Can film be non-narrative?" and question Jarman's own understanding of the category of narrative.[12] Their sophisticated analysis of Jarman in a recent volume on Jarman's *Caravaggio* will receive a more detailed discussion in later chapters. But their question—a theoretical question—can be answered now, in part, by providing a history of lyric film.

Thus we might first identify their question as an academic question, academic insofar as it does not wish to play the language game in which

Jarman places himself. In the 1960s, Christian Metz asked exactly the same question when he wondered whether Pasolini, in his essay "The Cinema of Poetry," understood what narrative was. In his own essay, Metz asserts that a nonnarrative or poetic cinema is a theoretical impossibility. Pasolini, it may be said, explicitly invited such theorists as Metz and Umberto Eco to argue with him in theoretical terms by setting out his essays in the language of academic structuralism. Jarman's loose, artistic language of poetry refers not to semiotics, but, I would argue, to the history of lyric cinema. Can we not attempt to join him in that field? "Nonnarrative" in Jarman's use points not to the works of Alain Resnais or Jean-Luc Godard, where Bersani and Dutoit turn in their discussion of Jarman, but rather to those of Jean Cocteau, Jean Genet, Pasolini, and Tarkovsky. To understand poetry in Jarman's films requires familiarizing oneself with the films and problems in this tradition.

And what, or where, is this tradition? Although the history of cinema is brief compared to that of poetry or architecture, its genres and traditions are of considerable complexity and are still being worked out. Tradition itself as a category or term in the history of art is not unproblematic. Yet in a pragmatic sense we can still speak of tradition and traditions; we can speak this way insofar as the term is critically useful. Jarman, as even he conceived of himself at times, might well be seen as a traditional artist, and he was always self-conscious of his place in history and of his use of history.[13] Lyric film is not a genre in the way that western or film noir is, it is true; but it does name a set of affiliations and issues that reach outward toward Jarman.

A few, infrequent films are overtly interested in poets: *The Barretts of Wimpole Street* (Sidney Franklin, 1934), based on a play about the courtship of Elizabeth Barrett and Robert Browning; *Total Eclipse* (Agnieszka Holland, 1996), with Leonardo DiCaprio as Rimbaud; *Il Postino* (Michael Radford, 1995), featuring Pablo Neruda in exile in Italy; and, of course, *Dead Poets Society* (Peter Weir, 1989), in which Robin Williams promotes poetry as a way of life. These films have poets in them, but the poets are not represented as being much different from other kinds of artists or exceptional persons; a film like *Dead Poets Society* sets the illusion of liberating creativity among the hoariest confines of Hollywood convention and plot.

Much closer to the sensibility in which we are interested are works inspired by poetry, like Wim Wenders's *Wings of Desire* (1987), which he says is founded on Rainer Maria Rilke's *Duino Elegies*, and Atom Egoyan's *The Sweet Hereafter* (1997), which cuts Russell Banks's novel out of chronological order and powerfully adds Robert Browning's "The Pied Piper of

Hamelin." Yet neither Wenders nor Egoyan works with poetry repeatedly; these are relatively singular manifestations of poetry in film.

And so it is a different story I will tell here, one more central to the case of Jarman's cinema. The directors that are most relevant here work repeatedly, even obsessively, with poems, poets, and lyric structure. In "The Cinema of Poetry" (1965), Pasolini argues that the films of Michelangelo Antonioni and Godard are more poetic than silent film. Yet each new generation organizes history in different ways, according to different landmarks. To my mind, Jarman's cinematic practice shows that lyric cinema has been around since the very beginning. (This was also part of Christian Metz's argument with Pasolini.) In this chapter I will examine some of the key practitioners of lyric film and identify some of the recurrent elements of lyric film. Lyric film is a splendidly arguable and movable genre, and the story I tell here would no doubt look rather different if I were not aiming toward Derek Jarman. In this telling, the tradition of lyric cinema goes back at least to D. W. Griffith, and so it is there, now, that we need to turn.

I. D. W. GRIFFITH AND THE CREATION OF ANOTHER WORLD

This is, I realize, mainly subjective; but it suggests to me the clearest and deepest aspect of Griffith's genius: he was a great primitive poet, a man capable, as only great and primitive artists can be, of intuitively perceiving and perfecting the tremendous magical images that underlie the memory and imagination of entire peoples.

JAMES AGEE[14]

Pasolini and Jarman, I suggest, take part in a cinematic tradition that emerges at the very origin of film history, a tradition that meditates deliberately on "poetry" in cinema. Surprisingly, this impulse exists even in the works of the "inventor" of narrative cinema, D. W. Griffith. Although Pasolini and Jarman might seem at first glance to work some light-years from this forefather, this late Victorian, as it were, the attraction to social outcasts and the creation of other worlds form a nexus where poetry and film join in the works of all three directors. As I hope to show, there are relatively clear links between a film like Griffith's *Broken Blossoms* and later works such as Pasolini's *Teorema* and Jarman's *The Garden*. Each director invokes poetry in the name of social responsibility and social transformation. I would claim, furthermore, that Griffith's deployment of poetry is much more self-conscious than has usually been assumed and that

Griffith deserves an originating role in the tradition of film poetry that this book seeks to describe.

Although Tom Gunning has shown that a cinema of attractions (the films of Georges Méliès, spectacle, pantomime, magic) offsets a cinema of narration at the origin of film history, narrative quickly becomes the major form of cinematic expression in America.[15] Griffith, at the influential center of narrative form, adapted story after story and novel after novel for his pictures; Gunning lists 1909 Biograph versions of George Eliot's *Silas Marner*, James Fenimore Cooper's *The Last of the Mohicans*, and Charles Dickens's *The Cricket on the Hearth*.[16] Griffith's films look much more like narrative stories than lyrical poems, certainly, but they do not exclude poetry out of hand. On the contrary, Griffith also filmed narrative poems such as *Pippa Passes* (1909, based on a long poem by Robert Browning), *The Golden Supper* (1910, based on an Alfred, Lord Tennyson poem), *Enoch Arden* (1911, Tennyson again) and *The Sands of Dee* (1912, based on a poem by Charles Kingsley). A title card for *The Avenging Conscience* (1914) says that the film is "suggested by Edgar Allan Poe's story of 'the Telltale Heart' [*sic*] and by certain of his poems of the affections."[17] At the beginning of *Judith of Bethulia* (1913), a card tells us that the film is based on the "poetical tragedy" by Thomas Bailey Aldrich. Poetry is not just one interest among many or a one-time concern; it is arguably at the heart of his cinema throughout the entirety of his career.

Poetry was always for Griffith a high art, a status that more and more he sought for his films.[18] It is no coincidence that the first film review ever published in the *New York Times* was for Griffith's version of *Pippa Passes*.[19] Despite, therefore, Griffith's propensity for narrative drive and novelistic adaptation, poetry also shares in his artistic and cultural distinction. The poetry quotation, or the prestige-bearing epigraph, was a key part of Griffith's ambitions for *film d'art*. The poetic quotation is a carryover from Victorian fiction, whereby a novel like George Eliot's *Middlemarch* asserts its own high status—despite its "provincial" subject matter and prose form—by providing, at the beginning of chapters, epigraphs from such cultural luminaries as Shakespeare, Cervantes, and Milton. The use of inserted poetry quotations to signal cultural status—a practice that is by no means simple or transparent—continues in Pasolini's first film, *Accattone*, where he provides a preliminary citation from Dante as epigraphic commentary on the neorealistic content of this film.[20]

Yet poetry is more than just another high art, a noble fiction with a compelling plot; it also appears in relatively complicated ways with respect to narrative. The contrast between poetry and narrative may be open to dispute by theorists, but major artists will continually attempt to work out, cinematically, elements of this vexed generic contrast. In works like *Intolerance* (1916) and *Broken Blossoms* (1920), which we shall examine in some detail now, Griffith seems to exhibit the contrast between poetry and narrative that will later be thought through by Deren and Jarman and disputed by Metz. Griffith is not as deliberate as Deren or Pasolini, but I do see his practice both as more self-conscious than it is usually credited with being and as bearing important affinities with the aesthetic and political practice of both Pasolini and Jarman.

Let us begin by noticing how Griffith deploys poetry in his masterpiece, *Intolerance*. *Intolerance* is certainly intended as both high art and spectacular film; it competes with European spectacles such as *Cabiria* (1914) and concludes by rising not only into breathtaking montage, but also, at last, into metaphysical allegory. Toward the end, to help underscore the plight of prisoners, Griffith cites lines from Oscar Wilde's "The Ballad of Reading Gaol":

> And wondered if each one of us
> Would end the self-same way,
> For none can tell to what red Hell
> His sightless soul may stray.

The ambitious, four-part structure of *Intolerance* (Babylon, the story of Christ, sixteenth-century Huguenots, and a modern-day setting) shows Griffith's clear pretensions to visual and literary prestige, and the Wilde quote can only further substantiate the artistic dimensions of the film.

As the poet and early film critic Vachel Lindsay helps us to see, the cultural prestige to which Griffith most obviously aspired was that of Walt Whitman.[21] Lillian Gish's observation that Griffith was never without his *Leaves of Grass* has often been noted. Miriam Hansen has given the most recent and convincing explanation of Whitman's relationship to the structure and ambitions of *Intolerance*.[22] For our purposes, let us note that the four narratives of the film are linked by the image of a mother rocking a cradle, over which Whitman's words "out of the cradle endlessly rocking" sometimes appear. The Wilde quotation cited above is inspirational and somewhat schoolbookish, but the Whitman quotation is central to the overall structure of the film. The Whitman phrase stands for repetition and rhythm, just as the film keeps returning to the mother and her cradle. Poetry thus stands in between the narratives, in an abstract, timeless space of sheer repetition. The Whitman phrase is thus clearly more than a nice quote or an amiable snatch of literature. It is a phrase that comments self-consciously on focus and pace; the lines and accompanying image form the point from which the centrifugal forces of the four narratives spiral out. The image pauses narrative in a generalized, motionless space with as much deliberation, contrast, and clarity as a diagram by Roman Jakobson.

This pausing and rhythm is even more characteristic of *Broken Blossoms* and speaks further to Griffith's intentional use of self-descriptive poetic language. In *Griffith: First Artist of the Movies*, Martin Williams calls *Broken Blossoms* a "film poem," and this characterization again has substance, is more than mere appreciation.[23] Like the scenes in *Intolerance* with Whitman's lines imposed over the intimate, interior spaces of mother and cradle, this film is noticeably quiet, unrushed, and closed-in. From the brutal world of the violent boxer, Battling Burrows (Donald Crisp), Lucy (Lillian Gish) escapes to the loving and glowing world of the Yellow Man (Richard Barthelmess). The ethereal soft focus of these scenes, in fact, proved a striking technical innovation at the time and strongly influenced soft-style photography in later films.[24] "Neither before nor later," writes Richard Schickel, "did Griffith do such a fully realized mood piece."[25] Schickel calls *Broken Blossoms* a "transitional film, not for him, but for movies, as a whole . . . the first memorable European film made by an American."[26] Martin Williams and Richard Schickel, two of Griffith's finest critics, well recognize the intimate, lingering poetic difference between *Broken Blossoms* and Griffith's more rambunctiously narrative or spectacular films, but they do not press this identification far enough.

Broken Blossoms is an early "film poem," and Griffith seems to know that it is. Yet Schickel, although finding some element of future artistic talent in a conventional early poem like Griffith's "The Wild Duck" (published in 1907, and reproduced in full by Schickel), cannot abide the exuberantly poetic intertitles of *Broken Blossoms*.

> And then there is the matter of the titles. Even the most passionate of *Broken Blossoms* defenders are uncomfortable with them. "Oh, lily flowers and plum blossoms! Oh, silver streams and dim-starred skies!" cries the heart of the Yellow Man as he bathes the face of his poor tortured love. And that says nothing about "all the tears of the ages" rushing over his heart when she dies.[27]

Compared to the grace and beauty of the pictures, the language of the intertitles does seem remarkably cloying, even ignorant of its own literary effect. But I think that we might cultivate a more forgiving attitude toward these titles by considering that in these poetic outbursts Griffith is signaling the generic form of his film in a way consonant with later critical identifications (i.e., a "film poem").

Note how deliberately and carefully Griffith adapts and highlights his source. In the Thomas Burke story from *Limehouse Nights* that provides the origin for *Broken Blossoms*, the Yellow Man is, although unconsciously, a poet.[28] The poetic outbursts in the film come almost directly from the story. In the film, it is implied that these rapturous poetic lines are from the Yellow Man's point of view, an implication aided by the little Oriental paintings on the backgrounds of the intertitle cards. These poems therefore are not really omniscient Griffith raptures, but rather outpourings from the mysterious and enthusiastic spirit of the Yellow Man. We are told that the Yellow Man's actions are conducted "with perhaps a whiff of the lilied pipe still in his brain." Such an editorial comment deidealizes the source of the poetry and allows, in fact, a skeptical response. Griffith uses the Yellow Man's enthusiasms to characterize the less-than-relentless narrative of his film. The intertitles name the language *as* poetry by self-consciously speaking of the "lyrical moon" and by calling Lucy "a poem" (both phrases, incidentally, from Burke). Griffith uses the intertitles, along with the soft focus and the relatively actionless narrative, to identify *Broken Blossoms* as a film poem. The flower is a conventional poetic image, and *Broken Blossoms* repeatedly uses the image of the flower to develop its own atmosphere of lyric beauty and tragedy. Thus, though we may agree that the intertitle poetry is, without a doubt, conventional, it needs also to be noticed to what degree the use of poetry is both self-referential (the poems name the film) and arguably deidealized (as poetry is located in the opium-smoking Yellow Man).[29]

Griffith's poetry in *Broken Blossoms* may be defended, then, for its self-consciousness, but it is considerably more difficult to defend his use or appropriation of the Yellow Man as an origin for that poetry. Griffith's reliance on a stereotypically effeminate Yellow Man as a source of poetry and beauty is an important issue, one related to how Pasolini will later be drawn to India and Africa for sources of poetry offering alternatives to capitalist Italy. The glowing, intimate world of Lucy and the Yellow Man is intended by Griffith precisely as a beautiful alternative to the violent, patriarchal world of Battling Burrows. The appearance of poetry in that context becomes a political gesture, although its politics may well resonate differently with audiences now.

The story deploys stock melodramatic figures, and both the passive, innocent girl and the exotic Chinese man are stereotypes that remain difficult to watch, difficult to accept. In a severe but important reading of

Broken Blossoms, Gina Marchetti finds that the "beauty and poetry" of the film serve only "to mask its perverse roots" in the realm of "pedophilic fantasy."[30] In this view, the Yellow Man gazing down at Lucy in his bed is caught up not in a dream of poetry, but a dream of child molestation. I think that Marchetti overreads the lust emanating from the Yellow Man, but it would be impossible to contend that the scenes of Lucy in Cheng's bedroom are devoid of erotic drama.

Here, defending Griffith against his use of stereotypes is probably a vain effort. Instead, we might at least see Griffith's poetry and politics as part of a cinematic tradition that attempts to create another world of poetry and cinema to hold against a vision of capitalism and machinery. Pasolini was accused of stereotyping the third world, and he had seemingly much less excuse. Both Griffith and Pasolini, unlike as they are, seek alternatives to the brutalities of industrial capitalism, and in works like *Broken Blossoms* and *Appunti per un Orestiade Africana* (*Notes for an African Orestes*) problematically represent that alternative in the form of an exotic other.[31] Griffith more or less admitted the difficulties of such a representation by concluding *Broken Blossoms* with the deaths of all three main characters.[32]

In the end, it may come to seem that there is no acceptable alternative to industrialization, hateful as it is; thus, the prevalence of emptiness and desert in both Antonioni and Pasolini and the recurrent ruined landscapes in Jarman. It is only by fatal accident that the careers of Pasolini and Jarman ended where they did, but there is still something of utmost importance about what each director's last film implies about the possibilities of alternative worlds and representation. Pasolini concluded with *Salò*, one of the most gruesomely unwatchable films ever made, whereas Jarman concluded with *Blue*, an unwavering screen of blue. These two films are wholly different from each other in effect, but are similar exhibitions of a deep hopelessness with regard to the possibilities of visualizing another world.

II. SOVIET POETIC FILM FROM DOVZHENKO TO TARKOVSKY

In "The Modern Cinema and Narrativity" (1966), Christian Metz repeatedly questions critics and theorists who perceive a decline in narrative in modern films, represented by the work of such directors as Resnais, Godard, Antonioni.[33] With a deflating skepticism that we have come to associate with Michel Foucault, Metz asserts that these various descriptions of and claims for the "breakdown of narrativity" are at their foundation part of a "great libertarian myth" (p. 186); that is, the supposed "freedom" of antinarrative is gained only by categorically mistaking what narrative actually is. Metz accuses the mythologizers and critics not only of poor semiology—that is, not knowing what narrative, and thus antinarrative, is—but also of poor cinema history. Thus, Metz questions, for example, the association of a "new cinema" with "poetic cinema" in Pasolini's "The Cinema of Poetry" by querying Pasolini's semiotic terms and, more vigorously, his sense of cinema history. Is it not the case, argues Metz, that Pasolini and his contemporaries have it all the wrong way around? Hence, instead of imagining a history in which contemporary films break down or disrupt an inherited tradition of narrative, is it not the case that film today seems even closer to fiction and that previous eras were in fact much more open to poetry than we are now? Wondering about moments of lyricism in film, Metz recalls Abel Gance's *Napoleon* and *La Roue*, the slow motion in the dormitory scene in Vigo's *Zero de conduite*, the "accelerated filming in the scene with the black coach in *Nosferatu*, and the incredible aerial travelling shot in the beginning of Murnau's *Faustus*" (p. 206). In Metz's semiotic view, a film "cannot be a poem"; in Metz's historical view, "the period in which one believed that a film could be a poem is that of the old cinema rather than that of the new cinema" (p. 206).

As Metz suggests, the silent film in many ways seems much more redolent of poetry and lyricism than the films of Resnais and Godard. The examples that Metz collects come mostly from German expressionism and French impressionism. The periodical criticism associated with French impressionism, by writers such as Léon Moussinac and Jean Epstein, often treats cinema in poetic terms and categories; these writers, as Metz helps us to recall, did in fact believe that a film could be a poem.[34] Double exposures and dissolves, along with the use of curious phrases and calligraphy in the intertitles, give rise to many lyrical effects in early French films, some of which even feature poems and poets.[35] Similarly, as German expressionism sought to represent the complexities of internal psychology and expression through distortions of exterior physical reality, early German films, above all the work of the masterful Murnau, often look far more poetic than prosaic or realistic.[36] Tom Gunning and Miriam Hansen, two of the finest scholars of early cinema, have recently investigated ways that the cinematic language of silent film is inherently symbolic—"hieroglyphic" in Hansen's terminology (the term taken from the poet-critic Vachel Lindsay)—and therefore may merit a hermeneutic approach formerly reserved for poetry.[37]

Jarman was interested in hieroglyphics and Egyptian motifs, as well as secret codes and forms of the occult, from John Dee to Carl Jung. Jarman's films often operate more like silent films than sound films in that the dialogue is often, by contemporary standards, drastically reduced. But for the more limited purposes of this introductory chapter, I need to put early French and German film largely in brackets and focus on a foreshortened tradition of directors in Soviet film—Alexander Dovzhenko, Sergei Paradjanov, and Andrei Tarkovsky.

Although Jarman ultimately made a short film in direct reference to Sergei Eisenstein (*Imagining October*), I would place Jarman in closer affiliation with this set of Soviet filmmakers. These directors more explicitly, consistently, and rigorously employed the language of poetry. The personal yet overtly political impulses of these Soviet films share similarities with the urgency felt in Pasolini and Jarman, and both Jarman and Paradjanov find in Pasolini a source of inspiration and energy. Thus rather than dividing film history into old narrative and new poetry (as in Pasolini), or even into old poetry and new narrative (which would be one way of reading Metz), we might attribute less importance to early and late, silent and sound, and rather see constellations of film poets, from impressionism to modernism, from classical cinema to the avant-garde.

Let me note also that this trio is connected more figuratively to Jarman than are the other directors in the poetic tradition that I describe in this chapter. Jarman often commented on Pasolini, Cocteau, and Genet; a tradition or context that includes their work does not need to be argued into existence, only studied. But I am not aware that Jarman ever mentions either Dovzhenko or Paradjanov in his extensive prose, although he does refer to Tarkovsky. I think that the parallels which can be drawn between Paradjanov's work and Jarman's are remarkable and critically rewarding, but one can prove absolutely only that both Jarman and Paradjanov found a central font of creative inspiration in Pasolini—that is unquestionably where the branches of this tree join.

One of the key figures in cinematic poetry is the Ukrainian director Alexander Dovzhenko, and one of the most highly regarded of all cinematic poems is Dovzhenko's *Earth* (1930).[38] As the title of an English translation of his selected works—*The Poet as Filmmaker*—suggests, Dovzhenko often considered his own films in poetic terms.[39] In his autobiography, Dovzhenko writes:

> The few films that I did complete I made with love and sincerity. In these films lies the primary meaning of my life. They are meant to be poetic films, and contemporary life, with the common man at its center, is their chief subject.[40]

The poetic sensibility and structure that Dovzhenko intended has been felt from the very beginning. In *The Rise of the American Film* (1938), Lewis Jacobs called *Earth* "a luminous contribution to the realm of lyric cinema" and considers that "Dovzhenko, perhaps more than anyone else, can be called . . . the first poet of the movies."[41] In *Film Culture Reader*, an important collection of articles and documents treating American avant-garde film of the 1960s, Ken Kelman's essay on *Earth* moves toward comparing Dovzhenko's nonnarrative impulses with those of directors such as Stan Brakhage, Maya Deren, and Gregory Markopoulos—that is, the creators of what P. Adams Sitney calls "lyric cinema."[42] And Dovzhenko's poetic practice is a recurrent reference point for Tarkovsky, as evidenced in this celebratory paragraph:

> Think of Mandelstam, think of Pasternak, Chaplin, Dovzhenko, Mizoguchi, and you'll realize what tremendous emotional power is carried by these exalted figures who soar above the earth, in whom the artist appears not just as an explorer of life, but as one who creates great spiritual treasures and that special beauty which is subject only to poetry. Such an artist can discern the lines of the poetic design of being. He is capable of going beyond the limitations of coherent logic, and conveying the deep complexity and truth of the impalpable connections and hidden phenomenon of life.[43]

For our purposes, as we aim toward Jarman, Dovzhenko's crucial importance in the history of poetic film resides in his implicit investigation of the relationship of the lyrical to the collective. Ordinarily, lyric is regarded as characterized by the subjective and the psychological (classically exemplified by such figures as Sappho and Catullus), but ancient poetry elsewhere does not distinguish so readily between lyric individuality and lyric collectivity (as in Pindar and Horace). It is in the twentieth century that we see most clearly the deliberate adoption of radical stances of subjectivity in poetry of all varieties. Yet at the same time, poetry breaks from convention and even communication in the name of politics. Avant-garde movements often speak in deliberately arcane ways, again in the name of political community. Just so, Pasolini and Jarman repeatedly negotiate the expressive territory between "I" and community, between the individual, suffering speaker and political activism. The subjectivity of poetry in a charged political realm will be an especially crucial problematic in both Pasolini and Jarman.

In Dovzhenko's *Earth*, the relationship between subjective lyricism and collective expression is theorized by the relationship between the death of

Basil (Vasyl), the communist, and the triumphal conclusion of the film. In a scenario for *Earth* (written retrospectively in 1952), Dovzhenko writes that the nightfall following the harvest contains poetry in itself—a poetry that changes the world:

> The apple tree, the willows, the pots on the fences, the old elm tree—every object had become unfamiliar, taken on quite a different nocturnal shape and begun to live a life of its own. It was as if a poet had taken ordinary, everyday words, arranged them into celebratory lines, and transformed them into poetry full of new and exciting meanings.[44]

In such a night, couples are seen one after another, sleeping quietly or simply together. And then, from out of this quiet, we see Basil walking down a darkened lane. He begins to dance with joy, kicking up bright, moonlit dust. Finally, at the end of this extended, deliberate sequence, lovely by any accounting, Basil is shot, and drops to the ground. We see at once the tragic contrast between Basil's premature, sudden death and the peaceful, natural death of Grandfather Semyon amidst the apples, with which the film began.[45]

Yet, equally, we are meant to see the relationship between Basil's nocturnal, dreamy, solitary dance and the song sung by the marching community at the end of the film. Basil's private moonlit dance comes to a sudden, murdered halt, and out of his death comes the image of bright, open song and poised, deliberate march. The difference between the moonlit dance and the sunlit march is the difference between private and public, lyric and ode. In a solitary, nocturnal dream, the world is transformed and magical, as Dovzhenko tells us, and the world is charged with communist hope at the end of the film as well. But Dovzhenko's montage at the conclusion of *Earth* analytically explains what is left out of moonlit, lyric poetry in order to obtain enlightened song.

Earth's final montage cuts from the singing marchers to three other images: Father Gersaim in an "empty room" (as the scenario says); the ceaselessly running Khoma (killer of Basil); and the anguished, naked form of Basil's wife, Natalka, beating the walls in protest and mourning. This montage analytically separates spheres of transcendence and heightened emotion from the labor songs of the commune. Basil's beautiful, lyrical dance gives way to procession and march, which has nothing to do, the montage implies, with the empty sky of religion ("the empty heavens to which the spiritual strength of people had been directed for centuries in the shape of prayers, supplications and sighs"),[46] the feverish madness of acting against community, or the fervor of subjective eroticism and passion. The montage works to describe what is at stake in the funeral procession and to refine our sense of what sort of changed world this is.

Dovzhenko's *Earth* gives the impression of lyricism through both content and style: through a virtually plotless narrative joined by dream more than cause and effect; through the ethereal pictures of sky, fruit, and rain; and through its rhythmic patience and deliberation. Indeed, the film is notable for its formality as much as for its atmosphere, light, and manner of proceeding. The formality of *Earth* is all the more remarkable, perhaps, given its rustic subject matter, and is a main contributor to the film's poetic effects. Poetry has often been defined as speech more formal than ordinary speech, and even though Dovzhenko, Pasolini, and Jarman eschew convention and, often, narrative, they do not fail to employ all manner of artifice and formality. In Dovzhenko the key stylistic formalism might be called the "turning head," where a posed face turns to one direction or another. In a splendid discussion of *Earth*, Barthélemy Amengual speaks of Dovzhenko's "living statues" and compares their stillness to the photographs in Chris Marker's *La Jetée*.[47] This rhythmic, formal stillness and turning is central to Dovzhenko's lyrical style; it is related to the formal tableaux in Paradjanov and to Pasolini's famous frontal style of photography. The artifice, poise, and deliberation of the *mise-en-scène* and editing throughout *Earth* culminate with the logic of poetry in the collective song of the funeral march, which is both enthusiastic and ordered, both heartfelt and formalized.

This description brings us directly, then, to another remarkable creator of cinematic poetry, the Armenian director Sergei Paradjanov. Dovzhenko himself signed Paradjanov's diploma from the Moscow Film Institute in 1952, and in answer to the question "Why do you make movies?" Paradjanov replied, "To honor the grave of Tarkovsky." Although he outlived Tarkovsky, Paradjanov was born eight years earlier, in 1924, and so I will treat him second in this triad of Soviet film-poets; in reality, their careers overlap at many points. Because his works are in Armenian, and so are less accessible than those in Russian, there is scarcely any scholarship on Paradjanov in any language. For the narrow purposes of this introduction, I will focus on *The Color of Pomegranates* (1968), a version of the life of the Armenian poet Sayat Nova, and on Paradjanov's cinematic relationship with Pasolini. As noted earlier, I do not see that Jarman cites Paradjanov in his journals, but as I also observed at the beginning of this chapter, I believe that Jarman "quotes" *The Color of Pomegranates* in *The Garden* and that Jarman's attitude toward artifice and form is illuminated by comparison with the work of Paradjanov.

Derek Jarman and Lyric Film

Patrick Cazals's Cahiers du cinéma book on Paradjanov contains many interviews with and quotations from the director; from these we can attempt to elucidate the sources of inspiration that Paradjanov drew from Pasolini.[48] Cazals himself names a "golden triangle" of directors for Paradjanov ("triangle d'or paradjanovien"): "Pasolini, Tarkovsky, Fellini." (p. 92). Pasolini is a repeated point of cinematic reference for Paradjanov, who summarizes their relationship most generously in this homage (all translations from Cazals's book are my own):

> Each time I view Pasolini, I am struck by the same standards. His principles, his spiritual attitude with regards to the Bible, he elevates to the rank of a mission. . . . he makes me discover, astonished, aspects of the world, from antiquity, Rome, Arabia, or simply contemporary life. (p. 137)

Pasolini's exotic settings in works like *Medea* or *The Arabian Nights* are undoubtedly related to the poetic projects in Paradjanov's *The Color of Pomegranates* or *Ashik Kerib*. Cazals also links Paradjanov's use of asynchronized sound to Pasolini; in both cases, the noticeable unrelatedness of sound to image heightens artifice and defeats realism (p. 83).[49] Most important of all, perhaps, is the link to painterly composition. Paradjanov is a brilliant practitioner of the art of collage, as the illustrations in Cazals's book (including a fragment from the collage "homage à Pasolini" [p. 42]) show. Painting is used not only as an abstract or postmodern reference (as in Antonioni's *Red Desert* or Godard's *Passion*), but also as a formal means of lyricizing film.[50] Cazals compares Pasolini's frontal cinematography with Paradjanov's and further suggests that an affinity for tableaux joins the two men (p. 45). Like the halt of narrative in the abstract space of Griffith's rocking cradle, painterly cinema pauses and disrupts narrative. It is no coincidence that poetic filmmakers often focus their attention on painting—Tarkovsky in *Andrei Rublev* and Derek Jarman in *Caravaggio*.

The Color of Pomegranates proceeds as a series of tableaux framed by an unmoving camera. The style of the film crosses back and forth between silent cinema and sound: the camera does not move, there is scarcely any dialogue as such, and there are frequent intertitles. Yet at the same time, the screen is saturated with glorious color, and the sound track is equally full of Oriental instrumentation or monastic chanting. Each picture is carefully framed and still, yet at the same time full of life and movement. Water flows, the pages of books flap in the wind, a high-stepping horse struts by. The formalist aspects of Dovzhenko's *Earth*, where statuesque faces slowly turn, are taken over here and multiplied. Each frame plays out a contrast between formal opposites: linear and arabesque, solid and fluid, horizontal and vertical, covering and revealing, round and flat, empty and full. The images illustrate the words of poetry that are scripted—and scripted beautifully—onto title cards, but clearly the poetry (and the poet, for that matter) is less the subject of the film than an opportunity to visualize objects and people in a poetic manner. Like Dovzhenko's *Earth*, the film works mythically rather than realistically. Artifice and exoticism are clearly meant to help us transcend the everyday world and see deeper into the flowing essences of life.

The poet's vision is pure and perfectly framed, but passive—offering itself rather than forcing itself. The film repeatedly shows us images of victims, chickens and sheep above all. At one point, the poet digs a grave in a church filled with sheep, and at the end, headless chickens flutter around the prostrate body of the poet. Poetry is not mythologized as salvific or monumentalizing; instead, there is such elegy and suffering that Patrick Cazals writes, "The procession of tableaux appears as an abridgement of a sublime life grasped at the threshold of death, the slow hemorrhage of a suicidal poet" (p. 110). Paradjanov is less activist in his politics than Pasolini or Jarman (although he was perceived as sufficiently nationalist to warrant repeated imprisonment), yet this "suicidal poet" is their kin. As we shall see, twentieth-century cinematic poetry most often turns against itself. Tellingly, the final image of the angel of resurrection is in profile. She is beautiful, and yet she also looks away from us, to one side. We shall return to images that recall the collages and formal gestures of Paradjanov throughout this book.

Andrei Tarkovsky is the most articulate spokesman for the theory of cinematic poetry in the Soviet tradition. Jarman's desire to elaborate discursively and extensively about the meanings and intentions of his films is most clearly reminiscent of texts by Cocteau and Pasolini, but not so far away from the somewhat less voluble Tarkovsky. Tarkovsky's spiritual inclinations may seem to contrast harshly with Jarman's political and sexual concerns, but we will find ourselves at key moments in Jarman's career turning to Tarkovsky for reference. As we shall see, the mirror is a central image for both Jarman and Tarkovsky, serving repeatedly in each case as an almost archetypal figure for the focusing and refracting power of the camera. That Jarman knew Tarkovsky's biography, prose, and films I extrapolate from a complaining remark in *Kicking the Pricks*: "If Tarkovsky had had the misfortune to be born in Great Britain, I doubt if he would have been able to make a single film; in the Soviet Union he worked with difficulty, but he worked."[51] Jarman would have, I think, been drawn to the language of poetry in which Tarkovsky casts his philosophy of film as well as to the practical difficulties that the Russian director faced when making his films.

Tarkovsky's ideas about cinema are seriously and intellectually thought out, and the most important statements are collected in *Sculpting in Time*. His aesthetics, which often recur to the poetic, have been well summarized elsewhere, and so, for the most part, I will discuss concrete examples from his practice.[52] A characteristic piece of Tarkovsky's prose goes as follows:

> But to return to our theme: I find poetic links, the logic of poetry in cinema, extraordinarily pleasing. They seem to me perfectly appropriate to the potential of cinema as the most truthful and poetic of art forms. Certainly I am more at home with them than with traditional theatrical writing which links image through the linear, rigidly logical development of plot. That sort of fussily correct way of linking events usually involves arbitrarily forcing them into sequence in obedience to some abstract notion of order. And even when this is not so, even when the plot is governed by the characters, one finds that the links which hold it together rest on a facile interpretation of life's complexities.[53]

Tarkovsky reads poetic cinema as both more contingent and more truthful than linear, cause-and-effect narrative, which once again overlaps conceptually with Deren's idea of "vertical" poetry versus "horizontal" narration. Tarkovsky does not wish to essentialize poetry, so he shortly qualifies his description: "When I speak of poetry I am not thinking of it as a genre. Poetry is an awareness of the world, a particular way of relating to reality."[54] Cocteau, Pasolini, and Jarman would all agree, in fact, that poetic cinema is not just poetry, not lineated, metrical writing, so we should not limit our ideas of lyric cinema to conventional, literary forms of poetry. Nonetheless, all of these directors revise our sense of what poetry and poetic cinema are by continually referring to recognizable poems. Their lyric cinema tells us that poetry is not what we think it is, but they also repeatedly use recognizable poems and poets in their work. Thus Tarkovsky's films not only include many dream sequences and follow the logic of dreams, but they also, like Jarman's films, include many interpolations of actual poems. Although the role of poetry in Tarkovsky's *Stalker* (1979) and *Nostalghia* (1983) could just as readily be discussed, for the purposes of this chapter, I will limit myself to *Mirror* (1974), a film that will come up as an important reference for the autobiographical element in Jarman's later films.

Tarkovsky's *Mirror* is autobiographical to the point of obscurity, and in its personal obliquity shows some affinity with a film like Jarman's *The*

Garden. Just as Jarman films his actual garden, in the midst of an industrial-fringed prairie, Tarkovsky rebuilds the actual house in which he grew up and contemplates the relationship of that inner space to the psychological and social world around it. In his prose, Tarkovsky always attacks overtly polemical and political films, and in this regard he seems to be an aesthetic contrast to Pasolini and Jarman. But few twentieth-century aesthetics, as we have seen, work entirely in formalist or "art for art's sake" terms, least of all in Russia, and Tarkovsky's personal reminiscences are always linked to wider social, national, and even global concerns. Although seemingly cryptic autobiography, *The Mirror* is as insistent, even tendentious, in its social commentary as his parable of nuclear holocaust, *The Sacrifice* (1986).

Mirror features four poems by Arseny Tarkovsky, the director's father. These poems self-consciously signal the poetic structure of the film, much like the intertitles of Griffith's *Broken Blossoms* or Paradjanov's quotations of Sayat Nova. These poems also heighten the autobiographical nature of the film, and are in fact spoken by Arseny himself. In *The Cinema of Andrei Tarkovsky*, Mark Le Fanu writes that "the tone of Arseny's poems is, like Pushkin's, that of thrilling, lofty affirmation." After quoting from Arseny— "I am one of those who haul the nets / When a shoal of immortality comes in"—Le Fanu says further, "It is a splendid definition of the poet and film-maker."[55] Le Fanu characterizes Tarkovsky as a metaphysical opposite of Godard: a spiritual creator contrasted with an ironic one, a believer in the creative power of the word compared to an agnostic.

Yet Tarkovsky's *Mirror* is about broken homes and a broken world, and I would suggest that Tarkovsky substantially deidealizes his (absent) father's poetry. Arseny's first poem, "First Meetings," is indeed, for the most part, glorious affirmation:

> Every moment that we were together
> Was a celebration, like Epiphany,
> In all the world the two of us alone.
> . . . .
> You awoke and you transfigured
> The words that people utter every day,
> And speech was filled to overflowing
> With ringing power;
> . . . .
> Ordinary objects were at once transfigured,
> Everything; the jug, the basin—when
> Placed between us like a sentinel

Stood water, laminary and firm.
We were led, not knowing whither,
Like mirages before us there receded
Cities built by miracle,
Wild mint was laying itself beneath our feet,
Birds travelling by the same route as ourselves,
And in the river fishes swam upstream;
And the sky unrolled itself before our eyes.[56]

All this affirms, indeed, a transfiguring, poetic vision of the changed world of love. But the poem ends:

When fate was following in our tracks
Like a madman with a razor in his hand.

Arseny's poem furiously doubles back on itself at the close, and Tarkovsky has the poem read over the lonely, reflective mother, her children quietly with her, and a notion of her crying at the end. The poem captures a happy memory with a brutal, sudden closure, but the director makes everything in the poem palpably absent, pathetic, estranged. This effect, which emphasizes the razor more than the mint, is also reproduced when the next poem is read, as the mother walks down a hall in the printing plant. Here we realize that her hurried, crazed search for a typo in the latest edition of the newspaper acts out a displacement of broken love, and this realization is confirmed when one of her fellow workers starts to lecture her about her personal life. The love poem again marks an elegiac memory, but not an affirmative prophecy. In general it seems to me that Tarkovsky's pictures do not illustrate or substantiate the poems as much as they interact complicatedly with them.

Arseny's third poem provides the most affirmative claim and forms the basis of Le Fanu's characterization.

I don't believe forebodings, nor do omens
Frighten me. I do not run from slander
Nor from poison. On earth there is no death.
All are immortal. All is immortal. No need
To be afraid of death at seventeen
Nor yet at seventy. Reality and light
Exist, but neither death nor darkness.
All of us are on the sea-shore now,
And I am one of those who haul the nets
When a shoal of immortality comes in.[57]

Derek Jarman and the History of Lyric Film

Yet Tarkovsky projects beneath these words documentary footage of the Red Army crossing Lake Sivash. As immortality is extolled, we see soldiers tramping through mud. Tarkovsky knew that many of these soldiers would die on this mission, and there is not a very obvious sign of immortality anywhere around. Of all the visual backdrops that Tarkovsky could have chosen for his father's poem, this one seems as bleak as possible, as far from an affirmative heroism as possible.[58]

And when the poem continues, it draws the same bridges between past and present as the film does.

> Live in the house—the house will stand.
> I will call up any century,
> Go into it and build myself a house.
> That is why your children are beside me
> And your wives, all seated at one table,
> One table for great-grandfather and grandson.
> The future is accomplished here and now[.][59]

Arseny's poetic house disputes linear time and gathers together families beneath its vast, welcoming roof. Tarkovsky's film also refuses chronological sequence and joins together past and present (most remarkably at the end, when the two little boys from the beginning of the film are seen walking with the "old mother"—a historically impossible scene). Film and poetry each have the power to invoke absent figures and to juxtapose disparate regions of time, but Tarkovsky's gliding, fallen world seems fundamentally elegiac rather than celebratory. Tarkovsky does not idealize the powerfully synthetic capability of poetry, since the world, both personally and historically, is too ruined to fix. The film's final picture of the "old mother" with the children imagines a breathtaking revenge against time, but it is also transparent fantasy, and the camera retreats away from them into dark woods. At the end of *Ivan's Childhood* (1962), we enter a dream in which Ivan frolics with his sister on a paradisaical beach, but this too is sheer wish fulfillment, since Ivan has been killed by the Nazis.

As critics have noted, *Mirror* begins with a kind of set piece of poetic vocation, when the stuttering student suddenly finds his voice: "I can speak!" Yet at the end, the narrator seems to be dying of strep throat. *Mirror* is lyric cinema, in Tarkovsky's terms and in our own, but as a parable about poetic vocation or the power of artistic creativity, *Mirror* is complex, not idealized. *Mirror* invokes poetry as an enabling contrast to prosaic modes of proceeding, but it does not do so triumphantly or self-righteously.

This nonidealized, unselfrighteous turn to poetry has much in common with Jarman's own assumption of the poetic.

Critics have noted on various occasions that both Paradjanov and Tarkovsky use over and over again the image of water, in particular the image of running water. Rain and dripping water enable various kinds of visual and sonic effects, no doubt, and critics often explicate these watery images with reference to nature; as homages to Dovzhenko (as the dream of apples and rain in *Ivan's Childhood* surely is); or as related to oceanic maternity.[60] In Paradjanov's *The Color of Pomegranates*, I take the liquid movement of water and other fluids to be setting up a relatively formal contrast to the symmetrical and stationary elements in his collages, as formal contrasts to the unbending and unmoving picture frame. In Tarkovsky's *Mirror*, I take the running water to emphasize the elegiac, gravitational pull of the earth: we feel, there, both chance and inevitability. When the camera tracks through the rooms of the house toward the burning barn in an early scene, "a bottle falls off the table for no apparent reason."[61] The fence breaks beneath the mother and doctor in the first scene; the children give spilled milk to the cat; the barn burns. The slow, fluid tracking shots and the imagery of falling, falling toward the earth, are emblematic of Tarkovsky's magical and also fatalistic cinematic poetry.

Usually, Tarkovsky's cinema is seen as martyring itself on the altar of truth in the face of unsympathetic authorities and distributors, and Tarkovsky's prose certainly enforces this idealizing image. But in my turn I would want to underscore the degree to which Tarkovsky's poetic cinema is not burned at the stake by uncomprehending law, but rather burns itself at the stake as a witness to the destruction of the twentieth century and as an embodiment of the laws of twentieth-century poetry. Once again, this is poetry that rejects serial narrative, but does not reject it scornfully; it brings unlikes together, but does so in mourning, rather than in salvific unity. Through the course of this book, we shall return to the examples set by Paradjanov and Tarkovsky for the illumination they may shed on the cinema of Derek Jarman.

III. EGOYAN, COCTEAU, AND THE POETIC ACCIDENT

A great film is an accident, a banana skin under the feet of dogma.

COCTEAU[62]

If there is an apparently "aesthetic" director of cinematic poetry, then it is not Paradjanov or Tarkovsky but Jean Cocteau. Cocteau happily speaks in terms of "poetry" and "beauty" through all his writings, and he seems to have been even less politically motivated in his mid-century France than Oscar Wilde in his late Victorian England. Yet like Wilde's plays, Cocteau's films have been retrospectively read into a tradition of gay aesthetics, and like Pasolini, Cocteau becomes a recurrent point of reference for Jarman. It is the accidental that is a main element in Cocteau's varying descriptions of the poetic, and he explores this aspect quite deliberately (the paradox of the intentional accident runs throughout his discussions) in both prose and film. In this third section I will focus on Cocteau's fable of poetry, *Orpheus* (1949), and continue to meditate in some detail on the notion of the poetic accident. In the chapter's fourth and concluding section, I will then examine Cocteau's *Testament of Orpheus* and its relationship to other lyric cinema by homosexual directors such as Pasolini and Jean Genet.

Because poetry for Cocteau is not premeditated (he always complains against those who self-consciously attempt poetic effects), he welcomes the accidental: "So I hope, with all my heart, that Hollywood will associate a minor branch to the great enterprise of film-making, one that will not be protected against routine by any insurance, but invite accidents to happen."[63] The accidental defies premeditation, but ultimately comes to serve as a revelatory sign, or a bridge to truth, just as the raindrops in Tarkovsky trace a pattern that is both accidental and inevitable. Poetic cinema materializes in images the truthful arbitrariness of its progression—through falling bottles and spilled milk in Tarkovsky and through, on a larger scale, fatal accidents in Cocteau. It is no coincidence that Kieslowski's *Trois Couleurs*—often characterized as "lyrical" and "poetic"—begins with a car accident in *Blue*. As seen above all in the coincidences and contingencies of colors, the metaphysical aesthetic of Kieslowski's film is held together by supernatural chance.[64] The thematic embodiment of poetic accident is exemplified also in Atom Egoyan's *The Sweet Hereafter*, to which we need briefly to turn.

24   *The Sweet Hereafter*, an atmospheric, otherworldly film, is adapted from Russell Banks's 1991 novel. The novel shows us a community's response to the tragic crash of a school bus off an icy road into a river. The book moves through five monologues, spoken successively by Dolores Driscoll, the bus driver; Billy Ansel, a Vietnam vet and widower who loses his two children in the event; Mitchell Stephens, a New York City lawyer who seeks damages for the accident; Nichole Burnell, a teenage girl who is crippled in the accident; and lastly, Dolores Driscoll once again. The modern perspectivalism effected by the lack of an omniscient narrator is

matched by the novel's bleak resolution: the lawyer can find no cause, no explanation for the accident. The hardheaded lawyer, Mitchell Stephens, returns empty-handed. The accident merely happened, therefore; there is no great metaphysical conclusion or consolation to be found.

Yet even as the novel metaphysically and existentially rejects the lawyer's determined search for causality ("There are no accidents," says Mitchell Stephens),[65] the logic of the novel does not coincide with the usual mechanisms of fictive explanation. There are no deep explanations for accidents, the novel says, bleakly, but the novel itself, in spite of its potentially relativistic perspectivalism or decentering, still obeys conventional contracts between writer and reader. Thus, characters perform their actions and come to their own conclusions for reasons that are clearly articulated within the novel itself. For example, a key obstacle to the lawyer's pursuit of explanation (and money) is the testimony of Nichole Burnell. She lies, claiming Dolores was speeding (no one wants to sue Dolores), in order to revenge herself on her sexually predatory father. The motivation for her lie and the consequences of her actions, as with other motivations and consequences in the novel, are made perfectly intelligible to us. Thus, for all of its angst or formal modernizing, there truly are no narratological accidents in the novel by Russell Banks.

Egoyan's cinematic version of *The Sweet Hereafter*, then, not only reduces and eliminates aspects of the novel's plot and character—usually necessary when condensing the thickness of a novel to ninety minutes of screen time—but it fundamentally changes the generic mode of the story's representation. One need not be overly essentializing or idealizing about generic form to claim that Egoyan's cinematic version has transformed novelistic causality to poetic accident. Egoyan now frequently cuts back and forth chronologically, as Tarkovsky does in *Mirror*, so that characters are seen well and whole *after* the bus crash. The most poignant example of this comes at the end when Nicole (her name is spelled thus in the film) reads a bedtime book to Billy Ansel's two children; they fall asleep, and she walks away to look out a window, which fills with light. Since the children will die and Nicole will never walk again, the scene is a fantasy—although technically a flashback—a fantasy that takes place in heaven, in another world where all is well. Unlike Banks's title, which is sheer, unforgiving irony, as critics noted in their book reviews, Egoyan applies the same title to an authentically reimagined space, the changed world of poetry—the sweet hereafter. If Egoyan's title is not brutally ironic, neither is it sentimentally utopian. The last scene of *The Sweet Hereafter* recalls, in fact, the last scene of Tarkovsky's *Mirror*. Both are scenes that dally with time's distress (although one is fact, the other fancy); both unify nostalgically, but undermine themselves elegiacally in the same gesture.

Egoyan's reductions of plot not only collapse for the sake of abbreviation, they eliminate the very explanation that constitutes narrative. Egoyan resees the crash according to a lineage of poetic cinema. He highlights the accidental nature of events, not only in the plot, but also in the form, the telling. If, as David Bordwell has argued, classical narrative is fundamentally concerned with causality, then Egoyan's manner of proceeding reduces explanation by highlighting the contingent. The central pivot of the entire plot, Nicole's invented testimony, now has no clear causality; a reviewer in *Sight and Sound* calls it "inexplicable."[66] The relationship of father and daughter is not so straightforwardly portrayed in the film—we have only a lyrical fantasy from her point of view to suggest her father's abuses.[67] What is more, Egoyan expressly and self-consciously announces the generic alteration of the novel into poetry—the cutting back and forth in time, the reduction of causality, the atmospheric, brooding music—by adding a poem, "The Pied Piper of Hamelin" by Robert Browning. This is the bedtime story that Nicole reads to the two Ansel children, and it organizes thematically and rhythmically the totality of the film. Like Arseny Tarkovsky's lyrics in *Mirror*, the Browning poem names *The Sweet Hereafter* as part of the tradition of cinematic poetry.

Cocteau repeatedly emphasizes the accidental in true poetic creation. He insists that one cannot analytically interrogate poetic form, and this is why both Heurtebise and the Princess tell Orpheus to ask no questions. Poetry is related to dreams, to self-consciousness, thus accounting for the seemingly random structure and continuity of *The Blood of a Poet* (which is not surrealist, according to Cocteau). Cegeste's accidental death brings the underworld into the mundane, and Orpheus finally dies when a gun accidentally goes off in a scuffle. All of these accidents also have the force of inevitability, however, as we know that it is death's stormtroopers who are running down their victims. As elsewhere in the tradition of poetic film, these accidents are characterized both by chance and by a deeper truth.

Cocteau contrasts the mundane, everyday world with the poetic underworld, but slyly, self-consciously (one of the clubs where Orpheus may be found is called "The Two Worlds"). The normal, unpoetic world is found, first of all, in Orpheus's bourgeois household, decorated with tasteful furnishings and framed engravings. Cocteau's film savages the ideals of romantic love at the heart of both the Orpheus myth and middle-class marriage by showing Orpheus and Eurydice as a squabbling, quarreling couple.

Derek Jarman and Lyric Film

The myth's poignant prohibition—"Do not look at your wife!"—becomes an intolerable inconvenience to Cocteau's Orpheus. This Orpheus does not turn to look at Eurydice out of the yearning of infinite passion, but rather glances up at her in a car's rearview mirror, accidentally. In addition to this tedious and impatient middle-class household, the other characteristic space of the unpoetic world in the film is, tellingly, the café where all the poets hang out. Here, where fashion and convention reign, is premeditated poetry, and so not poetry at all, as Cocteau always maintains in his prose, along with Tarkovsky.

In contrast both to the walled, middle-class household, with its garage, garden, and classical statuary, and to the trendy club, with its intoxicated fights and trendy journals (such as "nudism," a book of empty pages), Cocteau imagines an underworld—the poetic otherworld—a space of ruins and night. Using relatively few special effects (eschewing mists and double exposures), Cocteau creates a space of slow, timeless absence. The worldly irritability and time-consciousness of middle-class home and literary club give way to slow motion, silence, and a deliberateness suggestive of eternity. Not that Cocteau creates a world that is entirely alien or remote from the human. For the helmeted motorcyclists still stand around like Nazi stormtroopers, and the tribunal of old men performs a readily identifiable interrogation and show trial. The Princess smokes, and asks for a pen. This Orphic underworld is a deserted, ruined contrast to the bourgeois and the trendy, but it is also connected through the logic of dreams to the real world, to the visual imaginary of our historical world.

The archetypal logic of the original Orpheus myth (as may be found in the narrative at the close of Virgil's *Georgics*) shows the relationship of the poetic to transcendental emotion and experience: Orpheus can charm the rocks and trees, is able even to charm Hell and win his wife back from the confines of Death. The power of poetry overwhelms itself and the poet himself as well when the frenzied bacchantes shred Orpheus limb from limb. Yet in many versions of the myth, poetry is so powerful that the decapitated head sings out even while it floats down the river.

Cocteau deidealizes this myth of transcendence and ecstasy in a number of significant ways. Orpheus himself is not particularly likable, and his quarrels with Eurydice seem trivial and fussy, rather than heroic resistances in the name of art. Once again, therefore, the rejection of what is not art or not poetry is not self-righteous. This Orpheus is inspired by a car radio in the garage. Cocteau certainly aims to demystify conventional, more obviously Parnassian sites of poetic inspiration, but the image of Orpheus obsessively bent over the radio, copying down numbers, removes from him

27

all trace of the heroic or the transcendent. This Orphic creativity appears secondhand, and poetic madness just looks kooky in these scenes. This waffling Orpheus does not know what he wants, Eurydice or Death; he does not know where creativity resides. Yet this may be, Cocteau implies, a truer Orpheus after all; instead of one rapt with power and creative will, this irritable, indecisive Orpheus may be a truer conduit of the truly poetic—the poetry that occurs obliquely through accident and chance.

Cocteau's homosexuality means that his cinematic representations of poetry can be retrospectively related to representations of sexuality. Cocteau's films do not overtly represent homosexuality, nor, for the most part, do Pasolini's, but they can be related to traditions of homosexual art that directors like Jarman eventually drew from. The theme of the marginalized criminal, for example, can be seen to link directors such as Genet, Pasolini, Cocteau, and Kenneth Anger, all filmmakers with a formative influence on Jarman's work.[68] A film like Cocteau's *Orpheus* can be read retrospectively as a gay text, though most overly particularized interpretations do not seem very convincing.[69] There is no doubt that Cocteau radically disrupts the Orpheus-Eurydice couple on which the myth is found, but it seems that his target is as much middle-class respectability as it is heterosexuality. Yet Pasolini often makes the same strike: that is, he does not necessarily represent homosexual relationships with the positive, visual force that we find in Jarman's films, yet his attacks on middle-class norms and attitudes, as in *Teorema*, certainly attempt to remove a main obstacle to sexualized judgmentalism.

Among Jarman's various references to Cocteau's *Orpheus*, the following passage provides the most comprehensive explanation and context:

DEAD TO THE WORLD

Part of my interest in the magician John Dee was his preoccupation with secrets and ciphers.

Why this obsession with the language of closed structures, the ritual of the closet and the sanctuary? The prison cells of Genet's *Un Chant d'amour*, the desert encampment of *Sebastiane*; [Kenneth] Anger, insulating himself with magick, screening himself off; Cocteau's *Orphée*, an attempt to steal through the screen into the labyrinth and usurp the privileges only the cabal of the dead may confer; the wall of unreality that girds the house in *Salo*, and its victims, who are told: What is about to take place here will have never happened, you are already dead to the world outside.[70]

Jarman does not read homosexuality into Cocteau's *Orpheus* through character, but rather through theme and image: the thematics of secrecy and the imagery of enclosure. It may be that Jarman's queer poetry is born here, at the junction of the accidental and the secret. How is one part joined to another? We don't know: it is a secret; we do not know: it is an accident. Does the act of reading (of viewing, of interpretation) lead to a kind of freedom—the secret expressed? the truth exposed? What is the nature of poetry and symbol when it has to do not with the formal relationships of aesthetics, but with the socially problematic expression of same-sex desire? We will begin to address these questions by looking, in the final section of this chapter, at several films that are, like Jarman's, both contributions to the tradition of lyric film and also clear expressions of homoerotic sensibility.

IV. GENET'S *Un Chant d'amour* AND THE INVISIBLE UNDERGROUND

By setting Jarman next to Cocteau, Pasolini, and Tarkovsky, rather than Anger, Deren, and Jonas Mekas, I am following Jarman's sense of his own context and audience. Once he began to make feature-length films, he always insisted on the relatively traditional nature of his work. The films are low-budget, necessarily, but art-house, not alternative. Certainly, after *Sebastiane* one would not imagine that Jarman made underground films. Yet in both their antinarrative impulse and their representation of homosexuality, Jarman's films may be seen as rerouting underground themes into the feature-length light of day. Each of his feature-length films may be read as a parable of the visionary (and of visibility) in which poetry and homosexuality, which often make for short films or private showings, now appear to be jostling for feature-length attention, no longer satisfied with their relegation to the avant-garde. In this concluding section of the chapter, we need to fill out our sense of lyric cinema by looking at film that is more apparently to the scale of lyric poetry and by focusing especially on one of the most famous gay movies in history, Genet's *Un Chant d'amour* (1950).

By rebuilding the underground aboveground, as it were, Jarman continues the interest in poetic cinema embodied by a number of mid-century American filmmakers and definitively described by Sitney in *Visionary Film: The American Avant-Garde*.[71] Filmmakers like Deren and Brakhage not only seem to be visionary, lyrical filmmakers in Sitney's terms ("the lyrical film postulates the film-maker behind the camera as the first-person protagonist of the film"), they use the language of poetry throughout their own

29

extensive prose works.[72] We have noted earlier Deren's important contribution to the symposium on "Poetry and Film"; her *Collected Works* includes many poems and also elaborates the interest in ritual and the occult that led to her film on Haiti.[73] Brakhage's numerous prose works, including *The Brakhage Lectures*, cannot but remind readers of prose by Charles Olson or Robert Creeley.[74]

Brakhage's film *Thigh Line Lyre Triangular* (1961), for example, might be read as a lyric poem that self-consciously renders the invisible visible.[75] The "birth film" is, by genre, a species of underground film; one does not show, in any detail, the birth of a child to the public; on the contrary, the showing is necessarily private, restricted. Brakhage's birth films are home movies taken of his wife, Jane Brakhage, giving birth to their children. But these private images, especially those of Jane Brakhage's body, are taken into the realm of imaginative poetry and art. The delta of Jane's vagina becomes an Orphic lyre, inspiring the painterly filmmaker with color and emotion. Thus the film becomes more than a documentary revelation of a nude woman giving birth; it renders Stan Brakhage's wild responses to the event, as paint flies over and around the pictures. The act of projection in itself may thus be said to signal a liberation from oppressive distinctions between public and private. Whereas *Window Water Baby Moving* records a birth with conventionally beautiful images and without too much artificial mediation or postproduction interference, *Thigh Line Lyre Triangular* attains the complexity of a lyric poem by balancing subjective, painterly vision with emancipatory, documentary effect. Formal consciousness ("line," "triangular") is balanced against social consciousness, making for an uneasy viewing experience.

Genet's *Un Chant d'amour* (*A Song of Love*) also embodies, and may be said to perform, these paradoxes of underground visibility. Genet made the twenty-five-minute film with money from producer Nico Papatakis, nonprofessional actors, and professional film technicians.[76] Genet intended the film for private viewings only, although it eventually found its way into various avant-garde and alternative theaters. The slow progress and controversial itinerary of the film (sometimes leading to arrests and always to polemics) make it a true underground film, one of the most famous in cinema history. For the book jacket of Jane Giles's *The Cinema of Jean Genet: Un Chant d'amour*, Jarman writes, "There's no smoke without fire; *Un Chant d'amour* is a communion in which Jean Genet takes us into the prison in order to liberate us from it."

Un Chant d'amour buries itself in the underground two times over, through its cinematic lyricism and through its explicit representation of homosexuality. The film makes itself more incomprehensible through its manner of signification at the same time that it makes itself less socially acceptable by showing men's desires for one another in graphic detail. Where the film's plot is expected to be clear, it is obscure; it unfolds through symbolism rather than narrative. And where the film is expected to be obscure—in its representation of sexuality—it is explicit. Like Brakhage's *Thigh Line Lyre Triangular, Un Chant d'amour* is more than a documentary liberation—here we are shown the repressed, physical body in all of its joy—since the expression of naked love is organized and framed in an obviously subjective, artificial way. Hence Jarman in the above quotation speaks not only of liberation, but also of "communion"—the ritual of art.

Why are there symbols in *Un Chant d'amour*? For these are not symbols of sexual implication; these are not the (simple) sexual symbols of, say, Alfred Hitchcock—the fireworks in *To Catch a Thief* or the train going through the tunnel at the end of *North by Northwest*, where the symbol in each case stands for a sexual act. *Un Chant d'amour* does not need phallic symbols since it already shows us, quite clearly, the phallus. At the beginning and end of *Un Chant d'amour* an arm swings a bouquet of flowers back and forth out of a window; at the end of the film, the bouquet is finally caught by another arm. The image of the flowers is in part used to frame the film, to provide it with structure in the absence of concrete narrative; so that finally, at the end, we feel a kind of consummation or success. The flowers also substantiate the title, assuring us that this is a poem, a song, and a song of love. One way of reading the flowers is that they help compose and dignify what may otherwise be jumbled images of erotic desire; they help us see art and civilization rather than chaos; they help us see love rather than lust.

Yet in all of his works, Genet's figuration readily deconstructs; no wonder he is one of the two heroes in Jacques Derrida's *Glas* (the other is Hegel). As Edmund White points out, "Genet declared that he liked only works of art that destroyed themselves, that were both player and target in an artistic shooting gallery."[77] Lyric symbolism—the flower, the dance, the song—does not exist in order to raise the material into art or to add beautiful imagery to otherwise bleak regions. For the flower in Genet is inextricably, one might say dialectically, related to filth, as beauty is to ugliness, poetry to prose. The flower is born of the prison. Were there no prison, no obscure gesture would be needed; the men would need not to exchange cigarette smoke through a thin straw. Were all the walls down, there would be no need for figurative communication—communication that is both joyful and desperate, ecstatic and onanistic. The contrary energy of poetry and symbol does not perfect a good world; it comments desperately on a bad world, enclosed and oppressive. In poetry here we do not return to the primitive expressions of prelapsarian men. Instead, poetry itself signals the fall: communication has been reduced to gestures and images that may travel no further than cell to cell, window to window, private theatre to theatre.

Without much interpretive strain, *Un Chant d'amour* may be read as entirely self-reflexive, that is, as an allegory of underground film. Like many of Jarman's films, *Un Chant d'amour* models explicitly relationships between viewer and the viewed, thereby providing analogies for cinematic experience, for the relationship between film and audience. *Un Chant d'amour* unfolds as an exercise in voyeurism: we do not just objectively see the prisoners in their cells, at a distance; rather we see from a point of view that is aligned throughout the film with the spying guard.

It has been noted that the voyeuristic observer who looks in on one cell after another is reminiscent of the poet in Cocteau's *Blood of a Poet*; we know also that Cocteau watched the filming of *Un Chant d'amour* and that he provided the setting, although probably not actual assistance.[78] The two voyeurs do look superficially similar, but turn out very differently in the end. Cocteau's poet is a passive, floating viewer in a hotel hallway; his exotic visions (opium smokers, a hermaphrodite) appear through the keyhole like strange, short films—magical, but rather dead, without affect. Cocteau toys with the idea of poetic inspiration and the marvelous, but demystifies the mythology as soon as it appears. Although not idealized, Cocteau's approach still aligns the viewer with the poet, and our creative participation with the images and hieroglyphics in the film is certainly encouraged.

In Genet, however, creative expression is squarely on the side of the prisoners in the cells, and the viewer is aligned with the police. We watch, fascinated and perhaps even intrusive, as the guard steps through the door and into the room. The film is intentionally underground, private, but it reenacts in its development the interruption of its private spectacle by an intrusive public, an audience that both judges and participates. The underground is already visible from the moment of filming; there is no hiding place. The underground is not a place of safety, of hiddenness, but always a space where public and private share tenuous borders, where visibility becomes a necessary tool for liberation, but one that occurs only through contention and fight.

The tradition of lyric cinema that leads toward Derek Jarman is a many-branched tree, multifarious and always changing. As we have seen, even the directors who most deliberately invoke the lyrical also often substantially undermine it. These lyric films are self-conscious to the degree that they include actual poems and poets. Yet this self-conscious artifice is often attended by irony, pathos, and subversion. Another film historian may well dispute the existence of such a tradition; with different purposes in mind, with a different goal, the films brought forward here would certainly be seen differently. As I confessed at the outset, these brief descriptions of lyric cinema form a rather tentative narrative that aims tendentiously toward Jarman. The names assembled here are partly those directors that Jarman mentions himself (Pasolini, Cocteau, Genet), on whom he has intentionally modeled his work, but also those that I feel are rewardingly placed nearby (such as Paradjanov). I will have occasion to invoke these filmmakers throughout the rest of this study, and the reader can expect other names as well, which they might very properly have expected in an overview such as this: Fellini, Buñuel, and Anger.

Jarman's feature-length films work themselves out from the underground, from short films and *Sebastiane* to *Edward II* and *Blue*, yet still bear many of the problems and themes associated with visibility and representation that we have touched on in Genet's *Un Chant d'amour*. Genet's image repertoire in his lone film and throughout his novels repeatedly draws on the figure of the criminal—the prostitute, the prisoner, the thief. Jarman's imagery may be more idiomatically connected to the light and the light-writing that is cinema, but it is equally suited to the complex analysis of homosexuality that takes place in his art. The imagery that his films and prose return to, over and over again, has to do with the mirror and the sea, and it is to an extended discussion of those images that we turn to now.

The Mirror and the Sea: Jarman's Poetry and Queer Mirroring

Most critical discussion of Jarman's artistic production centers on the films, and then perhaps juxtaposes those films with selections from his art, his books, his journals. He is known primarily now as a director, but also as a painter and, indeed, even as a gardener. We know that Jarman thought of his creative output as highly interrelated, and so there is, not surprisingly, much productive overlap between the films and the various texts. Yet his lone poetry book, *A Finger in the Fishes Mouth* (1972), has received practically no critical commentary at all. To a degree, this is quite understandable: it appears in the career to be a one-off (a single instance) and a piece of juvenilia—not at all obviously a great work—and so perhaps better left forgotten and unread.

2

Yet I would suggest that as a first element in a terrifically interesting career, the book is worth our attention. Since our focus is on the poetry in Jarman's cinema, it makes sense to look at this collection of his early poems. In fact, he published the book only four years before making *Sebastiane* (1976), and we know that Jarman was experimenting with home movies and short films well before the release of his first feature. *A Finger in the Fishes Mouth* is part of that artistic evolution. Poetry will always be part of Jarman's cinema, and the poems in this early book are clearly related stylistically to poems found in both his films and journals during the rest of his career. This book of poems may be seen as foreshadowing many of the concerns of future films and as looking ahead, in particular, to the way poetic language is juxtaposed with visual imagery in his more mature cinema. Even though the book was published at a time when he was far more a painter than a film director, the impulses and aesthetics of the book look forward remarkably toward films not yet created.

This second chapter will divide evenly into two sections. To begin, I will describe the styles and effects of the poems in *A Finger in the Fishes Mouth*—I will "close read" the book and characterize its poetics. Then, drawing on this description of the poems, I will generalize more theoretically about the imagery that appears in Jarman's films and prose throughout his career. With these discussions and the descriptions of lyric film in the previous chapter, we shall then be ready to travel through the body of Jarman's work in the following five chapters.

I. POSTCARDS FROM THE SKY: *A Finger in the Fishes Mouth*

April 16, 1946 (Tuesday)
Blustery but pleasant—an exceptionally fine atmosphere—(magical, theatrical).

JOSEPH CORNELL[1]

In his splendid biography of Jarman, Tony Peake gives this description of *A Finger in the Fishes Mouth*, a collection which would go on to receive "no publicity" and would soon vanish from view:

> As a token of friendship with Jarman, Michael Pinney of Bettiscombe Press had used a photograph of a gathering at Bankside on the front cover of *Nota Bene*, his most recent collection of poetry. On the back, in Jarman's own handwriting, was Jarman's phrase "Thru the Billboard promised land." Pinney now offered to publish a matching volume of the somewhat portentous poems Jarman had written in his

early twenties. Like *Nota Bene*, *A Finger in the Fishes Mouth* would have a silver cover and feature Jarman's handwritten phrase on the back. On the front would be a Wilhelm von Gloeden photograph of a young boy with his finger in the mouth of a flying fish.[2]

The Bettiscombe Press, which printed *A Finger in the Fishes Mouth*, was a small-press publisher in Dorset, active from the late 1960s to the mid-1970s. The press seems to have specialized in poetry books with illustrations, such as *Night Flight* (1969) ("words Michael Pinney; photography by John Miles") and *Orion's Sword* (1971), words and photographs again by Pinney and Miles.[3] Jarman's *A Finger in the Fishes Mouth* also follows this "house style" (if such it is), as every poem is accompanied by some sort of illustration. Yet from our retrospective point of view, the use of visual imagery in contrasting relationship to the text also seems idiosyncratic, unique, already a Jarman signature. The pictures and poems together seem to foreshadow the editing and stylistic sensibility displayed in the films. Because of the strengths of and interest in the career, then, this "portentous" first book is definitely worth a look.

There are altogether thirty-two poems, whose titles are listed in a "catalogue of poems" at the back of the book in a European-style table of contents. The "catalogue" titles themselves are set across the page from a photograph of an elderly, dignified artist wearing a smock and beret. The artist is surrounded by walls packed with framed pictures of male youths and hunky men. By naming the list a "catalogue" of poems, Jarman imports a term associated more readily with an art gallery (a "catalogue of paintings"). Even in the table of contents, then, the book is already playing intellectual games. The conventionally hierarchical relationship between (primary) poem and (secondary) illustration thus turns, straight away, into a more equal and fluid relation.

Now, an old artist surrounded by all these framed pictures of young men is a visual gesture simultaneously veiling and revealing. Jarman in 1972 is not a white-haired old man, and the poems themselves do not have much overt homosexual content. Yet there they are in the picture, walls of men, as if they themselves embody a "gallery of poems," now complete with a catalogue. This final illustration serves as a kind of signature—an announcement of identity—but not in any straightforwardly autobiographical sense. The subjectivity of this artist figure is thus rendered both stunningly truthful and also amusingly mysterious. The artist in the picture is, in fact, the Victorian painter G. F. Watts, and the postcard is a parody version of Watts in his studio at Limnerslease (in Compton, Surrey), where he is surrounded by his own paintings.[4] For Watts's own works, the parodic postcard substitutes a bevy of beefcake.

But although Jarman frequently attaches himself to Victorian subjects (*The Last of England* is also the name of a painting by Ford Madox Brown, and that film's original title was *Victorian Values*), the relationship here is not simply parodic or subversive. For Jarman's poetry is in some ways straightforwardly equated with this mysterious artist figure, the first of many such figures with whom Jarman potentially aligns himself. John Dee in *Jubilee* and Prospero in Shakespeare's *The Tempest* will soon follow.

Like the way the framed pictures are stacked haphazardly all over the walls (as in Victorian galleries), the arrangement of the poems is intentionally random. The first poem is "Poem II" and the third to last is "Poem I." "Moon II" comes five poems before "Moon." There is even another poem called "Poem I 1965." Mostly titles are place-names or dates, which gives the flavor of a diary or a journal. There are also poems called "Words written without any stopping" and "Word Poem Fragments March 64." The monumentality of the catalogue of framed pictures is undermined by the offhandedness of the sequence and the titles. At least the collection ends politely with an ostensible gesture of closure, "Poem VII Farewell."

In this book Jarman teases and plays with ideas of the literary, with conceptions of what poetry is supposed to do. Compared with the poems of his more well-known contemporaries of the 1970s, such as those anthologized in *The Penguin Book of Contemporary Poetry* (1982)—namely, Seamus Heaney, Tony Harrison, Douglas Dunn, Derek Mahon, and Tom Paulin—Jarman's poems are noticeably uninterested in complex psychology or sophisticated, "literary" language.[5] He toys with literary topoi—dedicating poems to "Rembrant," Coleridge, and "Marc" Rothko—but he undercuts the seriousness, even in the misspellings.

The offhand tone and random sequencing potentially suggest the beatniks, perhaps Frank O'Hara, Paul Blackburn, or Ted Berrigan (American authors of classic texts published by Grove in the 1960s), but Jarman's poems notably lack any charismatic self-presentation, any quasi-protagonist "I," such as one would find in many American poems, either "square" or "beat." "The Billboard promised land," after all, is America, the home of Allen Ginsberg, Jack Kerouac, and Lawrence Ferlinghetti. Yet important as these figures are for Jarman, his poetry takes a very different stance from theirs, exhibiting an entirely distinct sense of the egotistical "I."[6]

The first poem, indeed, provides the context for a set of speakers whose "I" is vaguely indeterminate, speakers who are intentionally not captivating or garrulous:

POEM II
Now I am sailing on this rocking chair
back
back
to where tomorrow
washes the pavilions of today

This poem serves as a kind of quiet invocation to the collection, conflating traditional images of the poet in his boat with those of the poet in his chair. The poem is languorously surrealistic, paradoxically playing with time, but without much palpable tension or contradiction. Jarman's use of the poetic line is remarkably consistent throughout his career; he is almost never interested in the felt intensities of enjambment. Lines tend to be relatively discrete phrase units where punctuation is largely unnecessary and usually absent. In this book, a poem such as this is given an entire page. Visually, we see not very much poetry in a large field of blank white.

Yet the felt openness of this poem on the page is partly contradicted by its facing picture—two boats sailing through an underground cavern. Here, at the beginning of a book of poems, this picture, too, participates in the invocation, since the cavern calls to mind classic images of prophecy and origin, such as the Sibyl's cave in *Aeneid* 6 (with the boatman Charon) or Dante's related descent into the underworld at the beginning of the *Inferno*. Jarman's surrealistic poem in juxtaposition with this picture recalls these famous pieces of literature, but his quiet, offhand poem (in a "rocking chair") seems neither ostentatiously literary (celebrating its own cultural prestige) nor easily mocking. This complicated effect, where the "I" is unclearly located and where the tone of satire is multivalent rather than univocal, is a crucial feature of many of Jarman's films.

The "sailing" metaphor not only prepares us for a ride in the poet's boat, it also initiates a kind of travel narrative (the second poem is "Patmos-Delos"). Many of the "illustrations" contribute to the atmosphere of traveling, since the pictures are all reproductions of postcards, complete with captions. The picture of the boats in a cavern constitutes an allusion, more or less, to illustrations we might find in a more obviously ambitious book, such as a Doré in Dante or a Turner in Samuel Rogers's *Italy*.

But the fact that the illustration *is* a postcard makes for a more playful, self-conscious effect, and terms like "camp" and "postmodern" are not too far afield here. Jarman's book toys with ideas of the Victorian: the second-to-last poem is called "A Victorian Poem"; the last picture alludes to the crammed walls of Victorian art galleries. The idea of the illustrated book comes down to us, in fact, from the copiously illustrated gift books and annuals of the Victorians, which are filled with engravings by some of the finest artists of the time, along with lots of poems. A poetry book filled with postcards self-consciously transforms the masterful Victorian engraving into a nickel reproduction. Art contemporary with *A Finger in the Fishes Mouth* often depends on appropriation, reproduction, and parody, usually with the effect of disturbing the distinctions between high and low art. Postcards signal tourism and collectibility, not monumentality and prestige, and are usually accompanied by the briefest message. Jarman's small-press, often small-scale poems (which will not be very often "consumed," even if resoundingly successful) are juxtaposed with these overtly commodified images of travel, and the effect of the poem-image contrast is therefore always interestingly complex.

The poem-picture juxtaposition works in many different ways throughout the course of this small book. Just as a film's sound track can potentially either substantiate or contradict the visual image it accompanies, pictures and poems here interact sometimes in parallel and sometimes at cross-purposes. "Writ on the Presidio S.F." looks like a poem from San Francisco, but the postcard standing opposite—allegedly the illustration—turns out to be an absolutely standard one of the "Lincoln Memorial, Washington, D.C." "The Devil Old Junk Man" looks like a kind of urban street poem ("the fruit box woman collecting / fire in orange boxes"), but the postcard opposite is of an extravagantly outfitted king. "Poem IV to Rembrandt" (now spelled correctly) sits across from an old postcard filled with portraits of the "reigning sovereigns and principal royal personages of the day." The poems just by themselves are surrealistic and nonrepresentational, but juxtaposing them in various nonobvious ways with the pictures introduces yet another strange trajectory or level of comparison. Jarman's cinematic propensity for juxtaposition—to crosscut between two sets of visual narratives and to line up his sound track in strange ways with the visual images on the screen—is heralded in the visual construction of this book, page by page. 39

Clearly Jarman uses the book to question what a book is. This idea is reflected in the presentation and typography of the book. Instead of page numbers, each poem is numbered; but the large number is printed in between poems. The sequence runs thus: a picture on the left side, a poem on the right; then a blank white page on the left, and a (poem) number on the right. There are vast expanses of blank pages, then, defying utilitarianism and connoting emptiness and openness. The impulse behind these blank pages (which cynically may be regarded as merely filling out the book) is not so far away from the boundless expanse of blue in Jarman's last film,

Blue. This book does not behave itself: it does not bring us page after page of words; *Blue* does not conduct itself according to our expectations: it does not bring us frame after frame of moving images. The book empties out the book, then, as much as it brings the book forward.

Jarman's poems, like many post-1950 poems in America and Britain, do not cooperate with Cleanth Brooks-style "close reading"; they are not dense or well-wrought poems. Nonetheless we can begin to describe Jarman's style and intent in these poems by attending in some detail to a single and rather typical poem. Insofar as this poem is representative of effects elsewhere in the book, the discussion will allow us to generalize and survey beyond the specific poem.

The third poem in the book, "From Gypsy Mar 1 66," is quoted here in its entirety:

I had a dream
through the mirror of the morning
I walk where the image scatters on the silver
laps and ebbs in pools monotonously
I had a dream
in the dawn light
The clouds reflecting the fire of the billboard promised by
stalking the violet sky
floating the highways of delight
to new storms
tears tears tears
always floating above the houses
down each street
caught momentarily
between rows of poplars
a flying scarlet apotheosis
ascending the skies
    now two
or at this corner three
    float by in the dawn

The title is the most overtly epistolary of any in the book, but many of the poems, along with the postcards, construct a narrator who travels from one point to another, restlessly, a latter-day Byron. "Gypsy" in this poem is the humorous signature for the wanderer and implies, in concert with other poems, that the speaker is much more likely an alien, an exile, than one who feels himself at home. The date is interesting, too. This is the most specific date of any poem (March 1, 1966), but there are other poems with dates for titles: "July 64," "April 64," "Christmas 64," "March 64" (and again, of course, chronological sequence is not adhered to). Even though the poems appeared in 1972, there is the mysterious impression that many of the poems were written in 1964–1966 (Gypsy's response here is the latest date recorded among the poems). If we do not have personal knowledge of Jarman's biography, we can only ask, "What happened?" Are all the poems seven years old? Are these events so significant (although they don't seem so) that a present speaker continually recurs to them? No answer is given or suggested. In the end, the specific historicity of these dates is drowned out by the lack of determinable context and by the obliquely visible speaker, by mystery and silence.

The watery images in this poem are reinforced by the facing postcard, which shows an empty boardwalk next to an ocean (the caption is "Rough sea, Hovlake"). Water will become a repeated image in the book, from the title onwards. The first poem "sails" on the rocking chair, with a postcard of boats in a river cavern; "Venice April 64" ("we could see the rain drifting in from the dead adriatic") is attended by a male and female couple looking out toward a moonlit bay; the next poem ("Poem III," the fourteenth poem) repeats the first poem ("Now I am sailing on / this rocking chair"); "Myconos" is a brief haiku-like or imagistic poem ("now the fishing boats/ are back in the harbour / the wind is again on the beaches"), and the postcard shows sailboats offshore; the postcard for "Moon II" shows reflections on water; "Moon" is illustrated by a beachhead at night; "Word Poem Fragments March 64" ("Sea Minstrel") is illustrated by a sailboat seen through a tree-lined gate. Especially in the postcards, Jarman seems mostly interested in the beauties and languors of water. In his selection of postcards, Jarman cultivates a gentleness and naturalness (as in "Myconos") that is more relaxed than, say, the bright, pop laziness of the 1960s swimming-pool pictures by David Hockney.

Yet nature is always interesting in Jarman, who became an expert gardener; he named one of his films *The Garden* and one of his books *Modern Nature*. In the tradition of lyric film, which depends so much on self-conscious artifice, both Cocteau and Pasolini tend to denaturalize nature, to complicate the nature-art dichotomy until no "real" world seems left. Tarkovsky, on the other hand, is often thought of as a poet of the earth, who depicts the watery earth as people's true home. Jarman, working in the earth, might seem potentially to be more in the Tarkovsky line of descent, or to be following Wordsworth in the English poetic tradition. Yet in "Gypsy" the natural world appears out of a dream, out of the liminal place where "the image scatters on the silver." Beginning with the myth of Narcissus, the watery mirror has been an archetypical image of art, and it appears again in a later poem, "Death Comes Through Mirrors," a phrase clearly indebted to Cocteau's *Orpheus*. Since the clouds reflect "the fire of the billboard promised by / stalking the violet sky," the worlds of nature and art collapse in a hall of mirrors, of reflections.

As we would expect in any selection of travelers' anecdotes, there are numerous appearances of water, sky, sun, and moon, but *A Finger in the Fishes Mouth* always returns to the question of their representation and reproduction. The natural world is not experienced in an unmediated fashion; it is always reorganized, reordered. The four-line poem "November" shows form and color transposed onto nature, like the landscapes that Antonioni literally painted in his films:

> A glimpse of ones [*sic*] own exile
> radiating across green lawns
> passing geometric laughter
> someone had painted the oak yellow

Jarman's vision is attracted to strange and vivid colors: a "rouged automobile" ("Fargo 64"), a "flying scarlet apotheosis" ("From Gypsy Mar 1 66"), "the sky reached forth vermillion fingers" ("Marc Rothko's Dawn"). The numerous flowers in the poems seem there more to bear color than to embody natural fecundity: "I left blue flowers / by the phalloi of dionysus" ("Patmos-Delos"); "and he answered marigolds for malice" ("Freedoms [*sic*] a Drug That's Bought and Sold"); "he is a young man / with violets in his eyes" ("Death Comes Through Mirrors"); "and now the dandelion clock has stopped" ("Poem V"). The reproduction of nature is self-consciously evident in the varied style of the postcards—some of which are photographic or realistic, some of which are caricatured or sentimental—and, further, in repeated phrases such as "dreaming of a Kodak summer" ("Venice April 64") and "watched this city / recede like a Kodak dream" ("Manhattan"). The natural world is nearly always surrounded by signs of people, of art or technology:

> the mountains ring the edge of the world
> and the city watches
> the river flows from the mountains of
> the edge of the world

Derek Jarman and Lyric Film

through wild rose woods
and circles the city
punctuating its superhighways with bridges

"CALGARY JULY 64"

How directly does Jarman's book of poems represent the subject of homosexuality? One could look for signs of sexual dissidence in the accidental and surrealistic nature of composition embodied here, and that is certainly a point of lyric film—the refusal to play it straight. Jarman's multivocal, hard-to-dissect poems might be said to enact a sexuality that is polymorphous, promiscuous, or disobedient. The kinds of disrupted meanings and semiotic stresses that Thomas E. Yingling finds in Hart Crane's poetry might also be observed in Jarman's.[7] Yet Jarman is more explicit than Crane; he not only performs, stylistically, what might be considered a discourse of dissidence, but he also trains his eye more directly on the subject of homosexuality, on male homoerotic desire, itself.

We have already mentioned the gallery of hunky boys at the end, which transparently signals gay desire, but such transparency does not mean that the scene is simple to read. The appearance of homoerotic desire in the book's conclusion is not entirely without precedent in the book. For even the second poem is set thus in Greece:

I left blue flowers
by the phalloi of dionysus
thinking of the lions of
apollo

"PATMOS-DELOS"

With the gallery of the final postcard in mind, such Greek settings and images will necessarily acquire a homoerotic resonance. The "blue flower" in this instance is probably a delphinium—the flower that will conclude Jarman's meditations at the other end of his career, in *Blue*.

43

I place a delphinium, Blue, upon your grave.[8]

Mythologically, the delphinium is associated with the hermaphrodite, and so expresses "Greek love" from an otherwise conventional postcard.

The fourth poem, "November," is circumspect in language ("A glimpse of ones own exile"), but perhaps more open in image: the picture is a sphinx in front of a column in Alexandria. *My Alexandria*, as Mark Doty says in the title poem to that collection, is the beautiful and sensual Alexandria of

Constantine Cavafy, which Jarman, in his turn, makes his own by featuring his trademark sphinx, an embodiment of code and secret.[9] But not all the Greek poems have implications. "Myconos," for example, takes taciturnity to an extreme—pure image, haiku-like in both picture and poem.

> now the fishing boats
> are back in the harbor
> the wind is again on the beaches

Heterosexuality, in its turn, if not overtly sabotaged, is at least put through several bouts of indignity and ridicule. The fifth poem ("Stampede July 64") sits across from a postcard, perhaps from the 1920s, titled "Your Ideal Love Mate." Beneath a young woman's face framed in a heart, the quasi-astrological prose says:

> Your Ideal Mate may be a slim, brunette, plain and easy on the eyes; no matter, if the lady is a good sport and that everything she does is tempered with the saving grace of a sense of humor and fair play. Of course, she has the necessary feminine virtues of neatness, loyalty, intelligence, personality and appeal.

A contemporary audience will smile condescendingly at the archaic idealism, but in proximity to the homoerotic outlines in the book, this becomes an ideal attacked not just for a generic kind of backwardness, but for its heterosexual assumptions. The postcard's accompanying poem is more subtle and vague—performing as a poem across from this didactic prose—but it, too, presents a species of heterosexual mythology:

> Lady in an ashcan dress
>   seventy and a day
> pass polka dot lovelies
> corkscrew man
> loves Millie from Florida
> in cork mythologies
> man man
> I can supply you socks
> and she can have embroideries
> oh lady in the ashcan dress
> pass these electric roundabouts
>   and wurlitzer tunes
>
> "STAMPEDE JULY 64"

The conclusion does not insist very vigorously on a satiric reading, but the poem is playing with easy images of heterosexuality: the "corkscrew man" in "cork mythologies"—a Jarmanesque version of Alexander Pope's sex talk:

Men prove with child, as powerful fancy works,
And maids, turned bottles, call aloud for corks.[10]

Many of the postcards in the book are entirely devoid of people, which deprives the viewer of heterosexual imagery. The picture across from "Venice April 64" contains the only heterosexual couple in the book, and this picture is deliberately stylized, an elegant cartoon. The accompanying poem pitches this stereotypical image—the couple looks out over moonlit water— into a quietly mocked realm of dream, of fantasy:

[we wait and listen]
    in a drowning city
dreaming of a Kodak summer
and an important seduction
by a young girl
of a languid soldier
with lightning behind the houses

"VENICE APRIL 64"

The poem concludes with a seemingly enthusiastic moment of the sublime, but "an important seduction" is a very distant way of commenting on this erotic dream.

Sexuality courses through the collection of poems quietly, quasi-randomly, and without clearly defined persons or subjects to convey it. Even the title, A Finger in the Fishes Mouth, carries sexual innuendo along with its surrealism, but not with any further sense of sexual orientation or description. The most overt sexual image in the book is also unusually tactless; as Tony Peake describes the situation: "Unfortunately, the printers chosen to print the collection were Christian and baulked at the postcard selected for 'Christmas 64': that of a priest being pleasured by a nun. The offending image had to be put inside an envelope and inserted afterwards."[11] Thoughts of the commercialization of Christmas always brought on extreme responses from Jarman, both in his journals and in films like The Garden, and there is nothing like this postcard elsewhere in the collection. The change in tonality occasioned by this postcard is not unlike

45

the sudden outburst of musical theatre at the end of *The Tempest* or the staged interruptions in *The Garden*. In the poetry book, as in later films, Jarman is happy to break up his own brooding atmosphere, to fragment the appearances of integrity and coherence. More typical of Jarman's approach to Christianity is the conclusion of "Assisi" (the facing postcard shows St. Francis with St. Clare, their eyes turned upward):

> At assisi then
> there's a dive
> to commemorate Francis
>
> . . . .
> decor by a host of Italian primitives
> of cribs and popes
> and a dame called clara
> who he never touched
> whose place is the other
> side of the town

Here Jarman's voice lapses into laughable beatnik-ism (I hesitate to say intentionally), but this relatively quiet ("cool") kind of comment on Christian repressiveness is more typical of *A Finger in the Fishes Mouth* than a bawdy postcard.

Among many poems that seem lazily sensuous and invitingly open, the most overtly sexual poem is "Marc Rothko's Dawn":

> By the time the dawn had shrunken
> After the time of coupling and uncoupling
> And the rapture among the sofas
> By the time the night had shrunken
>   with a small protest
>   and the skies had come stars in the universal orgasm
> After the trees had wept
>   their leaves amongst the sky scrapers
>   lamenting the transience of billboards
> After the phallus had fallen in the still sad stasis
> And the milkman had broken the silence
> By the time the night had shrunken
>   and the shadows were streaked with silver
> In the wholly miraculous interval
>   thy sky reached forth vermillion fingers
>   and quietly extinguished the light bulbs

The poem itself does not seem to comment on a particular Rothko painting, either early or late, and the postcard shows a rocky beach, like a moonscape. But the imagery might be seen as a reading of any number of Rothko's luminous, pulsating abstractions. The seriousness (literariness) of the poem is signaled by the capital letters running down the left margin, an almost unparalleled formal feature in this book. The merging of the apocalyptic and the domestic, which will later become so characteristic of Jarman's cinematic style, dwells at the heart of this poem. Sexuality is brilliant and radiant, but unclearly embodied ("coupling and uncoupling," "the universal orgasm"). An abstract masculinity is associated with the detumescence of dawn ("After the phallus had fallen in the still sad stasis"), but the poem posits a moment of "miracle" and wonder even after post-coital sadness ("the sky reached forth vermillion fingers"). The painting, the picture, and the poem are able to hold the luminous moment before us, but the later movies will move on. How these films proceed, and how they represent, will focus our attention for the remainder of the book.

II. THE MIRROR AND THE SEA: TOWARD A THEORY OF REPRESENTATION IN DEREK JARMAN'S CINEMA

Having described in some detail the workings-out of poetry and image in *A Finger in the Fishes Mouth*, I will in this section attempt to describe a model for the appearances of poetry and subjectivity in Jarman's cinema. How to characterize Jarman's cinematic subjectivity? What queer subjectivity and identity might entail more generally remains a crucial subject for ongoing critical discussion and interrogation. The term "queer" itself—in contrast to "gay"—signals a refusal to hold still, essentialize, submit to definition.[12] And cinematic subjectivity is also an extraordinarily rich and complicated topic, much discussed, with no end in sight. It is to be expected, therefore, that the models set forth in the pages that follow will be quite particular to Jarman. Self-conscious artifice and oceanic mobility will emerge as signature elements in this description. Taken together with the history of lyric cinema that we outlined in Chapter 1, these models should assist us in our discussions of the specific films that will occupy us in the remaining chapters.

The key to all of Jarman's works is the relationship between the mirror and the ocean. The mirror signals the replication of identity and models the desire for a like self. This desire for the same has often been seen as central to a queer aesthetics, and I will discuss some of the recent contributions to this theoretical framework. Yet the mirror in the original myth of

Narcissus is, in fact, water; nature and art potentially alternate. The mirror that dissolves into water no longer reflects, but absorbs. The object is not duplicated; instead, it is consumed or drowned. Sameness and oblivion, repetition and dissolution: these are the polar extremes that the narcissistic mirror holds within it.

The most recent and considerable contribution to the study of narcissism in relation to queer theory is Steven Bruhm's *Reflecting Narcissus: A Queer Aesthetic* (2001).[13] Bruhm's wide-ranging study, which emphasizes historical particularity and interpretive variation through motif, analyzes literary examples from European Romanticism (Friedrich von Schlegel, Samuel Taylor Coleridge, Lord Byron) through Oscar Wilde, past Hermann Hesse, Tennessee Williams, and Vladimir Nabokov, to conclude with a look at contemporary gothic fiction. Bruhm intends to recuperate Narcissus for positive models of homoerotic desire, models that are not burdened with egoism as a consequence. The readings of Narcissus are multiple rather than reductive, asking us "continually to rethink the erotic possibilities of narcissistic replication" (p. 79). The queerness of Narcissus exists in the way that desire is both repetitive and various, reduplicating and multiplying at the same time. As Bruhm writes in conclusion, "If there is a 'use' in Narcissus, it is in his dangers. Narcissus, who is said to aspire to that which is the same, is continually destroying the political safety promised by sameness" (p. 178). Although Bruhm does not emphasize the artificial or oceanic aspects of the mirror, which are crucial for Jarman, this way of speaking, which emphasizes flexibility and multiplicity, will be quite to the point in our characterizations of Jarman's representations of "homo-narcissistic" desire.

Jarman reproduces the image of Narcissus throughout his cinematic career, from *Sebastiane* to *Edward II*, and I will emphasize the varying significance of mirrors and doubling in nearly all of the works. There is no single meaning behind the mirror, but there is usually a network of related associations and motifs. Jarman himself is wary of the negative reading of Narcissus from the very beginning—that the desire for the same is flawed, egotistical, a kind of self-absorption. We have already noticed, therefore, how often Jarman empties out the "I" in *A Finger in the Fishes Mouth*; the poems cross through Beat territory, but without the voluble, self-satisfied "I" of Ginsberg or Ferlinghetti:

> I have seen
> serpent taxis
> jewly gemming
> winding through stainless steel corsets

narcissistically reflecting
and scratching the sky

"MANHATTAN"[14]

Watching reflections and shimmerings is signature Jarman, yet the
speaker acknowledges that these reflections are "narcissistic." The poem as
a whole walks into typically urban, Beat territory, but this "I" seems relatively nonjudgmental, nonparticipatory compared to the voice of Ferlinghetti or Ginsberg, and most of Jarman's poems are much less "I"-powered
than this. For example:

A smiling friendly image!
    neither harvest
    neither thro' a pane of glass
    neither crescent
    nor geometrical
    nor egocentric
    new image

"MOON II"

Interested in images and atmospheres rather than egos, Jarman's poems
remain aware of the egotism that may attend the mirror's reflection.
Although Jarman will not associate the mirror permanently with either
extreme—with celebration or condemnation—the moral reading of the
mirror is something with which he is often concerned, and again from the
very beginning.

Earl Jackson, Jr.'s *Strategies of Deviance: Studies in Gay Male Representation* (1995) is another recent and important contribution to the
theoretical modeling of homosocial narcissism.[15] Without distinguishing
too much between media, Jackson treats examples from both literature and
film and includes extended readings of texts such as Wilde's "The Portrait
of W. H." and a selection of works by Samuel R. Delany, in addition to
films by Pedro Almodóvar and, indeed, Derek Jarman.

"Specularity" for Jackson is sometimes literally Narcissus at the mirroring pool, but it usually takes on broader implications: "the 'specular'
refers to the demarcation of subject positions in relation to an image or
images and to the schematics of intersubjective differences (subject-object,
passive-active, knower-known, self-other) established in the direction and
'command' of the look" (p. 44). Jackson's readings are brilliant and sophisticated, but lose the focus that I would like to see on that mirror. Jackson's

49

ideas about the mirror and homoerotic desire can be rewardingly developed and particularized, since he chooses not to discuss a great many of the important examples in Jarman. Although the paperback cover of *Strategies of Deviance* shows a young man looking at himself in the mirror, the text contains no mention of the doublings in *The Angelic Conversation* or *The Garden*, mirrorings around which those films revolve. Yet as with Bruhm's study, we can use the many insights of Jackson's book in order to move beyond the examples he provides. *Strategies of Deviance* helps us understand and appreciate the complicated intersubjective space between "subject" and "object." Even though the mirror repeats, there are also reversals (looker-looked at) aplenty inside that space of mirroring.

Both Bruhm and Jackson model their readings on (and even in contrast to) Freud, and a key text for each of them is Freud's *Leonardo da Vinci and a Memory of His Childhood*. Working from Freud, Foucault, and others strengthens the quality of generalization in either case; we have a strong sense of how narcissistic figuration and specular identification works in twentieth-century gay writing. For my own purposes, I will particularize these approaches in a number of ways: by insisting on the specificity of the mirror; by reminding ourselves of the artificiality of the mirror (which is doubly emphasized by the cinematic medium); and by contextualizing that mirror not with Freud (i.e., modern thought), but rather with both lyric film (a subdivision of modern film) and Jarman's favorite, Jung. Whereas we may well be skeptical about the recurrent deployment of the mirror in general studies of psychoanalysis and cinema, we might be likely to trust specific references to analytical psychology, particularly when we know they have been intended by the author or director himself.[16] But before we arrive at mythmakers like Cocteau and Jung—clear predecessors to Jarman the filmmaker—let us tread once more, to some degree, down the theoretical hall of mirrors that leads toward the particulars of Jarman's practice.

A good place to start is with the French feminist writer Luce Irigaray, for whom both mirrors and the ocean are crucial images in her overall critique of patriarchal visuality. The mirror, for Irigaray, emblematizes the patriarchal attempt to focus, order, and rule. Man invents his own subjectivity by rendering woman as object, "as a bench mark that is ultimately more crucial than the subject, for he can sustain himself only by bouncing off some objectiveness, some objective."[17] Irigaray's conceptual contrast to the fixed, imprisoning focus of mirrors is fluidity, polyvocality, formlessness. Thus she follows *Speculum of the Other Woman* (*Speculum de l'autre femme*, 1974) with *Marine Lover of Friedrich Nietzsche* (*Amante Marine*, 1983).[18] In flowing, performative prose, Irigaray maintains that Nietzsche fears the fluidity and formlessness of the ocean. Irigaray desires to shatter mirrors and inhabit the ocean.[19] Judith Butler, among others, has criticized Irigaray for the global reach of her theories, which are in some respects as monolithic as the patriarchal systems themselves.[20] But for our purposes, Irigaray's rather archetypal, even mystical critiques of patriarchal systems of knowing and seeing immediately point to the conflicted center at the heart of Jarman's mirror.

The mirror functions in varying ways in Jarman's films, yet altogether its repeated appearances signal a contradiction characteristic of the theorizing of male gay relationships. Male gay desire and female desire cannot be modeled equivalently, even without taking into account the social positionings of race and class, which are so often the crux of discussions within gay studies and women's studies. Male gay desire originates from within the patriarchy, whereas lesbian desire is doubly oppressed. Seeking both to particularize the sense of polymorphous sexuality that "queer" tends to evoke and to argue against the self-erasure of the gay that seems to be the consequence of much theoretical argumentation, Leo Bersani writes that "male homosexuality has always manifested itself socially as a highly specific blend of conformism and transgression."[21] This certainly comes through in Jarman's films, full-length features that blend traditional art-house subjects with experimental techniques and gay activist politics. Jarman's films, in certain respects, take the side of French feminists such as Hélène Cixous and Irigaray, in that he might be said to write, cinematically, a kind of *écriture féminine* against the law, against the patriarchy. Yet, as a man, he necessarily also inhabits a position of power and control, of ideological focus rather than dispersal. Hence the pivotal images of the mirror and the sea: the mirror that Irigaray rejects, and the sea that she invokes. Jarman's cinema proposes both repetition and dispersal, and these images capture the seemingly contradictory impulses in his work—for and against tradition, inside and outside the law.

Jarman's first cinematic mirror inhabits a dream world, in his short film *Art of Mirrors* (1973).[22] Fire, now, not water, is the archetypal image with which the film begins, as we see flames dancing over wind-blown ashes. The art of mirrors seems to be an attempt to contain this destruction, this fire and this power, but the art, as we see piercingly before us, is fleeting, and blinding as well. The film consists almost entirely of figures who hold the same round disc toward the camera and use it to reflect light back into the camera, a light so blinding, in flashes, that it blacks out the entire screen. The world that these figures inhabit—one female, one male, and one strangely masked third—is located in the imagination. The figures pose or move in grey slow motion; images of bloodred pyramids are intercut twice to indicate mystery and otherworldliness. These mirrors, which shine out like stars in the darkness, do not reflect the figures. Hence these mirrors are not idiomatically narcissistic. The figures move horizontally, left and right across the screen, but the film concludes with the female figure holding the mirror and advancing toward the camera. The rhythm of the film concludes with this advance, which rounds out a meditation on light and form told in the language of a dream.

Art of Mirrors burns with the light of imagination, but not yet with the particularized outlines of sexuality. By contrast, in *The Angelic Conversation* these light-reflecting discs will be held aloft by male lovers, and the mirrors there truly indicate desire; but for now, in this early short film, the light is only light, or the light of a dream. Many of these early films are dreamscapes open to the interpretation of dreams.

Films, indeed, are dreams in the dark, and cinema and psychoanalysis therefore share parallel histories.[23] Since Hugo Munsterberg (*The Film: The Silent Photoplay in 1916: A Psychological Study* [1916]) and Siegfried Kracauer (*From Caligari to Hitler: A Psychological History of the German Film* [1947]), psychological analyses—of both individual works and cinema itself—have been numerous and influential.[24] In contemporary film studies, variations on psychoanalytic models hold sway in every quarter, finding an anchor in the film journal *Screen* and extending into some branches of feminism and queer studies. Since film projects a world of erotic desire and a world of the imaginary, it makes sense that both Freud and Jacques Lacan would be brought forward to analyze cinema, which we see in such famous theoretical works as Christian Metz's *The Imaginary Signifier* and Laura Mulvey's "Visual Pleasure and Narrative Cinema." In academic circles, certainly, Freudian- and Lacanian-inspired or -provoked analyses have vanquished Jungian readings entirely.[25] Yet many artists, Jarman included, find Jung a far more inspiring figure than Freud with respect to creativity and the imagination. It gives cause to wonder why theories and interpretations of cinema do not refer more often to Jung than Freud or Lacan. Freud and Lacan are no more rigorous scientists than Jung: all are storytellers, mythographers. Hence it is an important aside when Jean Mitry, in his difficult, cerebral *Semiotics and the Analysis of Film* overtly rejects the usefulness of Lacan:

> The mysteries of the expression to which the cinema constantly leads us may well lie in the unconscious, the collective unconscious, which is closer, in my view, to Jung's or Cassirer's ideas than Lacan's hypo-

theses, but any further investigation would divert us from the more general considerations of this present study.[26]

Nor do we need to propose a Jungian theory of cinema here, because of the more specific considerations of our study, but we might sketch out some ideas that might aim toward such a proposal, with reference to Jarman's own particular practice. Key Jungian texts for Jarman are *Seven Sermons to the Dead* and, especially, the *Alchemical Studies*.[27] At one point, Jarman also obsessively read the Jungian analyst James Hillman.[28] As we shall see, Hillman provides clear and suggestive guides to creativity and interpretation. By expanding and stimulating his interest in alchemy, Jarman's discovery of Jung's work complemented research he had already performed as set designer for Ken Russell's *The Devils* (1971). The alchemical tradition is centered on magic and transformation and "tends towards the heretical."[29] From a critical point of view, avant-garde, magical film might more readily be associated with the alchemical-Jungian than with the Freudian-Lacanian. This kind of association is embodied most clearly in the extraordinary films of the American director Kenneth Anger.

Anger takes an ecstatic, almost literal-minded approach to the alchemical possibilities of cinema. The worlds he envisions are uniquely his own, strange places to inhabit, charactered with figures straight out of alchemical tradition. Isis and Osiris walk around the pyramids in *Lucifer Rising*, and Anger himself plays "the Magus." *Invocation of My Demon Brother* elaborately enacts that conjuration. *The Inauguration of the Pleasure Dome*—perhaps Anger's most compelling work—performs rituals from Aleister Crowley, and Crowley's head even appears from time to time. Anger's films do not just consider the metaphors that cinema is *like* magic or *like* alchemy; they literalize those conceits and then proceed to act out both ritual and transcendental vision.

Jarman's films also import the literal magician or two (John Dee, Prospero), appropriate images from Egypt (Jarman's script for *Akenaten*), perform strange rituals (the women running their fingers around humming wine glasses in *The Garden*), and project dream images (*The Last of England*), but they do not so directly attempt to reproduce an alchemical experiment. Anger's more overtly heretical intensities ("Priapus shadowing Narcissus in ecstatic addiction, in sadistic fury")[30] should be contrasted with Jarman's more muted mythologizing. Although Jarman spends time in apocalyptic realms, he often balances these excursions with domestic spaces. Anger's exuberant cinema literalizes, therefore, the idea of the transcendental:

It was precisely this cinematic potential for expressing spontaneity that attracted me as a form of personal art. I saw its disruptive strength: a way of bringing about a change. This means of expression can transcend the aesthetic to become experience. My ideal was a living cinema that explored the dynamism of the visual communication of beauty, fear and joy. I wanted my personal cinema to transmute the dance of my interior being into a poetry of moving images that would create a new climate of spiritual revelation where the spectator, forgetting that he or she was looking at a work of art, could only become one with the drama. . . .

These prophets will restore faith in a pure cinema of sensual revelation. They will re-establish the primacy of the image. They will teach us the principles of their faith: that we participate before evaluating. We will give back to the dream its first state of veneration. We will recall primitive mysteries. The future of film is in the hands of the poet and his camera. . . .

Angels exist. Nature provides the inexhaustible flow of visions of beauty. It is for the poet, with his personal vision, to capture them.[31]

Anger's magical poetry of the image, as embodied in his films, is tremendously important for Jarman, but too idealistic and too relentlessly ecstatic for Jarman's sensibility and his times.

The embarrassments often associated with Jung are similar to those aroused by the feverish intensities of Anger. It is no shame to follow Freud, although that road is littered with guilt and difficulty, because Freud maps the territory of sexuality, desire, eros—those things that are part of our material lives. But for Jung, sexuality is a subtopic of spirituality. As Jung writes in *Memories, Dreams, Reflections*:

> One thing was clear: Freud, who had always made much of his irreligiosity, had now constructed a dogma; or rather, in the place of a jealous God whom he had lost, had substituted another compelling image, that of sexuality. It was no less insistent, exacting, domineering, threatening, and morally ambivalent than the original one. Just as the psychically stronger agency is given "divine" or "daemonic" attributes, so the "sexual libido" took over the role of a *deus absconditus*, a hidden or concealed god. The advantage of this transformation for Freud was, apparently, that he was able to regard the new numinous principle as scientifically irreproachable and free from all religious taint. At bottom, however, the numinosity, that is, the psychological

qualities of the two rationally incommensurable opposites—Yahweh and sexuality—remained the same.[32]

Even though the scientific aspects of Freud and Lacan have been continuously and invariably emptied out over the years, their skeptical, rational, atheistic approach has made them more worthy to follow, borrow from, or argue with than the "spiritualist" Jung, who recorded not only his dreams but his visions. But with a view toward understanding film, one need not necessarily believe in angels in some kind of naive, intoxicated way; one might, instead, believe in film, a rather more secular transaction and one that may still be subjected to sociological inquiry. "Both alchemy and the art of memory work within minimal space," writes James Hillman, using references of scale that would be important for Jarman; "we learn that one need not soar and plunge on grand shamanistic journeys in order to affect the soul to its depths."[33]

Here "soul" is one of those embarrassing words derived from Jung's spiritual concerns; "I believe with Jung that each of us is 'modern man in search of a soul.'"[34] Yet Hillman uses "soul" intentionally—where he might have chosen the more scientific-sounding "psyche"—for its religious resonances. Hillman's writing seeks unashamedly to inspire "soul-making" (a concept direct from Keats) and attempts in numerous places to define and contextualize this abstract and archaic term:

> First, "soul" refers to the *deepening* of events into experiences; second, the significance soul makes possible, whether in love or in religious concern, derives from its special *relation with death*. And third, by "soul" I mean the imaginative possibility in our natures, the experiencing through reflective speculation, dream, image, and *fantasy*—that mode which recognizes all realities as primarily symbolic or metaphorical.[35]

What soul may come to grasp, according to Hillman, is more than "the gift of speech" or "the gift of interpretation" but "the gift of faith in images, a psychological faith, which permits belief and enjoins conviction, a fervid animal faith in the depths, a dove in the belly that gives one the sense that the psyche is the first reality and that we are always soul."[36]

This ideal, optimistic language may well seem too abstract for critical use, and I believe that it is. But it does, positively, help lead us away from a Freudian theater of sexuality and sexual repression and take us toward a Jungian theater of spirituality and spiritual repression. On the cinematic landscape, one need not think here only of serious figures like Tarkovsky

55

and Ingmar Bergman over against Hollywood and exploitative consumerism. And a Jungian or spiritual attitude need not look toward only—to use Paul Schrader's examples—Yasujiro Ozu, Robert Bresson, and Carl Dreyer.[37] For Bresson and Tarkovsky, as well as Anger, may only be literalizing, in a way, the transcendental aspect inherent in all of cinema. The point is that it is not just visionary cinema by Anger or Brakhage that depends on an audience's desire for vision. As Bruce Kawin argues, even a mass genre such as the horror film does also:

> In this sense the horror film asserts the survival of "paganism" (the gypsies are right) and the inadequacy of science ("All astronomers are amateurs," a theme recognizable in *The Thing*)—a return to magic. Judaeo-Christianity represses, in this sense, the mystical unconscious that the horror-system allows to be expressed. (All this opens the possibility of a Jungian reading as well.) We may recall Van Helsing's pronouncement in *Dracula* that "the strength of the vampire is that people will *not* believe in him."[38]

The Jungian cinematic screen analyzes our faith in all images, in all kinds of film, and it expresses or represses the mystical unconscious. This mysticism may no more exist in reality than does the Lacanian "phallus," but it reroutes our critical attention, allowing us another way of speaking to what the cinema is there for and how it communicates.

Although an artist might well be interested in Jung, alchemy, or the soul, mysticism is not, it would seem, a critically viable category these days. Yet enlightenment reason having come under critical attack throughout the century (*The Dialectic of Enlightenment* by Max Horkheimer and Theodor Adorno is a well-known analysis), categories contrary to reason are more likely open to critical consideration. Thus Georges Bataille often writes about mystical sensibility; Derrida's deconstruction is sometimes thought of as a "negative theology"; and writers like Julia Kristeva and Irigaray have both written about mystics—all of them in search of alternatives to linear, centered (sometimes called patriarchal) discourse. In the wake of phenomenology, contemporary invocations of mysticism now emphasize its immanent rather than transcendent characteristics. Mystical experience is today more likely found *in* the body rather than out, and in the context of a multifarious deity rather than a unified one.

Since Gilles Deleuze posits his work in direct conflict with Freudian models (as set down most concretely in *Anti-Oedipus: Capitalism and Schizophrenia* by Deleuze and Guattari), his remarkable critical texts *Cinema 1* and *Cinema 2* might be read as species of rerouted Jungian criticism, where the emphasis has been drawn away from repetitive, patriarchal sexuality and moved toward the thinking and experiencing of the cinematic image. For example, Deleuze chooses "the crystals of time" as an image of cinematic projection and movement. These crystals may be mirrors (in Orson Welles's *The Lady from Shanghai*, "where the principle of indiscernibility reaches its peak") or ships, "caught between the two crystalline faces of the sea."[39] The image of the crystal conjoins a self-consciousness about the cinematic projection of light with ideas of fragmentation and fluidity.

Deleuze, it turns out, is quite happy to use the abstractions of spirit and body as long as they are set into a world of bodies (or body parts) and money (though not in easily identifiable socioeconomic language):

> Perhaps this is also the perspective from which to understand the splendor of the images in Herzog's *Heart of Glass*, and the film's double aspect. The search of the alchemical heart and secret, for the red crystal, is inseparable from the search for cosmic limits, as the highest tension of the spirit and the deepest level of reality. But the crystal's fire will have to connect with the whole range of manufacturing for the world, for its part stop being a flat, amorphous environment which ends at the edge of a gulf, and to reveal infinite crystalline potentialities in itself ("the earth rises up from the waters, I see a new earth. . . ."). In this film Herzog has set out the greatest crystal-images in the history of cinema.[40]

Deleuze returns over and over to the self-reflexive aspects of cinema, which might be read monolithically as elements of the ideological apparatus, but which he encourages us to read both archetypically, as fundamental building blocks, and also fluidly.[41] Deleuze's postmodernist descriptions often capture the seeming contradictions in Jarman's films, which turn between narcissism and dissolution, poetic tradition and aesthetic subversion, artificial self-reflexivity and passionately romantic ideology.

Cocteau, the profound cinematic theoretician of lyric accident whom we met in Chapter 1, is also, in his own inimitable manner, a great cinematic theoretician of renewed myth and modernist archetype. Cocteau always speaks of film in terms of the dream, as in his own prologue—spoken *in propria persona*—to *The Testament of Orpheus*:

> It is the film-maker's privilege to be able to allow a large number of people to dream the same dream together, and to show us, moreover, the optical illusions of unreality with the rigor of realism. In short, it is an admirable vehicle for poetry.[42]

Cocteau embraces the metaphors of cinema as dream and as poetry, but refuses the narrow readings of Freudian psychoanalysis. And so his prologue continues:

> My film is nothing other than a striptease show, consisting of removing my body bit by bit and revealing my soul quite naked. For there is a considerable public interested in the world of shadows, starved for the more-real-than-reality, which one day will become the sign of our times.[43]

Cocteau deliberately invokes a figure of marginalized sexuality (a "striptease show"), but directs the emphasis not toward a naked body, but toward a naked "soul." Despite his modernist tact and wit, Cocteau takes us away from the Freudian ironies of sexuality and toward a kind of refashioned, but still magical Jungian cosmos of dream and myth.

The veer away from Freud in this dream-film is explicit in several key moments. A little way into *The Testament of Orpheus*, the Poet (Cocteau) says to himself:

> Of course works of art create themselves, and dream of killing both father and mother. Of course they exist before the artist discovers them. But it's always "Orpheus," always "Oedipus." I thought that by changing castles I'd change ghosts and that here a flower could make them flee.[44]

Cocteau amusingly wants to escape both Orpheus, the poet to whom he continually returns, and Oedipus, the figure toward which all narratives and all dreams eventually descend. Yet even Cocteau's film runs into Oedipus, the blind Oedipus being led away from Thebes by Antigone. The parallel between old Oedipus, in the last play of Sophocles' trilogy, and Cocteau, in the last film of his Orpheus trilogy (his last film of all), is readily apparent. But in this scene both men are blind (Cocteau wears artificial eyes), and they do not see each other. We overhear Cocteau say, "The Sphinx, Oedipus
58 . . . It is possible that one day we can meet those we have been too anxious to know, and not see them."[45]

In Sophocles all paths cross, and all crossings fatalistically lead to death. In Cocteau, by contrast, paths loop around and diverge; figures pass, accidentally, and poets never die. The avoidance of Sophoclean and Freudian doom in *The Testament* is underscored by having Jean Marais— Orpheus himself—play the wandering Oedipus. Yes, it is always Orpheus, or Oedipus, but Cocteau himself moves on. Cocteau wants to inhabit a world of myth and dreams, but wants the interpretation of that world to be less narrow, less fatalistic than Freudian psychoanalysis might allow.

Cocteau continually returns in his films to archetypal and magical images, and he reads these flexibly, fluidly, and self-reflexively. Cocteau's brilliant use of the mirror is renowned, and in both *The Blood of a Poet* and *Orpheus*, Cocteau associates that mirror with water. In *The Blood of a Poet*, the living statue coaxes the poet into the mirror, and he falls in with a splash. In *Orpheus*, Heurtebise tells Orpheus that he will go through the mirrors like water ("comme l'eau"); the surface of the mirror becomes water when the magic gloves strike it. Beyond the surface of the mirror in *The Blood of a Poet* is a black void where the poet is lost in obscurity and darkness. In *Orpheus* the poet moves with unbearable slowness through a world of ruins and night. In Cocteau's films, a mirror's reflection repeats the image, but contains also chaos and oblivion. In Heurtebise's poetic interpretation: "Mirrors are the doors through which death comes and goes. Look at yourself in all your life and you will see death at work like bees in a hive of glass."[46]

Jarman wrote a script called *The Bees of Infinity*; another script centered on one of Cocteau's homosexual relationships through the imagery of Cocteau's mirrors.[47] Here the mirror opens out not into water, but into snow, as Peake writes in his biography:

> Jarman also started a script about another of his idols, Jean Cocteau, and his relationship with the young Creole writer Raymond Radiguet. It is 1963. The elderly Cocteau is in a lift. He stares at his reflection in the mirror. "Mirrors are the doors through which death comes and goes. Watch yourself all your life in a mirror and you will see death at work like bees in a glass hive." He opens the door to his apartment to find "a snow blizzard taking place in his room." His furniture is buried under drifts of snow. Giant icicles hang from the chandeliers. We are taken back in time to Cocteau's childhood and a dialogue between himself and Radiguet. Where Cocteau is hesitant and conservative, Radiguet is an utter rebel. Yet again, Jarman was probing one of his favorite dichotomies.[48]

Cocteau's taciturnity in film with respect to his homosexuality causes Jarman to regard him as conservative, but Cocteau's self-expressiveness still serves as a model for Jarman's autobiographical impulses. Hence this exchange in an interview from *Kicking the Pricks*:

> Why did you put yourself in the film [*The Last of England*]?
> I think film-makers should bring much more of their experience to their work than they do. I've never understood why so many are

59

content to be transmitters of the second-hand. It's epidemic in our film culture. I've always admired Cocteau's *Testament*. It's one of the bravest failures of the cinema. Welles worked that way, and Pasolini; they suffered for it.[49]

The representation of sexuality in Cocteau is usually archetypal and oblique, but in his autobiographical *Testament of Orpheus*, there are several figures that connote male erotic desire. Both are characters that blend animal and man: the horse-man and the dog-man. A horse-man leads Cocteau into the underground cavern at the beginning in a kind of seduction; the horse-man removes his horse's-head mask to reveal his beautiful human face beneath. The dog-men, on the other hand, are more comical than divine. Naked except for spotted swimming trunks (and dog's head—Anubis—and tail), one man grabs the other around the waist to make a dog, the way children might otherwise make a horse. The lady who sees the dog exclaims, "I must say, everything is topsy-turvy today," and Cocteau gets the last word on the beast—"What a strange dog."[50]

Mirrors repeat back the self (Cocteau runs into his double at one point), but they also invert the image, turn things around. "Mirrors reflect too much," says Cegeste; "They reverse images pretentiously and think they are profound."[51] But Cocteau is both the master of the statue and the master of reversal. The dream of cinema fixes the image and also lets images loose.

> Princess: What do you mean by "film"?
> Poet: A film is a petrifying source of thought. A film revives dead acts—A film allows one to give a semblance of reality to unreality.[52]

By creating another world, Cocteau repeatedly gives the impression of what it is like to live between two worlds. As the poet says during his interrogation:

> I would like to say that if I deserve punishment I cannot imagine any more painful one than being forced to live between two worlds, or to use your own words, between two realms.[53]

Reading the horse-men or dog-men as allegorizing in some respect this state of social betweenness—a betweenness that might be seen as related to a gay problematic—might well be too literal-minded a reading. But Cocteau's project in *The Testament* and elsewhere can easily be seen as pointing toward Jarman's more direct representations. The dream may be read not just as a universal dream of cosmic archetypes, but more concretely as the dream of homosexual doubling and multivalent sexuality. This is a dream that retires from Freud, but still returns to sexuality.

Derek Jarman and Lyric Film

Cocteau's mirror is one that both repeats and reverses. This is why so often the magic in his films comes from running the film backwards. Torn petals are reassembled as a flower; a fire burns backwards; Cocteau falls upward, alive again; Cegeste leaps out of the sea.

Cegeste: Aren't you an expert in Phoenixology?
Cocteau: What is that?
Cegeste: It is the science that allows one to die many times, only to be reborn.[54]

Cocteau's films perform the poetic accident of magical contingency and temporal reversal, but they potentially also announce the deliberate questioning of social norm and hierarchy that Jarman will come to reflect upon with his own mirrors and in his own abstract poetry.

From *Art of Mirrors* and *Sebastiane* to *Edward II* and *Blue*, Jarman's films return again and again to the image of the mirror. Nearly always, the mirror focuses our attention both on the reflection of light—on the technology associated with filmmaking—and on the doubling and reflection attending upon homosexual desire. Yet the image of the mirror is often also accompanied by a counterimage, as it were: the watery ocean, an image of dispersal and dissolution. The reflecting mirror and the shimmering ocean will appear over and over again in Jarman's films, but with different implications and different resonances, depending on the circumstances in which we find them. Eventually we will come to look upon the open expanses of *Blue*—as blue and endless as ocean or sky, but painted intentionally with Kleinian blue—as sheer, boundless artifice. For now, we will begin some sixteen years earlier, as Sebastian, the compelling focus of male gaze and desire, looks at himself in the archetypal pool of Narcissus.

Poetry and

Interpretation

in Three

Early

Features:

SEBASTIANE,

JUBILEE, *and*

THE TEMPEST

In many respects Jarman's first three feature films look very different from one another: (1) a Christian saint's tale, visually drenched in homoerotic display; (2) an up-to-the-minute, if apocalyptic depiction of punk culture in England; (3) a small-scale retelling of Shakespeare's culminating romance. *Sebastiane* (1976) is set in sun-washed desert; *Jubilee* (1978) takes place in some urban nightmare; and *The Tempest* (1979) unfolds not on an enchanted island, but in an empty, dark house. The overt homoeroticism of *Sebastiane* is greatly reduced in *Jubilee*, whereas *The Tempest* is even more sexually restrained.

3

Yet as different as the subjects seem, there are notable commonalities. For example, Jarman begins his career with a set of films that blend old and young, as if each film might be his last, a confluence most emblematically signaled through his early adaptation of *The Tempest*, with a young Prospero in the lead. Young and old at once: Jarman begins his career by forcing the underground up into the light of day in *Sebastiane*, where he aims his bevy of young boys toward the grim re-creation of a classic Christian painting. Old and young at once: he then journeys with Queen Elizabeth and John Dee into the inferno of contemporary punk.

Jarman, from the very beginning, occupies a radical and transgressive place with respect to cinema, and he is also interested, simultaneously, in relatively traditional questions of literary interpretation and artistic iconography. The graffiti world of *Jubilee*, where the punks read history books and the walls are scrawled with writing, exhibits visually the problems of communication and decipherability that one finds in both *Sebastiane* (spoken entirely in Latin) and also in *The Tempest* (where Prospero is surrounded by hieroglyphics). In this chapter we shall place particular emphasis on these questions of interpretation and readability, questions which are at the very heart of Jarman's poetic sensibility. We shall examine, furthermore, not only these three films, but also two unfilmed scripts from this period, *Akenaten* and *Neutron*. Like Jarman's early poems, these scripts have received almost no critical attention, but they too will help us understand the intentions and interrogations of Jarman's early art.

1. *Sebastiane, Akenaten,* AND THE CLARITY OF THE WORLD

Sebastiane is Jarman's first feature-length film, one already of historical significance as "one of the first independently gay-made feature films to get a wide showing (including, astonishingly and fortuitously, a commercial release in Britain)."[1] Jarman himself makes a similar and even stronger claim in *At Your Own Risk* (where he also declines to call it by its Latin name):

> *Sebastian* didn't present homosexuality as a problem and this was what made it different from all the British films that preceded it. It was also homoerotic. The film was historically important; no feature film had ventured here. There had been underground films, *Un Chant d'amour* and *Fireworks*, but *Sebastian* was in a public space.[2]

Jarman's retrospective emphasis is on political effect rather than aesthetic success: "Although it is flawed and lacks any of the finesse of professional film-making, it altered peoples lives."³ But as critics such as Michael O'Pray and Earl Jackson, Jr. have shown, *Sebastiane* merits thoughtful discussion and can stand up to some analysis. *Sebastiane* is brazen, polemical, and clumsy, but exhibits nonetheless many of Jarman's characteristic effects and elements. Jarman's recurrent imagery of mirror and sea occurs even here, and this imagery may be said, indeed, to constitute the structural center of the film.

This central scene, then, with resonances that reach throughout the film, has Sebastian looking into a pool. *Sebastiane* is strewn with classical references—some straightforward ("more beautiful than Adonis"), some humorous ("Oedipus" in the dialogue is translated by the subtitles as "motherfucker")—and here the visual allusion to the myth of Narcissus is transparent. Michael O'Pray describes the scene and its initial implications as follows:

> The scene cuts to Sebastian kneeling beside a pool looking at his own image and reciting his poems to God. Nowhere in the film is Sebastian's narcissism more explicitly imaged. The key homosexual relationships in Jarman's subsequent films often contain a narcissistic mirroring—the twins of *Jubilee*, the two gay "Christs" of *The Garden* and the more subtle "twinning" of Caravaggio and Ranuccio in *Caravaggio*. The main structuring device of this "mirroring" is the exchange of eroticised gazes through which characters become isolated from their surroundings and from one another. Invariably the "macho" masculinity of institutions and their representatives is brought into focus by their internal space created by the homosexual gaze.⁴

This is one of the few comments in the criticism on Jarman that takes into account the repeated image of mirroring, and O'Pray rightly links the image of the mirror with the varying homoerotic relationships in the later films. Although O'Pray also characterizes this narcissism as isolating and internalizing, he does not seem to condemn it out of hand, which, we recall, is the trap that Stephen Bruhm has warned us away from.

In this moment of inwardness and self-reflection, Sebastian does not just consider his own reflection; he speaks a poem. Even at the very outset of his career, Jarman substantiates his lyric cinema by composing around poems. From a journal entry written before the film went into production (February 1975):

> James wants an oil and vanilla film full of Steve Reeves muscle men working out in locker-rooms. Paul Humfress, who is to edit, wants a

64

very serious art film, slow and ponderous. I want a poetic film full of mystery. The debate rages as I write, and the script is caught in a tug-of-war between the grey mirrors of Sloane Square.[5]

The film clearly reflects all three sensibilities, although the difference between a "slow and ponderous" art movie and "a poetic film full of mystery" may not be readily obvious. Jarman assures himself of a poetic atmosphere by including actual poems, several of which are spoken by Sebastian. And, famously, everyone speaks in a different language.

The language spoken is Latin, a further crucial and risky realization of Jarman's desire to create poetry and mystery.[6] That everyone speaks Latin might be explained as a specific, utilitarian invention; since there was so little money available for costumes and props, how otherwise could any effect of historical distancing be achieved? But more generally, and seriously, the Latin is consistent with Jarman's antiprosaic impulse elsewhere. The exact re-creation of history is not a goal at the heart of Jarman's projects (although in *Dancing Ledge* he details how much historical research went into what few props there were in *Sebastiane*), but the refusal of the prosaic is. Peter Wollen goes so far as to celebrate *Sebastiane* just here, for the innovation of its Latin dialogue:

> What strikes me now about *Sebastiane* is no longer its place as a pioneering transposition into film of age-old visual motifs aestheticizing beautiful, tormented boys in a Mediterranean setting, but its "high camp" silver Latin dialogue track. To me, this makes the film like an opera, whose libretto is in a foreign language, foregrounding the role of performance and visual composition. Dialogue has always seemed an awkward necessity for Jarman, and he has increasingly been happiest with preexisting literary texts—*The Tempest* or *The Angelic Conversation*—or, as with *War Requiem*, musical texts.[7]

The dialogue of *Jubilee* or *Caravaggio* does sometimes indeed seem like "an awkward necessity," more perhaps because it shows Jarman reaching out toward conventional film than for its inherent clumsiness. Elsewhere Jarman's cinema often avoids dialogue through the use of silent gestures, with an emphasis on the visual, or by the incorporation of figurative language. Seen in this light, the Latin text may be thought of as foreshadowing his adaptations of Shakespeare and Marlowe, texts that are attractive not so much because they preexist, but because they are literary. *The Tempest*, *Edward II*, and *Sebastiane* each embody linguistic difference in the form of their expression.

The Latin dialogue in *Sebastiane* does indeed have its moments of camp,

65

to use Wollen's term, and probably not all of these moments are intentional. The clearest instances of these are jokes or crudities in the subtitles (as in the translation of "Oedipus" mentioned above), where the juxtaposition of "elegant" Latin with vulgarity makes for an amusing effect. But surely most of the Latin text is intended as relatively serious in effect, as conveying distance and perhaps even mystery. In a less generous view, the effect of the Latin is merely pretentious, but even that reading takes the Latin to be erring on the side of art rather than camp.[8] The ambient sound track by Brian Eno surely intends to convey an otherworldly atmosphere, mysterious through and through. Just as surely, the Latin dialogue is intended to work in concert with the sound track, to make strange this visual world.

Despite Wollen's comparison, then, the impression we have of the Latin dialogue is unique; whether from directorial genius or clumsiness, the effect is singularly not like that of watching an opera or a foreign film. The actors are not speaking a language that they know; it sounds positively unidiomatic in everyone's mouth, like a first-semester Spanish class. Once again, this could be taken as unprofessional or hurried awkwardness—and with some reason—but I more charitably prefer to take this delivery as purposefully signaling disorientation and difference. This linguistic disorientation is a species of poetry. The Latin works together with the appearance of actual poems in order to self-consciously contextualize *Sebastiane* as lyric film.

It is amidst all this Latin—and *in* Latin—then, that Sebastian speaks his poems, not so much as serious elements contrasted with camp, but as lyric monologues contrasted with quotidian dialogue.

> Hail God, of the golden sun
> The heavens and earth are united in gold
> comb your hair in the golden rays of light
> in your hands the roses of ecstasy burn
> the wheel turns full circle
> cooled by breezes from the four quarters
> the swallow has risen in the east
> > the doors are open
>
> your body your naked body
> initiated by the mysteries steps forth
> the beauty that is made with different colors
> comes into the world
> Hail golden fire
> Your beauty holds the heart captive

Derek Jarman and Lyric Film

This poetry supposedly originated in the time of St. Sebastian (d. 288), and might therefore recall early Christian Latin poets such as Prudentius, Claudian, or Fortunatus. But these lines are reminiscent of Jarman more than anything; this is Jarman's rather stereotyped idea of a romantic invocation, and we find similar passages in *Akenaten*.

Such poetry does not lay claim to poetic innovation through its language, but it does stage a bold revision of saintly love through its admiring address. The naked body of light stands for both a deified sun and Sebastian himself, so that the address seems to turn between a poem about self-love and a poem about love for a transcendent Other. Both Christian doctrine and Ovid's Narcissus would find this self-loving vain and delusive, but Sebastian's beautiful figure seems to incarnate Christ in a Blakean, revisionary sense—"the human form divine." This incarnation of physical and spiritual love amounts to a contemporary reading of St. Sebastian's iconography. No classical or medieval saint could be read historically in these terms, but with our post-Blakean, post-Whitmanian emphases, such a reading, although anachronistic, becomes almost unavoidable.

This crucial scene, which combines poetry and homoerotic desire and which powerfully reroutes both classical and Christian references, is structurally and thematically related to numerous other scenes in the film. It is by using this logic of association that Richard Dyer links two other watery scenes in the film, where scintillating light on water provides the *mise-en-scène* for a depiction of male homoerotic desire:

> The latter [Anthony and Adrian] provide an image of untrammelled eros in the beautiful central sequence of them making love, in the open air and in a pool. Slow-motion photography caresses their limbs and in the pool shows mesmerising streams of waterdrops glancing off and haloing their glowing bodies. The use of water to convey this dreamy eroticism links it to, but also distinguishes it from, the violent sexuality of horse-play and frustration. In an earlier sequence, Max leads the crude verbal by-play as the men cavort in the sea playing ball; when Anthony tackles Adrian, the latter, recognizing it as an advance, backs off and refuses to play any more; yet later we have the love scene between them, now whole-heartedly sexual, not uglified by the others' need to declare a heterosexual fuck mentality.[9]

67

Dyer's reading properly emphasizes the different forms that "'eros' (love, desire) can take" in the film,[10] and we may note further not only the varieties of desire that are represented, but also the way that these watery settings are always linked to one another and to Sebastian's set-piece reverie at the pool.

We are introduced to Sebastian, in fact, by way of another poem and another watery scene. The desire of the Roman soldier Severus is aroused when he watches Sebastian taking an early morning shower. As Sebastian pours water over himself, we overhear Sebastian's poem in interior monologue.

Hail messenger of dawn.
The young God has arisen.
The horses of dawn fly forth to conquer the Goddess of night.
The reeds sigh when the young God rises
The waters sing when the young God rises
Mankind awakens from sleep
The scarlet cock struts when the young God rises
The lily gives forth perfume when the young God rises
He is glorious in the dawn light
He sparkles like the gold in the sacred lapis
He sparkles like dew on the spider's web
His smile brings colour to the morning
The world is united in peace.

This is once more, as a poem, a string of classical cliches, but the effect of the whole scene taken together is still quite complex. Because of the close-ups that begin the scene, we know that the poem comes from Sebastian and not the Roman onlooker, even though we have not heard Sebastian's voice before. Once again this is a scene of innocent narcissism, where Sebastian celebrates the dawn with his ode, but also celebrates his own beauty. The beauty of nature and the male body are simply taken as givens. However, the viewer is put into the awkward position of looking at the scene along-side Severus, who clearly does not possess a poetic sensibility. Mankind is awakened, indeed, but not in any pastoral sense.

Such a scene is not only linked to other watery scenes, but may be said to contain the film's entire narrative. The whole plot of Sebastian's death-by-desire is implicit in this scene of washing, since we see Sebastian with his eyes closed and arms upraised in an exact duplication of his body lashed to the stake at the end of the film. Sebastian will be punished for arousing and then refusing the erotic will of Severus. Here Sebastian is at once associated with poetry, a stark contrast to the power-hungry gaze of Severus. The language of Sebastian's poetry is jeweled with reflections and mirrorings ("He sparkles like the gold in the sacred lapis / He sparkles like the dew on a spider's web"), even as his body appears in a sheen of watery light. But eventually this poetry will be stilled and silenced, crushed by lust and power.

Derek Jarman and Lyric Film

The homoerotic doubling implied by Sebastian's narcissistic reflection echoes through various scenes—from crowded play in the water to a solitary desert monologue—and culminates in the scene with Sebastian and Justin toward the end of the film. Severus in the introductory scene is no double for Sebastian, but Justin is. As Jarman describes the scene himself: "On a group of rocks Justin and Sebastian rest after swimming. The sunlight sparkles on the water, the scene is quiet and contemplative. Justin points to a shell which glitters in the water."[11] In this sequence, which directly foreshadows the shimmering visuals of *The Angelic Conversation*, Justin sees a "pearl" in the water, and both men look into the sea. Beauty is found in the water, and Justin brings the shell back for Sebastian ("Here, it is for you"). The shell is a lovely spiral, which the camera zooms in on, and they now listen to the voices of the shell. "I hear the old gods sighing," says Sebastian. After a moment, Justin can hear "a seagull crying and a great storm." Each man has another lover—Adrian for Justin, Christ for Sebastian—so the shell is an image that figures a loving relationship that is not simply reduced to sexual contact. "Sebastian! Much-loved Sebastian," Justin hears the shell sing. *Sebastiane* may be early and, in some respects, even unrecognizable Jarman, but these linked scenes of narcissistic reflection and homoerotic doubling will be continued in many different guises throughout the course of his career.

The execution scene powerfully summarizes the imagery and thematics of the scenes that have come before. Now there is no dialogue, nor any atmospheric Eno music either (until the very end), only the sound of wind whipping over the hilltop. Sebastian is already tied to a stake when the scene begins, and the soldiers slowly assemble, in a very long, effective single take. Then each soldier shoots an arrow into Sebastian. Sebastian's upraised arms echo the scene where we saw him the first time, when he doused himself with water. Now a slow-motion shot shows blood streaming out behind his head in a bathetic echo of the shimmering water earlier. Behind the soldiers, in a number of shots, we see the sea, wide and blue, and the sky also provides a clear blue backdrop, as if to continue the watery element. Whereas water originally sheened and focused Sebastian's beautiful body, now the blue ocean suggests only dissolution and vacuity.

Sebastian's pose copies well-known iconography from painting, but here without any postmodernist frisson, the shiver of wit that might accompany the resurrected paintings in *Caravaggio* or the poses in *War Requiem*, and flows through everything in Godard's *Passion*. The first soldier to shoot is entirely naked, giving perhaps a momentary sense of Cupid and his arrow, but otherwise this scene is devoid of the erotic. When he was staked out in the sun, Sebastian eventually showed that he enjoyed the sun's tormenting light, but there is no sign whatever that Sebastian is enjoying his martyrdom now. All desire for light and translucence is in the past, all passion spent.

Sebastiane is an important political contribution to the intellectual and emotional potentiality of art-house cinema, and so in some ways is a revolutionary gesture, but its imagery might be seen as relatively traditional. Jarman sets the film among the empty desert landscapes of Pasolini, and Tony Peake recalls *The Gospel According to Matthew*, although the relentless erotics of *The Arabian Nights* might be more to the point.[12] Pasolini's appropriation of third-world people to provide faces and bodies for his films is much more disturbing than Jarman's appropriation of a small space of Italian landscape for his friends, and as various as Jarman's discussion of the erotic might be overall, it seems much easier to read than Pasolini.

FIGURE 3.1
The recreation of classical iconography in SEBASTIANE

Visually, *Sebastiane* provides the occasion for a film that revels in the male nude. In an aboveground film, this remains remarkable, but in relationship to the history of art, for example, Jarman's male bodies are, more or less, classical. Jarman's swimmers might be compared to those in Thomas Eakins's paintings, swimming and sitting around on the rocks, although it remains an open question whether a Victorian audience would have seen the male nude in Eakins in a homoerotic context.[13]

Derek Jarman and Lyric Film

Although self-conscious and complex, Jarman's male bodies are not as transfigured as those in David Hockney's works, especially the paintings from the 1960s that also take the opportunity to picture male nudity in scenes of swimming, showering, or washing up. As Paul Melia convincingly argues, Hockney transfers the classical representations of male nudity associated with the Mediterranean seaside to the poolsides of Los Angeles:

> Hockney's painting also evokes the two hundred year tradition of educated English homosexuals who, often after social ruin or legal persecution caused by their sexual activities, were forced into exile. The Mediterranean, specifically southern Italy, was a favoured destination; not only did its history satisfy intellectual interests, it also supported a culture hospitable to their desires. As Robert Aldrich has shown, beginning in the 1750s a comprehensive utopian myth of southern Europe as homoerotic was produced and reproduced, which legitimated the type of sexual pleasures northern Europeans came to the region to enjoy. Desire was conceptualized as an aesthetic experience, justified by reference to both "Greek love" and an idealised image of antiquity.[14]

Whereas Hockney in the 1960s transforms this classical tradition by setting it in Los Angeles, Jarman in the 1970s chooses simply to continue the tradition of the homoerotic Mediterranean. The world that he creates here is conflicted and complicated, but also idealizing in its deployment of the male body. Though first coming to light in the deserts of Italy, where these young exiles manage to find a tropical home, Jarman's films will ultimately come to seem much more at home in the homelessness of England than in the mythical sands of Sardinia.

Sebastiane is a low-budget, intuitively thrown-together scramble of a movie in some respects, but there are central images that Jarman will return to again and again. The figure of martyrdom is one of these images, and we will see martyrs in different guises and tonalities in such films as *Caravaggio* and *The Garden*. Jarman has been criticized for his attraction to and identification with martyr figures, but it is a character that he adopts—when he adopts it—knowingly and self-consciously. The subtitle of *At Your Own Risk: A Saint's Testament* (1993) refers to his "canonization" by the Sisters of Perpetual Indulgence on September 22, 1991. From a press release that Jarman quotes himself: "The Sisters have created saints worldwide to recognize those who have achieved and struggled for the lesbian and gay community. These include Australian saints who have worked on gay prisoners' rights, for anti-discrimination legislation and on gay radio."[15] The saint's testament is the saint's testimony, a bearing witness. The "martyr" is literally a "witness" (from the Greek *martys*, meaning *witness*). In one of the last sentences of *At Your Own Risk*, Jarman explains, "I had to write of a sad time as a witness,"[16] which shows exactly where Jarman is placing the burden and duty of sainthood. The martyred saint is momentarily a victim, but he is much more powerfully a witness, a visionary who documents the realities around him.

Jarman's St. Sebastian embodies this kind of contemporary sainthood, then, as one who both suffers on behalf of others, selflessly, and as one who draws others toward his beautiful self. He is a saint who testifies with his eyes, as well as in his own beautiful flesh. Jarman's St. Sebastian is a narcissistic Christ who embodies all the paradoxes of those Christian male nudes in the history of painting, who absents himself in selfless love, but is anything but absent before our desiring eyes. The mysterious and poetic mood of *Sebastiane*, with its voice-over poems and disorienting Latin, intends to dislocate a simple reading of St. Sebastian's iconography. We can read the saint's death neither as straightforwardly Christian and orthodox nor as ecstatically homoerotic. Rather, we drift with the poetry and the music into a place where we must read the martyrdom in fundamentally contradictory ways.

A comparison of *Sebastiane* to the unproduced screenplay *Akenaten* will help further this description of poetry and communication in Jarman's early films.[17] According to O'Pray, the final draft of *Akenaten* was probably prepared while Jarman was working on *Sebastiane*, and the two projects show many overlapping impulses.[18] They both take us to exotic, archaic worlds where light and flesh are visually of primary consideration. The scrolling prologue to *Sebastiane* reads:

> In the summer of the year 303 the Emperor Diocletian's palace was ravaged by a series of inexplicable fires. The Emperor blamed the Christians, and as a result unleashed the last great persecution against them. . . . Later in the year Diocletian returned to Rome to celebrate his 20 years on the throne with a jubilee and games. The celebration culminated on the 25th of December with a party given by Diocletian for his family and favourite, Sebastian, the captain of the palace guard, to celebrate the birth of the sun.

Akhenaten, as Jarman tells us, is the story of a monotheistic sun-worshiping heretic (*A*, p. 3). Similarly awash in sunlight, then, that script opens with a voice-over by the Sphinx.

Sebastiane begins with "inexplicable fires," and *Akenaten* begins with the Sphinx; both projects foreground mystery from the first syllable. But *Akenaten* moves closer to the hieroglyphic landscapes of *Jubilee* and *The Tempest*. Both *Sebastiane* and *Akenaten* are relatively simple worlds, visually; for instance, Jarman writes of *Akenaten*: "This would be no *Cleopatra* [referring here presumably to the 1934 spectacular with Claudette Colbert]. It was to be as simple as butter muslin with fine white limestone walls, and perhaps a gold bracelet on a scarlet ribbon" (*A*, p. 3). At least in its script form, however, *Akenaten* broods more obliquely over its deserts and over its expanses of flesh than does *Sebastiane*.

Sebastiane is not simplistic in its various representations of desire—it ranges between the sentimental and the orgiastic, the tender and the repulsively brutal—but the narrative of persecution and martyrdom is relatively clear. The Romans blame the "inexplicable fires" on the Christians, and the film narrates the potentially inexplicable fires of human desire in a relatively familiar framework of voyeurism, exploitation, and exclusion. Although it is spoken in Latin, *Sebastiane* is usually not so difficult to read; it is a homoerotic fable of the spirit and the flesh that concludes in the familiar, though certainly not uncomplicated iconography of St. Sebastian. *Sebastiane* begins with a dance of painted men (bearing giant phalluses), but for the remainder of the film the flesh is not painted, not tattooed; it is laid open to our eyes and to all the labyrinthine mysteries of merely looking.

Akenaten is populated by desiring and light-seeking lyrics like those in *Sebastiane*.

Come forth O Sun
Come and look at me
Come and look at me
The days are long, the nights are peaceful
Time spins a golden diadem
For Nefretiti
My life is spent in laughter
Awake Egypt. Awake sleepers of Thebes.
See the fish which lies beautiful on my
Fingers in the dawn light.

(*A*, PP. 6–7)

But the narrative of *Akenaten* is not so familiar, or so clear in its intent. Where *Sebastiane* is divided into scenes that, for all their seeming looseness, still partition a story into motivations and consequences, *Akenaten* moves more elliptically, through ritual stages. Like Paradjanov's *The Color of Pomegranates*, *Akenaten* tells the story of a man's life in symbolic scenes from birth to death. Now poetry is aligned with ritual and ceremony, an artifice more ambiguous than sunlit desire and flesh. This world is characterized by burning incense, bowl carrying, bejeweled diadems, and painted boys ("suddenly over the horizon the wild nomadic boys of Akenaten appear, riding naked on black horses, they are painted blue," *A*, p. 11). The nakedness of this exotic world, with its arrowings of sexual desire, is cloaked by artifice and paint. The world of *Akenaten* is only as readable as color and less reducible to words.

Akenaten concludes with its hero punished for his heresy and driven into exile:

> Akenaten. I inhale the sweet breeze that comes from your mouth and contemplate your beauty every day. My desire is to hear your voice, like the sigh of the north wind. Love will renew my limbs. Give me the hands that hold your soul. I will embrace you. Call me by name again and again, for ever, and never will you call without response. [He stares motionless into the sun. We see that he is blinded by the sun. Slowly, as he is blinded, the light goes out.]

> (*A*, p. 40)

But we have much less sense of what Akenaten, compared to Sebastian, is being punished for, or how desire for the sun might correspond to anything in our real world. Jarman writes in his preface to the script: "I think if I made it now it would have no real necessity and would be merely decorative—perhaps not" (*A*, p. 3). Compared to *Sebastiane*, *Akenaten* may seem to be nothing more than a decoration, a set of visuals and poses without the erotic and political dimensions of *Sebastiane*. But the way it proceeds in loose sequences circulating around artifices and rituals is crucial to the way that Jarman's films will develop as time goes on.

74

1. *Jubilee, Neutron,* AND BLAKEAN APOCALYPSE

Here, too, we can usefully juxtapose an early film with an unproduced screenplay by looking at Jarman's second feature film, *Jubilee*, alongside the script for *Neutron*. *Neutron* emerged at about the same time as *Jubilee*, although Jarman continued to revise the script for *Neutron* until 1983. By genre, both works are species of science fiction and equally bathed in the tumultuous waters of apocalypse. Jarman will be drawn to apocalyptic regions throughout his career, and *The Last of England* is only his deepest and most remarkable immersion. Neither *Jubilee* nor *Neutron* contains any identifiable poems, in contrast to *Sebastiane* and *Akenaten*, but each still has much to do with the poetic themes of vision, communication, and interpretation. As the lyric cinema of Tarkovsky also entered the imaginary worlds of science fiction in such films as *Solaris* and *Stalker*, so too does the early Jarman, following now not the likes of Stanislaw Lem, but rather traveling in the line of the romantic poet William Blake. After focusing on the poetic elements of *Jubilee*, then, we shall go on to compare that film to *Neutron*, its unproduced Blakean brother.

Jubilee has often been regarded as one of the most authentic punk movies ever made, a document to a landmark moment in history.[19] Yet at the same time, *Jubilee* has been regarded as in some ways the most atypical of all Jarman's films, in that it focuses on punk (a movement about which he was fairly skeptical) to the extent that his own signature style and emphases may seem to be displaced. Although not a "slick" production, to say the least, *Jubilee* exhibits a certain opportunism: the attempt to get punk music on the screen at—it is hoped—a ripe moment does not convince one necessarily of the film's artistic integrity (a tired phrase, but almost never in question elsewhere in Jarman). For our purposes, despite the absence of actual poems, *Jubilee* can still be seen as working through poetry and associated ideas about writing in ways that will become more expansive and characteristic in later films. It is important to examine the ways that punk and poetry are related, though keeping in mind this caveat, as quoted by Greil Marcus: "Luis Buñuel once referred to some of those who praised *Un Chien Andalou* as 'that crowd of imbeciles who find the film beautiful or poetic when it is fundamentally a desperate and passionate call to murder.'"[20]

Jubilee began as an homage to Blake, with whose visionary sensibility Jarman felt much in common. "In an early note," writes Peake, "Jarman wrote that the film was dedicated to 'all those who secretly work against the tyranny of Marxists fascists trade unionists maoists capitalists socialists etc. . . . who have conspired together to destroy the diversity and holiness of each life in the name of materialism. . . . For William Blake.'"[21] Blake's work in both word and image, as well as his interest in mysticism and the occult, was compelling to Jarman. As O'Pray reminds us:

> Like Blake, Jarman was a Londoner who believed the city physically
> embodied the woes of its times—in sixteenth-century alchemical
> terms, it was a microcosm. Both created mythological systems span
> ning the personal and the national in which the social critique was

inseparable from the spiritual. . . . Both Jarman and Blake plundered the cabala, alchemy and the occult philosophies, finding in them a symbolic vehicle for anti-rationalist and anti-materialist sympathies.[22]

Jubilee is structured as what Jarman calls a "dream vision," and features Jarman's Renaissance hero of the occult, John Dee. One might readily view *Jubilee* as a kind of apocalyptic, visionary response to the world's turmoil and corruption, a contemporary outburst of energy and satire in the tradition of Blake's *The Book of Urizen*.

Blake's visionary poetry stands at the head of an important line of apocalyptic writing that has recently received splendid treatment by Edward Ahearn in *Visionary Fictions: Apocalyptic Writing from Blake to the Modern Age*.[23] Ahearn travels in his critical descriptions from Blake through Novalis and Gérard de Nerval toward André Breton (*Nadja*), Louis Aragon (*Paysan de Paris*), and William Burroughs (*Naked Lunch*). The apocalyptic sublime in surrealism and Burroughs "puts the reader in uncomfortable contact with all that is squalid in life: the people, the body, the world around us, language."[24] The "visionary" also "frequently involves a provocative view of the body, and an oppositional sociopolitical stance, all inextricably linked."[25] Ahearn examines the homosexuality in Burroughs and the lesbianism in Monique Wittig (*Le Corps Lesbien*), and concludes that "the body, and primarily in its sexual aspect, is consistently presented as the privileged source of the visionary."[26] This way of foregrounding provocative bodies, particularly in works of the contemporary sublime, has an obvious relevance to the sexual displays and naked performances in both *Jubilee* and *The Last of England*.

As Ahearn makes apparent, visionary sublimities continue to occupy twentieth-century writers, but in translated form. The transcendental becomes the immanent, the grotesque, the parodic. A Blakean Jarman makes for a rewarding conflation, then, a productive link, but we know that Jarman will incarnate Blake in his own image, just as Allen Ginsberg's Blake is equally his own.[27] In a film that is in some sense dedicated to him and inspired by his visionary stance, then, what does happen to William Blake? Let us look at the following scene for a preliminary indication. Two-thirds the way through, *Jubilee* finds itself amidst a party-orgy in Westminster Cathedral, which is now renamed "The Temple of Heavenly Delight" (so-called in the script; in the film, Angel calls it "the Palace of Heavenly Delight"). To put an orgy in a renowned church does not follow Blake's practice in specifics (usually the church kills sexual passion), but it might be said to follow a more general sense of Blake's ongoing reevaluation of

76

institutional types and conventions. What we see and hear, then, when we enter the cathedral-palace-temple is this:

> [In the crypt Christ and the twelve apostles perform a dance to a disco
> version of *Jerusalem*]
> Song: And did those feet
> In ancient times
> Walk upon England's mountains green
> And was the holy lamb of God
> On England's pleasant pastures seen?
> And did the countenance divine
> Shine forth upon our clouded hills
> And was Jerusalem builded here, etc. . . .

(*J*, P. 67)

Yet what sort of appropriation of Blake do we have here? The images of Christ and his disciples are grotesquely parodic and determinedly unfunny, like practically everything else in this grim landscape. Jarman himself describes the absence of humor: "A bitter chill blows through the film. For an audience who expected a punk music film, full of 'anarchy' and laughs at the end of the King's Road, it was difficult to swallow."[28] This redepiction of Christ arrives with the potential for humor and fun, however transgressive or troubling (think of Monty Python's *Life of Brian* or Pasolini's *Ricotta*), but the Christ actually before us on the screen is a pale, pathetic nonfigure.

Contemporary art and film often appropriate their materials, but Jarman's appropriation of Blake himself seems to confound all sense of value. Jarman's apocalyptic, visionary satire may in some ways seem Blakean, but Blake is undermined as a heroic figure or watchword as much as is "maoism" or "capitalism" or "socialism." "Do you remember any real hero? No, I don't," says Mad (*J*, 40). By the end of this section, we will want to determine what can possibly remain of Blake or culture, since in the chilly air of *Jubilee*'s punk nihilism, poetry is not likely to last very long in any recognizable form.

Yet there are two places where we may nonetheless look for poetry, in moments that will, later on, expand into entire films—films like *The Angelic Conversation* and *The Last of England*. Amid the brilliant "documentary" of punk, we see Jarmanesque "poetry" at least twice: in the frame narrative and figures and in the remarkable sequence known as "Jordan's Dance."

The frame narrative sets us down in a reduced, fantasy version of

77

Renaissance England, where Queen Elizabeth walks in a courtly garden with John Dee, her court astrologer. From here the film will time-travel forward into the present-day nightmare of contemporary England. England's Jubilee year of 1977 is Queen Elizabeth I's bad dream. The means for Elizabeth's visionary time travel is provided by Dee—astrologer, alchemist, and magician. Dee is a recurrent character in Jarman's prose writings and always stands for visionary transformation and cinematic magic. Dee is, in other words, a more serene Kenneth Anger. He is a creator, a figure of poetry, like the magus at the end of *A Finger in the Fishes Mouth* and like Prospero in *The Tempest*. *The Angelic Conversation* is, in fact, "the angelic conversation" of Dee, and *Jubilee* has no sooner begun than it invokes another world, a transcendental realm, a home of angels.

> Queen E: Our own Dr. John, our triumphant antinomy, our kingdom's eyes, this me pleaseth to see and have discourse with angels.

(*J*, P. 45)

Unlike Blake's poetry, which appears only to be deconstructed by disco, the naive archaisms of John Dee and Elizabeth seem to be stable, a source of antique pleasure set against everyday prattle. Just like the linguistic dislocation of *Sebastiane*'s Latin, the faux Shakespearean dialogue impresses us as being intended seriously. In costume and speech, Queen Elizabeth and John Dee stand potentially at the edge of parody and comedy, but the film somewhat surprisingly wants us to appreciate them as figures of tragic and even aristocratic dignity.

Jarman's lifelong interest in Dee is clearly related to his attraction to Blake and to thinkers like Jung, figures who worked extensively with symbols and emblems of the imagination. Dee is also a recurrent reference in the work of Frances Yates, to whose writing Jarman often refers. In the *Theatre of the World* (1969), Yates describes Dee's extensive travels in search of "forbidden knowledge," and the immense library he developed as a consequence.[29] Reference works in Dee's library—the *Hieroglyphica* of Valeriano, the *Mythologia* of Natalis Comes, and the *Emblems* of Alciati[30]—remind us that Jarman is often trying to construct films using similar resources: myths, symbols, and emblems. Jarman has an artist's interest in Dee rather than a scholar's. So whereas Yates mentions Dee's famous, or rather infamous, book *A True and Faithful Relation of what passed for many years between Dr. John Dee . . . and some spirits*, which "shows Dee in an extremely superstitious light,"[31] Jarman, in his turn, treasures that spirit, refuses so readily to judge rationally, and thus names his later film after Dee's book *The Angelic Conversation*. Yates's *Theatre of the World* links the magic of Dee with the thaumaturgical power of theater, and in *Jubilee* Dee emblematically embodies the cinematic power of Jarman's dream allegory.

Yates interprets the figure of Prospero in *The Tempest* as a staged version of Dee himself, and, indeed, when *Jubilee*'s Dee invokes angels and draws down celestial conversation, he calls into presence Ariel, who arrives directly out of Shakespeare's late romance:

> All hail, great master! Grave sir, hail! I come to answer thy best pleasure be it to fly, to swim, to dive into the fire, to ride on the curled clouds to thy strong bidding task, Ariel and all his quality.

(*J*, P. 46)

This cinematic Ariel is a glittering and remarkable figure, well suited to traverse the distant spheres of Jarman's visionary cosmos. As Dee describes him, Ariel is associated with poetry and light: "My angel flies with mirrored eyes leaving a sparkling phosphorescent trail across the universe" (*J*, p. 46). When we first see Ariel, he stands on a rocky ledge, and a mirroring light radiates out from his belt. Such mirrored eyes and mirrored waist may well seem to herald the creative power of sexuality. Yet for now, as in *The Art of Mirrors*, mirroring Ariel seems only to embody the fluidity and transcendence of poetic cinema; his mirroring does not seem, at this time, to imply homosexual doubling. He does hold sexuality within him *in potentia*, however, for Jarman will take this image of Ariel and his mirror straight out of *Jubilee* and splice it into *The Angelic Conversation*. In the later film this glittering image clearly does signal both the gathering light of lyric film and the doubling of homoerotic desire.

Jarman will continue to incorporate recognizable, if archaic-sounding, poetry into voice-overs and speeches throughout his career. As in Tarkovsky, recognizable poetry emerges to signal that this is, indeed, lyric cinema. But the poetic aspect of his cinema that is most idiomatically his own occurs in the nonverbal, emblematic performance pieces. *The Last of England* shares a similarly angry and apocalyptic atmosphere with *Jubilee*, but it conducts itself through a few spare voice-overs and one performance piece after another. *Jubilee*'s scenes are usually as full of dialogue as any conventional movie; it has, moreover, several song-length scenes of punk bands playing and entire musical productions (such as "Rule, Britannia"). But there is a scene early on in the film that proceeds in a manner that later films will help us to see as characteristic of Jarman's lyric cinema. This is

"Jordan's Dance," which Peake rightly calls "the most dramatic, disembodied, and perhaps most beautiful of its sequences."[32]

As is so often the case, Jarman's script clarifies aspects of this scene that an unassisted viewer could not be expected to determine. Jarman calls this "The Bonfire of Vanity," where Amyl "in a classic white tutu dances round a bonfire." Meanwhile "a boy with long golden hair circles the fire fuelling it with books"; the boy cuts his hair "until he resembles a shorn penitent" (J, p. 49). And Jarman continues the description, "the burning of the books, Savonarola's bonfire of vanity, contro i capelli lunghi, against long hair, a new puritanism" (J, p. 49). But would anyone without the script be able to decide that this fire was a "bonfire of vanity" or that this dance signaled a "new puritanism"?

The piece moves forward through incremental stages, adding elements to be interpreted, but without giving us much of a handle. We begin in slow motion, focusing on a ballerina who is not stereotypically lithe and overly made up with blue eye shadow and red cheeks. She pirouettes around a bonfire to "romantic" (Jarman's word) violin music. Is this the end of classicism? The last dance on earth? The ashes of the fire fly up around her. We wonder who the long-haired man is. When he throws a book into the fire, the book arcs through the air so marvelously that we do not name the moment as a species of "puritanism." Surely we read it, for now, as a visual gesture approaching pure form. An abrupt cut immediately after the book falls into the fire does not help us to reflect on the situation any further. On the other side of the cut the music continues, but the ballerina now stalks around prosaically, at ironic odds with the music. The sequence has set various archetypal images in motion—ballerina, fire, book burning—but the overall impression is contradictory and vague. We follow the music through fiery, apocalyptic images, but without a clear sense of our heading or of what might be at stake.

As we continue through Jarman's films, I will often gloss such moments, such emblematic staged performances, with the improvisations and open-form theater that is collectively known as performance art. The traditions of performance art provide important and rarely mentioned contexts for Jarman's gestural cinematic poetry. As an artist immersed in all forms of culture, Jarman was entirely familiar with the happenings and gallery performances around him, and in his journals he jots down opinions about Gilbert and George as often as about Francis Bacon. By the time of *The Last of England*, his cinematic poetry will express itself almost entirely in a series of set-piece performances.

How does performance art help us understand "Jordan's Dance"? Performance art often disdains temporal structure of any kind, as exemplified in Joseph Beuys's famous *Coyote: I Like America and America Likes Me*, which consisted of a sparse set of props and repetitive movements and took place over a week. But an equally well-known work of performance art, Carolee Schneemann's *Interior Scroll* (1975), was structured through incremental stages, culminating with the removal of a scroll from her vagina.[33]

Jarman's performance pieces are often highly repetitive (the cauliflower-eating scene in *The Last of England* comes to mind), but may also proceed by increment and crescendo (the restaurant tar and feathering in *The Garden* is an example of that). "Jordan's Dance" in *Jubilee* plunges us into a slice of apocalypse, where the dance and fire are repetitive elements, but the editing of the sequence adds elements piecemeal: here's another figure to contemplate, here's another. When the tempo of the music changes, we notice masked characters watching the dance. In the script, Jarman proceeds to name them: "Masked Figures representing art, Michelangelo's David, and death watch impassively" (*J*, p. 49).

Once again, however, it is unlikely that anyone scriptless will decide that all three of these characters represent these things—although "death" is likely, "art" is certainly not. Even if we have the script before us, there still remains the question of what it means, anyway, for *these* figures to be standing around and watching. Whereas often such explicitly theatricalized scenes allegorize the film-audience relationship, it does not make too much sense to think of ourselves as inhabiting either art or Michelangelo's *David*. If art is looking, what is it looking at? Perhaps there are two kinds of art. Perhaps we are to sense a contrast between the passivity and stillness of classical art, sculpture, and death, and an art of movement and life. Or, we might say, a contrast between monumental art and performance art.

Since one of the figures watching "Jordan's Dance" is Michelangelo's *David*, we should take this opportunity to meditate for a further moment on sculpture in Jarman. Contemporary sculpture is, in fact, intimately linked to ideas about performance art, since, more and more, sculpture *performs*—refuses to be installed quietly in galleries, refuses monumentality. As we shall so often see, in films such as *The Last of England* and *War Requiem*, Jarman's lyric cinema constantly stages a dialogue between performance and monumentality. Cinema, "moving pictures," might be said to have destroyed the monumental from the outset, loving to be associated with trains, planes, and rivers, and fleeing from anything like the paralysis of sculptural form. Yet early cinema staged numerous interpretations of the monumental, in works like Griffith's *Intolerance* and Lang's *Metropolis*. Monumental scale in the twentieth century was often associated with oppressive power and, more specifically, fascist ostentation, but cinema did not so easily give over its desire to impress an audience through power and scale. Despite the fact that movies move and despite the tyrannical associations of monumentality in the twentieth century, monumentality in film often makes for an open question rather than an easy and certain evaluation.

We usually think of Jarman's cinema as that of a painter, but he had significant training in architecture as well.[34] His paintings were sometimes three-dimensional, and his garden was given form by found objects sculptured together or arranged. In *The Last of England*, we see Jarman daubing paint on so thick that he's really making a sculpture as much as a painting. His architectural and sculptural impulses emerge most notably in his work as a set designer, particularly in his set designs for two films directed by Ken Russell.[35]

Russell is himself probably associated more readily with music than architecture, if we think of his cinematic lives of Tchaikovsky and Mahler and of his rock opera, *Tommy*. In order to point cinema away from its obsession with words and dialogue, Russell constantly determined to use music in original and foregrounded ways. "It's not often that British directors realize the power of music and image," writes Russell; "They usually rely on words, the stuff of radio and stage plays."[36] But Busby Berkeley musicals would not be much without the sets, and Russell's visual use of architecture and monumental form is often as arresting as his use of music. This is particularly the case in the two films for which Jarman was set designer, *The Devils* (1971) and *Savage Messiah* (1972).

The status of the monumental is of extraordinary interest in Russell's *The Devils*. The pomp, power, and spectacle enjoyed by Father Grandier (Oliver Reed) are substantiated in the monumental city and in the very walls that surround the city. The walls of Loudon are, in fact, at the center of the narrative, since the tyrannical Richelieu wants the walls torn down in order to ensure his grip over all of France. When, in the end, Grandier is burned at the stake, the walls are simultaneously blown asunder all around him. Grandier's epic magnificence is equated with the city and the walls; his power is aligned with the look of the city and the scale of the walls.

Jarman identifies his architectural sources for the "great white city" as Ledoux, Boulleé, and Piranesi; he writes in the *Dancing Ledge* journal: "All detail is sacrificed to scale as I want the sets as large as possible, and as forceful as the sets from an old silent."[37] The reason that the monumental is so

82

interesting in *The Devils* is because we do not, as it turns out, want the walls destroyed at the end. Yes, the priest is promiscuous and exploits his power, but the narrative makes us feel that he is human and completely innocent of the charges that the power-crazy Richelieu has brought against him.

Jarman's walls brilliantly embody the contradictions at the heart of Russell's epic theater. The walls of Loudon, although vast and impressive, appear surreal and entirely nonthreatening because of their white color and their undifferentiated lack of detail. Although Jarman compares his set to those of silent films, these walls are notably unlike the walls in Griffith's *Intolerance* or Lang's *Metropolis*, where the sculptures and parapets threaten, confine, and intimidate. Jarman's walls look vast but strangely steadying and peaceful, more like a set from *The Wizard of Oz*, perhaps, than Lang. When the walls are broken apart at the end and the camera cranes up over a huge pile of bricks, the effect is quite astonishing. These walls never seemed to be made out of anything; so that to rise up over these ruins, brick by brick, is like discovering an anatomically correct skeleton inside Casper the Friendly Ghost. Jarman's set exteriors in *The Devils* not only work perfectly in the service of the narrative's complicated exploration of power (religious, political, and sexual), but they also embody a kind of simultaneous experiment into the nature and evaluation of monumental design.

Jarman's role in Russell's *Savage Messiah* (1972) is less decisive, but the film deserves mention for its potential significance in Jarman's cinematic development. *Savage Messiah* is, in fact, a rendering of the life of Henri Gaudier-Brzeska, the modern sculptor. Jarman's contributions to the film are relatively slight compared to those he made in *The Devils* (he has an entire screen giving his credit for set design in the first picture, but he shares the screen with four other contributors in the second). His main design responsibilities for *Savage Messiah* were for a nightclub called "The Vortex," a dining room for the art dealer, Gorki, and a number of complicated artifacts, such as a giant Easter Island head and a marble torso for Gaudier to work on.[38] Jarman's sets are visually important, but not as stunning or 83 ever-present as the walls of the great white city of Loudon.

Savage Messiah, however, must figure as an important element in Jarman's maturing artistic sensibility, since the film also stages a feature-length discussion between monumentality and performance. Scott Antony's Gaudier is irrepressibly vital and ecstatic. At the beginning of the film, Gaudier poses mockingly on top of classical sculptures, and the old monuments seem to be no match for his ebullient spirit. But the film clearly shows us, almost didactically, how sculptures can demonumentalize and so carry life along with them. These sculptures follow Rodin, where imperfection and a lack of finish signal vitality and spontaneity, even in the weighted medium of stone. The film's remarkable conclusion takes us through a gallery exhibition of Gaudier's pieces, many of which we have seen earlier in the process of their creation. Gaudier has been shot and killed in the First World War, yet his sculptures seem as alive as he was. The sculptures turn and pivot, rotating magically, which adds to their energy and animation.

Hence the sculptures seem to carry on his spirit; they embody Gaudier, and, in their living quality, memorialize him in death. Finally, at the film's very end Russell's camera closes in on a block of stone that has only barely been worked. On its surface, an abstract drawing of a man enfolding a woman tells us what this sculpture would have become. The rectangular block of stone fills the screen to just the scale of a tombstone (Gaudier earlier stole his marble out of a graveyard), and the official death notice is then printed over the block ("Henri Gaudier-Brzeska, killed in action at 1:00 P.M. on 5th June 1915 at Neuville St. Vaast, France, Aged 23"). But as the final credits roll, annotating music turns from military celebration to a circus march.

All in all, therefore, the film itself becomes a living monument to Gaudier, poised on the brink of monument and performance. Gaudier runs directly into the horrors of war, but the film avoids building him a conventional war memorial. Similar meditations on modern sculpture and monument in the context of twentieth-century war are implicitly in the background of almost every film Jarman made, and most explicitly to the point in *War Requiem*.

As we refined our senses of poetry and mystery in *Sebastiane* by comparing its sunlight and its deserts with those in *Akenaten*, so too might we sharpen our senses of apocalypse and mythic structure in *Jubilee* by comparing that film with *Neutron*. Both *Jubilee* and *Neutron* structure their apocalyptic worlds around extreme contrasts. *Jubilee* contrasts the idyllic garden world of Queen Elizabeth and John Dee to the chaotic urban world of the punks. *Neutron* contrasts the idyllic world of Aeon, with his country house and garden, to the nightmarish urban world of Topaz, who lives in a derelict porn shop amidst a landscape of wrecked factories, hotels, churches, and supermarkets. In *Jubilee* there is no interaction between the two worlds. The time-traveling Queen Elizabeth remains a shocked spectator who reacts in horror to the barbarities she sees before her, but she is essentially unable to dislodge herself from the frame narrative. On the other hand, the plot of *Neutron* works in just the opposite respect, since Topaz and Aeon are doubled figures who reverse positions by the end. Just

84

on this basic level of structure, *Neutron* seems a more satisfactory narrative because it blends together its Manichean contrasts. *Jubilee* never allows the bright world and the dark world to really meet, and the retreat to archaic dialogue and nostalgia at the end feels less convincing, somehow, than simply leaving us in the wrecked, nihilistic world of the punks.

Neutron begins with a technological conflict in which a "blank white paper" falls through space, "past mountains of disused machinery" (*N*, p. 149). Over a radio we hear: "2000 calling I know your works repeat I know your works. Do you hear me? I know your works repeat you have the name of being alive but you are dead" (*N*, p. 149). Throughout the film the radio speaks an updated version the Book of Revelation: "I will feed you [static] I will lead you to fountains of living water [static]" (*N*, p. 158). In contrast to these spoken words—from something more like an all-surveilling Big Brother than a consoling deity—are the words produced by the typist. The blank white paper falls into a typewriter, and we see

[A hand catches the paper and places it in a typewriter. . . . There is a brief silence then the words:
    "Who if I cried would hear me
    Among angelic orders"
are typed aggressively over and over. There is the sound of a crash as the typist hits the keys so hard they tangle and jam.]

(*N*, P. 149)

The moment may be compared to the earlier contrast between Sebastian's poetic monologue and Severus's power-hungry gaze. The typist here counters the radio's propaganda with the beginning of a poem, namely, the first lines of Rilke's *Duino Elegies*. Poetry attempts to emerge from the wreck, from the confines of ruin and dogma, but it runs over itself and collapses in the course of its own transcription. In contrast to the poetic figures of John Dee and Ariel in *Jubilee*, who have magical powers (although they cast a bleak vision), the typist in *Neutron* is a destroyer of poetry from the very first sentence. Poetry is as much a victim as every other aspect of culture in this bombed-out world.

What Aeon does in the course of the film is continue to type. We see him in a "derelict office of [a] deserted factory" where he "sits at a table looking at the decaying table top and the rusting typewriter and its yellowing paper" (*N*, p. 152). He doesn't manage to actually type here, but a few scenes later he is back at the country house, in the garden, where he "sits under a huge cedar tree in the sunlight. He is typing out a manuscript" (*N*,

85

p. 154). But then a gang of children tramples through the garden, breaking his concentration.

In the good old days, Aeon was a member of the cultural elite, wealthy and having the leisure to write. Thus Topaz accuses him:

> Some of us picked up guns and turned on them. We knew who the enemy was. While you sang about the end of the world we fought to save it.
> [Aeon slumps back in his chair and begins drumming his fingers on the table].
>
> (N, P. 160)

And here the script's stage directions enact a dissolve to what must be a figurative confirmation of what Topaz says—that Aeon did sing the world, perform the world, even as the world crashed into blackness.

> Aeon watches as his face flickers on a dozen screens, and the sound of his drumming fingers becomes the rhythm of a song, which shows the world's leads, and marching feet, missiles, tanks, interspersed with dancers who dance at the edge of time to Aeon's immaculate performance.
>
> (N, P. 160)

The "rhythm" of poetry here, which escalates to the march of fascism, can be compared to the meditations on rhythm in *The Tempest*, where Ariel monotonously sings on a rocking horse. Poetry and the concerns of poetry—vision, imagination, and rhythm—appear in strange places in Jarman, but they constantly appear.

By the clarity of postapocalyptic lights, we can see that Aeon's writing is figuratively compelling, yet associated at the same time with the machines of destruction. In a "derelict factory" Aeon and Topaz "sit by the dying embers of a fire"; Topaz says that they are "waiting for the archaeologists" (N, p. 163).

> [Topaz carries on boxing. He pretends to knock himself out. Aeon carries on typing, talking to himself.]
> Aeon: There was a lull which seemed an eternity. Such total silence. Then the church bells started to ring as the fiery glow sucked up the city like a passionate kiss.
>
> (N, P. 163)

86

What Aeon says is what he types. This prose is what now passes for and stands for writing, and for writing figuratively. Here we cut immediately to scene 39, "the bomb and the city": "In an intense white light an image of a great metropolis glimmers briefly and turns to ashes" (N, p. 163). After his inability to transcribe Rilke at the film's opening, Aeon's prose finally emerges into a voice, and he speaks it out loud, and in similes: "like a passionate kiss." But the poetic language is aligned with the light of a bomb. In the following scene, Aeon continues his figurative history: "A lion had escaped and lumbered out the pools of steaming water in the shadows of the underground" (N, p. 164). As a member of the cultural elite, Aeon remembers and records the disaster for which he was responsible. In scene 68, toward the end of the script, we cut to a flashback where "Aeon receives public recognition for his work at a glittering reception" (N, p. 174). While receiving a "thunderous" ovation, he "sits in his chair and looks at the bronze statuette in his lap. Its design is vulgar, rather hollow" (N, p. 174). What Aeon's cultural contribution is, exactly, is left open, but we are given to understand here that it is all hollowness at the core.

In an equally emblematic sequence, Aeon and Topaz are connected through a set of mirrors. Scene 54 is an interior set in a "factory lavatory":

Aeon stares at himself in a mirror. Behind him smashed basins and mirrors litter the floor. In one corner a sinister and large pile of bones. The room resembles a stone age lair. Aeon idly turns on a tap. After a series of rumbling noises and splutterings, rusty water spurts out onto the floor. Aeon looks around and finds an old galvanised bucket which he fills. He peers at himself in the shattered mirror. In the corner he sees the reflection of Topaz. He then slowly peels off layer and layer of clothes. He takes a T-shirt and tears it in half. He picks the bucket up and leaves the bathroom.

(N, P. 168)

In a room full of mirrors, Aeon sees the reflection of Topaz in the corner of a mirror. This image functions as a metaphorical explanation for what happens. Literally, Aeon now takes off his clothes; more figuratively, Aeon and Topaz reverse positions. In the good old days, we know that Aeon was associated with a nice suit (we see him in suit and tie again in scene 58, at his town house), and there are flashbacks to Aeon and Sophia making love in the garden. We meet Topaz in a pornography shop, and in scene 55 Aeon watches "in a detached manner as Topaz jacks off" (N, p. 168). The cultural high and low of Aeon and Topaz are thus apparent, so

87

that when Aeon takes off his clothes, he figuratively descends into the realm of Topaz. This figurative reversal is precisely what happens in the plot. It will be only a few more scenes before Aeon turns himself in to the authorities, who are the last signs of order in the world and the producers, as well, of those dogmatic radio signals we hear over the course of the film.

The plot reversal is this: whereas (typing) Aeon has given over the cultural reins, now (boxing) Topaz himself runs the world and produces its culture ("To Aeon's horror he sees that it is Topaz. He is now exquisitely polished and manicured," N, p. 173). Aeon's poetic figurations rested on cultural privilege and led to disaster, but the cultural productions of Topaz are dictatorial propaganda. The radio thumps a generic Bible, and the television force-feeds utopia: "The television relays the illusion of a perfect and visionary idyll of *Life on Earth* constructed around the central image of Topaz" (N, p. 175). What is the difference between blind figuration and tyrannical propaganda, between poetry and rhetoric? The script collapses and complicates the distinctions brilliantly and devastatingly.

The plot concludes with another mirroring scene when Aeon assassinates Topaz. The dictator Topaz plays the role of Christ, surrounded by twelve disciples and a crowd that shouts "Hosannah! Hosannah!" (N, p. 181). But after shooting Topaz, Aeon "seems to have been transformed. The gun has fallen to the floor. He stares at the palms of his hands. He has received the stigmata. An open bleeding wound" (N, p. 182). Aeon becomes a kind of Christ, but he is a bloody killer Christ; a hero, but a hero on the side of blind culture. The contradictions of the mirroring scene cannot be unraveled, for they speak deeply, indeed mythically, to our contemporary travails.

And so *Neutron*—like *Jubilee* and like so many delusive idylls in the tradition of poetic cinema—jumps out to a fantasy conclusion:

94. Ext. Aeon's Countryside. Sunny Day.
We are back in time when the old house was built new. Aeon is a medieval pilgrim with a palmer's wide-brimmed hat and a shepherd's staff, sets out on a brilliant sunny day. He is surrounded by white doves which flutter around him in slow motion.

(N, P. 182)

A brilliant closing description, indeed, in a brilliantly desperate escape to regions of nostalgia and purity. A beautiful image, which concludes a script that questions in every scene the consequences of creating beautiful things. Both *Jubilee* and *Neutron* remove themselves from violence and distance to pastoral fantasy at the end. But the sheer genius of *Neutron*'s invention, the sudden and completely unexpected appearance of idyll (the nostalgia that one could never remember), makes *Jubilee*'s return to the strange costumes and sad speech of Dee and Queen Elizabeth pale in comparison.

It is a pale return in *Jubilee*, but extraordinarily telling nonetheless, since it aims us toward the light and secrecy of Jarman's next film. Instead of a dark urban world of noise and miscommunication, the concluding pastoral world in *Jubilee* is full of beautiful secrets and flowery codes.

> Elizabeth. The sea remindeth me of youth. Oh John Dee, do you remember those days? The whispered secrets at Oxford like this sweet sea breeze, the codes and counter codes, the secret language of flowers.
>
> (*J*, P. 76)

And Ariel consoles his listeners with the rhythms of his poetry ("there and back"), but he also foresees a tempest.

> Ariel. There and back.
> There and back.
> The white cliffs stand against the void
> We gaze seaward contemplating the night journey. . . .
> In the south at Tillywhim a picture of wind on the sea
> In the west a vision of silver dew falling into a chalice
> Flowing on a sea of pure gold
> In the east a black hoarfrost
> The sun eclipsed by the wings of a phoenix
> In the north a howling chaos into which a black rain
> Falls without ceasing
> Now is the time of departure
> The last streamer that ties us to what is known parts.
> We drift into a sea of storms.
>
> (*J*, P. 76)

Ariel is *Jubilee*'s figure of poetry, but one who sees destruction as much as creation. And so the film ends with bright Ariel at the ocean side: "I am the mirror, the fire that consumes all that is created. I bring the winter of thy flowers and the frost that secretly destroys the temple" (*J*, p. 74). Jarman's next film will open up and elaborate this mirroring, poetic aspect of magic Ariel.

III. THE MARRIAGE OF PROSPERO AND ARIEL
IN *The Tempest*

After *Jubilee*, where Ariel arrives splendidly and strangely from another world and Queen Elizabeth and John Dee reflect elegiacally on the disastrous landscape of the future, it is only logical that Jarman expands upon the Renaissance framework of *Jubilee*, on the dream and the archaisms; and so *The Tempest* emerges in its entirety. Although Shakespeare's final romance had produced numerous offshoots by 1979, such as *Age of Consent* (Australia, 1968), *Forbidden Planet* (USA, 1956), *Love Story* (UK, 1944), *The Yellow Canary* (UK, 1943), and *Yellow Sky* (USA, 1948), no one had at this point filmed a direct adaptation.[39] But the magical, imaginary world of Shakespeare's *The Tempest* is clearly Jarman territory, and his adaptation carries on his interest in the hieroglyphic occultism of John Dee. Jarman aligns himself once again with the tradition of lyric cinema by conceiving the entire play as Prospero's dream and by drastically reducing the dialogue. Even though Jarman lauds Heathcote Williams—

> He is an ideal Prospero, [who] performs sympathetic magic, who destroys the poetry and finds the meaning. I've rarely heard lines spoken with such clarity.[40]

—Jarman's *The Tempest* contributes to his ongoing discussion of poetry's role in film, which will continue throughout his career. Indeed, when Jarman again turns to Renaissance drama in Christopher Marlowe's *Edward II*, he will write "Fuck Poetry!" in the preface to his notes on the play. But Jarman likes to undermine poetry as much as to flaunt it, and I will argue in my final chapter that *Edward II* still possesses poetry in abundance.

Williams may well "destroy poetry," in the sense that he refuses to speak theatrically or ostentatiously, but Jarman's whole play is arranged as poetic cinema. It takes place in the form of a dream; it values atmosphere over narrative, and figurative or pictorial language over verbal language; and, of course, it is spoken in Shakespearean poetry, in contrast to everyday, contemporary speech. Like Cocteau, Jarman always treasures magic and wants to destroy poetry, that is, the poetry that is ordinarily conceived of as poetry. But Jarman notably cuts out those lines where Prospero promises to break his staff and drown his books, and this can only give the impression that Prospero's magic continues and that poetry is not destroyed.

Although *Sebastiane* is an exterior world surrounded by desert and *The Tempest* is an interior world surrounded by sea, each film equally centers on the double-edged image of mirror and ocean. In my second chapter, I describe a theoretical model to account for those interrelated images—a model that attempts to speak to both the medium of film and some general formulations of queer identity. As with *Sebastiane*, then, this is a good place to start, by looking at the ways these images appear in *The Tempest*, and this focus will bring us directly to the signature features of Jarman's adaptation.

Choosing to film *The Tempest* allows Jarman to immerse himself once again in watery imagery. But what do the water and the storm mean in the context of the play? Prospero is the creator figure on the island, the magician with power over nature. Classic interpretations of the play read Prospero's magical control over the elements as being akin to the relationship of art

FIGURE 3.2
Prospero's glassy, hieroglyphic staff in THE TEMPEST

and nature; recent interpretations have often sought to emphasize the imperialist aspects of Prospero's power. How has Jarman conceived of and represented Prospero's magic and power?

When *The Tempest* begins, we see a figure in bed who is clearly dreaming the storm. The storm itself is rendered immediately as part of an imaginary world, an effect that is enforced by the obvious use of stock footage for the storm-lashed boat, footage that has in addition been run through a blue filter. The sound track is not ocean waves, but rather electronic music added to sounds of human breathing. In this way, the storm is instantly denaturalized. This ocean is all imagination and art, and then collapsed onto a single, breathing human. But the human figure is not seen here as controlling and powerful, but rather as writhing and disturbed. It is evident from this dreamer's body that to dream such a storm is to dream a nightmare.

At first, because there is a cloth draped over his head, like a sail blown awry, we cannot recognize the figure in bed as male or female. But when a male figure, Prospero, is revealed as the dreamer, the breaths become more urgent and desperate. The cloth then falls across Prospero's mouth as a kind of gag. This last image suggests that his power to find a voice, to speak out, is somehow qualified, and that is certainly the effect of the whole sequence. Notably, the first words of the film that Prospero seems to articulate—that he does not just hear in his head—are "we split," and we hear that phrase echoed and repeated through the rest of the scene (many more times than in the text of the play itself).

And so Prospero wakes up from his nightmare. This Prospero is a "split" authority from the very beginning. He is a powerful dreamer, but one whose dreams are not entirely in his control and one whose identity is immediately open to question. By beginning with this dream, filmed in this manner, and by cutting out Prospero's farewell lines later on, Jarman creates a Prospero whose power is self-divided. From his journals and through his references to Dee and Jungian alchemy, it is clear that Jarman must feel an affinity toward figures like Prospero. But the figurehead of Shakespeare's last play is also noticeably altered from what we might expect.

Jarman emphasizes the decentering or even deconstruction of Prospero's character by certain choices in casting and filming. A deliberate and strikingly original choice, for instance, is to cast Prospero as relatively youthful. That he is Miranda's father is not an outright impossibility, but their conversations seem much more collegial than cross-generational. Jarman also connects and equalizes his characters through laughter. When Prospero laughs at Ferdinand after one of the tests, Caliban immediately laughs too, an echo. That Caliban repeats rather than opposes Prospero potentially undermines hierarchy. A similar doubling appears when Ariel pokes his head out of a sawdust heap: the camera frames the now almost exactly similar heads of Prospero (who has "big hair," to say the least) and Ariel, who sports a woodchip wig, which looks just like his master's. This doubling of Prospero, like the splitting of Prospero in his dream, once again decenters the magician, and these effects appear numerous times in the film.

Derek Jarman and Lyric Film

In "Magic in the Last Plays: *The Tempest*," Frances Yates contrasts the good magic of Prospero with the bad magic of Sycorax.

> Shakespeare makes very clear in *The Tempest* how utterly different is the high intellectual and virtuous magic of the true magus from low filthy witchcraft and sorcery. Prospero is poles apart from the witch Sycorax and her evil son. Indeed, Prospero as the good magus has a reforming mission; he clears the world of his island from the evil magic of the witch; he rewards the good characters and punishes the wicked. He is a just judge, or a virtuous and reforming monarch, who uses his magico-scientific powers for good.[41]

Jarman is a great student of Yates, and would probably concur that *The Tempest* should be placed in the intellectual context of John Dee and Giordano Bruno.[42] But as much as he is drawn to this emphasis on magic, he would, I think, want to interrogate the clarity of Yates's hierarchies. The contrast between Prospero and Sycorax or between Prospero and Caliban is not so readily apparent in Jarman's adaptation.

By cutting away a good deal of act 5, including the epilogue, for example, Jarman significantly reduces Prospero's role as judge. Further, compared to Jack Birkett's Caliban, with his always compelling banter, Prospero is played as rather a bore, and his magic has no charm. Sycorax is invisible in the play, but visualized quite spectacularly in the film, an enormous naked woman giving suck to an adult Caliban. The good magician-bad witch opposition, which may hold for a Miltonic reading of Shakespeare's play, is deconstructed in this new visualization, since our eyes probably wonder at, rather than judge, this Sycorax.

The destabilization of Prospero's colonial authority is effected most crucially through his relationship with Ariel. In a terrific but brief description of Jarman's emphases in *The Tempest*, Colin MacCabe writes: "Jarman's *Tempest* concentrates on the relationship between Prospero and Ariel with its barely suppressed sexual undertones."[43] This remark is spot on, but needs to be developed. The most striking doublings in this film occur, in fact, in exchanges between Prospero and Ariel. The casting again rather deconstructs the conventional relationship, since instead of an old Prospero and young Ariel (recall for instance John Gielgud as Prospero and all the little boy Ariels in Peter Greenaway's *Prospero's Books*), we have now the relatively young Prospero and the older-looking—at least, thin and haggard, David Bowie-ish—Ariel. Moreover, even as he upsets conventional expectations, Jarman structures the film to focus more intently on Ariel and Prospero. The film ends when Prospero discharges Ariel after the masque, and their scene together thus becomes the last in the film. In addition to the amusing visual doubling mentioned above (they share hair), Jarman goes as far, at one point, as to put the two of them in front of mirrors, thereby asking us to contemplate, once and for all, the pair of them as reflections of each other: now, perhaps, not servant and master so much as brothers. This mirroring scene is worth our detailed attention.

Jarman takes a dialogue between Ariel and Prospero from the first act of Shakespeare's *The Tempest* and moves it ahead almost two-thirds the way through the film. In Shakespeare the scene explains the relationship of Prospero and Ariel; it serves as etiology (Ariel was confined in a tree by Sycorax before Prospero arrived), background, and exposition. In Jarman's version the scene is structurally and visually much more dramatic, even climactic, than expository, and it suddenly brings before us imagery of glass and mirrors that we have not seen to this degree. This "glassy" scene is so striking and so significant that Jarman will ask us to recall it again in his preface to the script of *Wittgenstein*.

But first Ariel needs to talk himself into his confrontation with Prospero, like an employee asking his boss for a raise. Ariel looks into a mirror and works out his lines: "Let me remember thee what thou hast promised, / Which is not yet performed me" (I.ii. 243–244). Notably and weirdly, while Ariel repeats the lines several times he plays a little game of "rock-paper-scissors" with one hand. This mysterious gesture, so typical of Jarman, suggests that Ariel and Prospero have perhaps a playful or randomly hierarchical relationship (the game is based on pure chance) rather than a relationship characterized by anxiety and tyranny. Perhaps the gesture also implies that Ariel is self-divided, his hand not knowing what his head is doing. But overall it contributes to an atmosphere of humor—quiet, *tired* humor, since Ariel always looks to be a few naps short of a good night's rest—but humor nonetheless, in contrast to an atmosphere of imperial surveillance and terror.

For the moment, however, Prospero refuses to release Ariel, and he argues for his authority by reminding Ariel of past favors. Now instead of showing Miranda her young self in the circular glass, Prospero suddenly thrusts Ariel's past before us—a grotesque scene of a naked Sycorax nursing a fully adult Caliban. Just as the postcards in *A Finger in the Fishes Mouth* do not always match the poems facing them, the images we see on the screen do not always match the words (which is another reason why this Prospero may not strike us as threatening, even when he says threatening words). When Prospero reminds Ariel that he was imprisoned painfully in a "cloven pine," the flashback shows Sycorax hauling Ariel over to herself by a chain. And when we cut away from this bizarre memory (which must certainly have influenced both the cinematic technique and visual content of Greenaway's *Prospero's Books*), we find before us Prospero face-to-face with Ariel in front of a receding, duplicated set of Ariels and Prospero. They stand before mirrors.

Prospero threatens Ariel, but the image suggests a continuity rather than a hierarchy; the image suggests that these men do, in fact, mirror each other. When Prospero snaps his chalk (he scrawls his occult symbols on blackboards and all over the floor), Ariel suddenly finds himself trapped in a glass cabinet of some sort. We saw a chain instead of a "cloven pine" in the flashback; now there is an upright glass coffin instead of an oak ("If you more murmur'st, I will rend an oak / And peg thee in his knotty entrails" (I.ii.294–295). Ariel becomes meek and submissive—we look upon a blurry Prospero from what must be Ariel's point of view—but at the end he exhaustedly repeats his original line once more ("Let me remember thee what thou hast promised, / Which is not yet performed me") and collapses. Ariel's stubborn repetition (and Jarman's cut-up rewrite) refuses to grant Prospero an easy victory and declines equally to make himself a victim. Prospero threatens his servant with concretely visual power, but Jarman resees the scene nonetheless as divided in its power relationships, the hierarchy unbalanced rather than clear.

The doubling relationship between Ariel and Prospero is complex and runs throughout the entire film. Each character is a creative figure—Prospero as magician, Ariel as fairy sprite—but each one taken by himself seems isolated and repetitive. It is their union that leads to fecundity and light. In Greenaway, Prospero's books are literally alive, moving and flowing across the page, instinct with magic and exotic color. In Jarman, Prospero's books seem inert; the books and symbols are not filmed to suggest excitement or power. Attached as Jarman is to the strange symbols of Prospero's staff or the signs on the wall, the symbols seem dead on film—quaint, curious, but, as Thomas Carlyle would put it, Dryasdust. We see Prospero studying, wearing spectacles, looking at a globe, but compared to the ebullience of Miranda (bright shells dangling over her face) or the bathetic craziness of Caliban, Prospero appears to be intentionally uncompelling.

Ariel, in his turn, is played deadpan, exhausted, wizened. He is a connoisseur of repetition for its own sake. His rock-paper-scissors game, which we see him play before the big interview with Prospero, continues a series of rather vacant demonstrations of repetition. In one sequence, the camera starts with a little skull, whose jaw Ariel snaps shut several times, and then pans slowly up to show Ariel's mouth, his teeth clacking. A rather bleak analysis of rhythm is the impression. In another early scene, Ariel appears to Miranda on a rocking horse, where he delivers lines from the song of Juno and Ceres in the masque from act 4 (IV.i.106–115). Out of context, the lines mean nothing. Ariel simply recites the poetry, showing no enthusiasm whatsoever. But taken altogether, Ariel's strange mannerisms may be taken as curious relics or allegories of poetry. That he delivers his lines while on a rocking horse—a traditional image of metrically unsophisticated poetry—shows that Ariel is being used quite self-consciously as a figure of poetry. The hermeneutic mysteries of Prospero or the rocking-horse lyrics of Ariel are aligned with poetry, but by themselves they are bleak, vacant, amounting to naught. When Ariel and Prospero join forces, however, then a spectacular creation is the result.

Surely the marriage that Jarman's *The Tempest* celebrates is the creative relationship between Ariel and Prospero, not the forthcoming marriage of Miranda and Ferdinand. Jarman's refusal to celebrate the marriage of the young lovers is transparently evident. The masque of the goddesses from *The Tempest* is dropped entirely and replaced by a sailors' dance, where Elisabeth Welch sings "Stormy Weather." "I don't want to bless the union as Shakespeare did," said Jarman, "because the world doesn't see the heterosexual union any more as a solution. Miranda and Ferdinand may go into stormy weather."[44]

The dance of the sailors, by contrast, is clearly the creation of Ariel, and praised immediately by Prospero ("my trixie spirit"). Ariel welcomes the young couple to the ballroom with a flourish and the broadest smile we've yet seen. During the dance, he sits calmly by the side, watching with, we can only imagine, pride and contentment. Miranda and Ferdinand are clearly at a loss to respond to such an apparition, but finally Miranda says, "How beauteous mankind is! O brave new world / That has such creatures in it!" In Shakespeare these lines are Miranda's response to the discovery of Gonzalo and the rest of the shipwrecked company in act 5; during Shakespeare's masque only Ferdinand is given lines ("This is a most majestic vision, and / Harmonious company" [IV. I.118–119]); Miranda is entirely silent. Jarman transposes the lines in order to make the dancing sailors appear marvelous, admired by Miranda, where by contrast, the heterosexual male, Ferdinand, appears amiable but dim.

The dance of the sailors may be seen quite readily as the creative offspring of the mirroring collaboration between Prospero and Ariel. As will happen in Jarman's films repeatedly—think of the black-tongued Judas hawking credit in a satirical advertisement in *The Garden*, or even of the musical number toward the end of *Blue*—the mood of the film changes abruptly, and the heterogeneous resources of Jarman's cinematic palette are suddenly revealed. Yet although the scene seems to appear from out of nowhere and embodies by far the most radical revision of the entire adaptation, there is also a logic, at least a figurative logic, out of which this dance of men is born—since the dance is born from Prospero and Ariel.

The dance itself is, by turns, dignified, poignant, and silly. There are close-ups of the young men smiling at one another as they turn about, which seem documentary in their recording of mutual happiness. The dancing is graceful, but not ostentatious; there is even a moment of intentional clumsiness, when the sailors duck out of the way of a cartwheeling colleague. The sailors run about with arms raised, do patty-cakes and a few vaguely Russian calisthenics. Altogether, then, a dance for nonprofessionals. They end up in pairs, one sailor raised in the arms of another, which calls attention to the ways that conventional male and female roles have evaporated. The music borrows a flute or whistle from a reel and plays what is at times overtly childlike music in both major and minor keys. The whole effect is happy, innocent, and ridiculous. Jarman removes the masque of Juno, blatantly refusing to bless the marriage of Miranda and Ferdinand, but his alternative celebration, although clear in its oppositionality, is not self-righteous in its critique.

Elizabeth Welch's "Stormy Weather," which follows, is also a perfect and subtle nonblessing for Miranda and Ferdinand. If the audience can shift gears, the song works in a straightforwardly successful way, as a beautifully sung musical standard. Yet the lyrics, as Jarman intends, conflict with the marriage celebration and even with the song's performance. Welch is splendid and smiling, radiating and golden in her costume, but the blues song is concerned with what happens when "my man is away":

> Life is bare
> Gloom and misery everywhere
> Stormy weather
> Just can't get my poor self together
> I'm weary all the time.

("STORMY WEATHER," LYRICS BY TED KOEHLER)

When the song ends and Welch vanishes, we cut back to a darkened house, only Ariel and Prospero remaining. The clear division between interior house (the cerebral realm of Prospero) and exterior beach and ocean is now collapsed, since the house is strewn with leaves. The inside is an outside. Ariel smiles at Prospero, who is asleep. Ariel's smile conveys both pride—what a great show that was—and also the knowledge that he is free. Ariel sings "Where the bee sucks, there suck I"—first cheerily, then in a more melancholy mood—as if in continuation of the song that we have just heard. Then Ariel spirits himself up the stairs and vanishes. Finally, on a close-up of Prospero's sleeping face, we hear his final voice-over, which concludes, "We are such stuff / As dreams are made on, and our little life / Is rounded with a sleep." And thus the film ends by reminding us that everything was indeed Prospero's dream. The final scene, too, continues the focus on the two men, Ariel and Prospero, who now might be regarded not so much as master and servant, but rather as independent collaborators.

In his poem "The Sea and the Mirror: A Commentary on Shakespeare's *The Tempest*," W. H. Auden reverses Shakespeare's emphases by allowing the bulk of the program to Caliban. The mirror in Auden's poem is one that reverses what it sees and also calls attention to its own artifice. In his essay "Balaam and his Ass," Auden writes: "*The Tempest* seems to me a manichean work, not because it shows the relation of Nature to Spirit as one of conflict and hostility, which in fallen man it is, but because it puts the blame for this upon Nature and makes the spirit innocent."[45] In "The Sea and the Mirror," Auden remedies both the "manichean" contrasts and the victimization of Nature by allowing Caliban his extended comment on artifice and the stage. Auden's disillusioned, post-*Tempest* commentary aims from the exhausted spirit of "Prospero to Ariel" in part 1 to the reality of "Caliban to the Audience" in part 3. Auden's work probes the limits of the imagination, but also self-consciously makes the audience aware of the performative aspects of this theater of disillusionment. The mirror's reversal of emphasis may seem to be a necessary correction, but it stands, at the same time, as an artificial device.

Jarman would disagree, presumably, with Auden's corrections, in that we can see that the limits of Prospero's art are his own and have nothing to do with Caliban. Jarman removes the dramatic interruptions of Caliban into the masque ("I had forgot that foul conspiracy / Of the beast Caliban and his confederates / Against my life [IV.1.139–141]") that brings Greenaway's version to a stunning, evaporating silence. Although Colin MacCabe finds that Jarman "makes clear how Prospero's reign is one of terror,"[46] many of Prospero's more threatening lines have been excised, and the delivery of the lines that remain is far from furious or tyrannical.

Jarman is interested in the magical figure of Prospero, no doubt, but the magic—like Blakean energy—results from the mingling of contraries, from the energetic reflection of Prospero and Ariel, from the heterogeneity of styles implied by both Prospero's dream and Caliban's carnival. Poetry, as Cocteau always says, is not where you expect it, and the same goes for Jarman's magic. The magic of *The Tempest* exists not so much in the glittering light of Ariel (which is how he appears in *Jubilee*) or in Ariel's beautiful lyrics (delivered completely deadpan by Karl Johnson), as in Ariel riding the rocking horse or playing his rock-paper-scissors game or smiling proudly at his happy sailors' dance.

Or instead of reading *The Tempest* as a kind of Blakean synthesis or meditation on doubling, we might view the film through the eyes of Stanley Cavell:

> How do movies reproduce the world magically? Not by literally presenting us with the world, but by permitting us to view it unseen. This is not a wish for power over creation (as Pygmalion's was), but a wish not to need power, not to have to bear its burdens. It is, in this sense, the reverse of the myth of Faust. . . . In viewing films, the sense of invisibility is an expression of modern privacy or anonymity. It is as though the world's projection explains our forms of unknownness and of our inability to know. The explanation is not so much that world is passing us by, as that we are displaced from our nature habitation within it, placed at a distance from it. The screen overcomes our fixed distance; it makes displacement appear as our natural condition.[47]

A main critical problem: we know that Jarman reads *The Tempest* as being about magic, yet this film is really not a magical *Tempest*. Not only are all the animated, Walt Disney kinds of special effects eschewed, but even the simple, ordinary kinds of magic that Cocteau used in *Beauty and the Beast* are not employed. Where is the magic? In the weird music? Is not Cavell's sense of cinematic magic at work here? The potentially showy, scintillating magicians, Prospero and Ariel, are nearer to invisibility than we can possibly imagine. In contrast to a *Tempest* that meditates explicitly on colonial power and patriarchal rule, Jarman's Prospero dreams quietly in a house, privately, nearly anonymous. The magic for Cavell surrounds the private audience, each viewer by himself in the dark theater, and Jarman's Prospero, alone in a dark house, may be more like the audience, or a reader, than a master of the occult. The magic, like the poetry, is not where you expect it.

Poetry

and the

Dislocations

of Sound in

THE ANGELIC

CONVERSATION

and WAR

REQUIEM

For the first and only time in this book I will break with chronological order
so as to emphasize a grouping of films. *War Requiem* (1989) follows both
Caravaggio (1986) and *The Last of England* (1987), but I will set it next to
The Angelic Conversation (1985) in order to foreground their similar structures, particularly their use of dislocated sound. The sound track is almost
entirely asynchronous in both films; sound is almost never used, therefore,
to substantiate three-dimensional space. I will describe the sound track and
the consequences of this dislocated sound in some detail.

   These are also films that read and sing out poems from beginning to
end. Although they were constructed in almost antithetical fashion—*The*

4

Angelic Conversation begins with images and finds a sound track; *War Requiem* begins with a sound track and then discovers the images—both films are *tour de force* experiments in lyric cinema in which not only are many conventions of cinematic continuity, such as dialogue, narrative causality, and representational acting, set aside, but poetry supplies the words of the sound track to an almost entirely unprecedented extent. As we noted in the first chapter, films have featured, on more than a few occasions, the appearances of poets or the readings of entire poems, but no other feature-length film, to my knowledge, orders up its images to attend so extendedly on a series or sequence of poems, which is what we see in both *The Angelic Conversation* and *War Requiem*.

I. LIGHT AND DISSOLUTION IN *The Angelic Conversation*

If we are in the mood to pursue and attach significance to definitions, *The Angelic Conversation* is perhaps the purest example of lyric cinema in Jarman's oeuvre. The title itself suggests the transcendental realm of lyric. The images before us focus on two male lovers to the exclusion of almost anything else. There is little plot, only segments and episodes with different moods and atmosphere. And the only spoken language we hear in the film are the voice-overs spoken by Judi Dench of fourteen sonnets by Shakespeare. Like Paradjanov's *The Color of Pomegranates*, *The Angelic Conversation* is, as Michael O'Pray describes it, "made up of a series of ritualistic actions." O'Pray adds that "Jarman thought of the different films that make up *The Angelic Conversation* as poems."[1]

This is an extraordinary film, "one of the most moving and beautiful of Jarman's works," as O'Pray says,[2] and in order to particularize this triumph, it is worth attempting to describe in some detail the episodes and actions that make up the film. Although the film, like other Jarman films such as *The Last of England* and *The Garden*, began without a script and proceeded by improvisation, there is structure and coherence by the end. As Jarman wrote during his editing of *The Garden*, "Today the film took off—a pattern began to emerge out of the chaos."[3] In what follows I will attempt to indicate and evaluate the significant patterns of *The Angelic Conversation*.

The film developed toward its present form in fits and starts, but poetry and ideas of poetry organized the project from the very beginning. Originally, Jarman began shooting film simply to get footage of Paul Reynolds. As Jarman writes, "When we started the film, I had no idea I was going to make it a love story! The initial attraction was mine for him."[4] While the film evolved, Jarman thought of the pictures as a visual accompaniment for the Anglo-Saxon poem *The Wanderer*. But eventually Shakespeare's sonnets came to seem to be the fittest pairing for these images. Along the way, then, the poet and the poetry changed, but the intention to join pictures to poetry was a constant. Thus Jarman describes his own film using not only the archetypes of Jung, but also the rituals and symbols of poetry:

> The descent into darkness—that is like Rimbaud—the descent into the other side is necessary. Then I saw the swimming sections as ablution, the ritual washing of the world. . . . and the sunlight comes out and one is out in the fresh air. I saw the section with the emperor as service for others. It's based on the first poetic elements of our culture—the wanderer, the giver of dreams.[5]

As is characteristic of Jarman, only now more so than ever, the nature of the film is figurative, metaphorical, evocative.

Every aspect of the film accumulates to project a dream world. Dench reads the sonnets, not in a clear BBC voice-over, as will be the case with Nigel Terry in *The Last of England*, but rather as if out of an echo chamber, ghostly. The music by Coil is ominous, brooding, atmospheric, quietly gothic. The most striking technique is the freeze-frame effect of the pictures, moving forward slowly, stroboscopically, "like a series of moving slides," as Jarman puts it.[6] The freeze-frames of *The Angelic Conversation*, combined with a restricted color palette, evoke the ghostly chiaroscuro of silent film, the sense of these people as being somewhere else and in some other time. Voice-over, music, slowly moving "slides," and archetypal images all work together to build up a haunting, ethereal world of vision and desire.

In what follows I will describe, in more or less chronological order, the most important passages of the film. We may be tempted to leave alone a film originally so personal and intuitive, to let it create its atmosphere, to quietly follow it through to its "romantic" conclusion. But many works of art evolve in fits and starts or emerge in personal and obscure circumstances, yet once rounded off and finished, they may well require critical discussion of their elements and structure. *The Angelic Conversation* is a brilliant amalgamation of symbol, imagery, and poetry, and it deserves a detailed commentary that fully appreciates its beautiful patterns. I will focus in particular on the relationship of the poems to the images, on the structure of the film, and on the archetypal imagery that Jarman deploys, imagery that once more, in fact, centers on the mirror and the sea.

Although there will later be large stretches of film where we hear no voice-over, no sonnet being read, the first sonnet, sonnet 57, starts immediately after the epigraph. This sonnet is one of the many time-conscious sonnets in the middle of Shakespeare's sequence, and it begins: "Being your slave, what should I do but tend / Upon the hours and times of your desire." Even before we hear Dench's echoing voice, we hear the ticking of an old clock. Unlike the voice-overs in *The Last of England* or *The Garden*, the voice-overs in *The Angelic Conversation* will often also be tracked together with other sound effects, effects which look forward to the "radio program" sound track in *Blue*. On the screen before us is a man waiting at a paned window, a setting which immediately controverts the iconography of waiting in nineteenth-century painting, where so often a woman waits at a window (John Everett Millais's *Mariana* is a famous example of this topos). We see mostly the man's face in close-up; the camera's intimate look thus interprets the space of poetry as a space of solitary inwardness. Sonnet 57 provides a logical place for *The Angelic Conversation* to begin: the clock ticks, the man sits at a window, and so we start out in something like the real world. Soon we will see the radar station and the overturned car, a few more details of reality, before we plunge into more obviously otherworldly realms.

Immediately after the sonnet is over, there follow two main images that will govern the course of the remainder of the film. We see a man holding a ball of light that shines out brightly, although he himself fades to black and then reappears. This ball is in reality a round mirror, and we will see this image in numerous later scenes. The round mirror that reflects light into the camera is a technique carried over directly from *The Art of Mirrors*, but there it implied only self-conscious artifice and experimental cool. Here the light not only comments self-consciously on the light of the camera, but also performs the light of love's eye in Shakespeare's sonnets. This mirror is the mirror of homoerotic desire.

After a brief shot of the rotating arms of the radar tower, we cut to look over the back of a man walking down the road; sound effects make it seem as though he is walking through water. It is immediately clear that both mirror and water have everything to do with the relationship of the walking man and the man holding the mirror. That the men visually mirror one other will be repeatedly emphasized in the composition of later scenes. Homoerotic desire is once again figured as a mirroring in *The Angelic Conversation*. The men are not twins, though physically very similar, as is most conspicuously evident in the fight sequence. Jarman tells us that he chose a female voice to read the sonnets in order to assure that one male would not seem to dominate over the other.[7] Their relationship is therefore one of equality, of reciprocity. Like desires like, and mirrors the other, but may also lose itself in love of the other. Thus the related imagery of water comes to be associated both with the amalgamation of self as well as with its dissolution.

The psychic landscape we enter now is difficult, laborious. This is no idyllic garden of love, although eventually the film will, indeed, end in a garden. The terrain is strewn with giant boulders—a hard, strange world. One man carries a barrel on his shoulder, his head sunk down beneath the weight. We see a number of other similarly ponderous images here: next to a smoking car, a man carries a large post over his shoulder. The slow-moving men carry burdens and seem in need of respite from their labors. We hear harassed breathing, reminiscent of Prospero's breathing at the beginning and end of *The Tempest*. To dream is also to labor. At the exact moment when we see that the walking man carries a torch in one hand, we hear sonnet 90. This sonnet begins:

> Then hate me when thou wilt, if ever, now,
> Now while the world is bent my deeds to cross,
> Join with the spite of fortune, make me bow,
> And do not drop in for an after-loss.

In this way, the images we have seen—of a man bent under his burden, of obstacles thrown in men's way—are given verbal reference. The poem is loosely illustrated. In most cases the images in the film will not correspond to the words of the sonnet with greater specificity than this. Also charac-teristic is that we stay focused on a single image or object over the course of the sonnet. There is thus some sense of the preeminence of the poem, as if the film has paused for a moment to listen to it. Or there is the related sense that the figure before us—for there is nearly always a man present when a poem is read—is thinking the poem. Yet even as the poem focuses the images, Dench's voice-over does not replace but rather joins the restless and noisy sound track, and the sense of difficulty and obstacle continues.

Form is marked out clearly at the conclusion of this extended sequence, since the film now returns to the setting with which it began, the man wait-ing at the window. It is as if we have returned to the surface for a moment before a plunge toward even greater depths. Again the clock ticks—the sound of time is associated with this space—but now Dench reads sonnet 43, a sonnet where the speaker dreams of his beloved: "When most I wink, then do my eyes best see." The descent into dreamscape, into a more dis-tant realm of the unconscious, is made apparent when the camera breaks away from the waiting man over the course of the sonnet. At line 10, the picture cuts abruptly to a blackboard that is seemingly covered with line after line of Latin. This alludes, more or less, to Prospero's blackboards in

Derek Jarman and Lyric Film

The Tempest, and signals a moment of learned magic. Presumably, we will need some good magic to make our passage into the other world. Finally, the couplet is given its own illustration: a man holding a brilliantly lit round mirror over his head.

> All days are night to see till I see thee,
> And night bright days when dreams do show thee me.
>
> (SONNET 43)

After some wandering and difficulty, therefore, we have entered a dream world.

Jarman often links together sequences of light images (as, for instance, when Jarman's cigarette becomes a torch in *The Last of England*), and here we descend to a cave of darkness by twisting between light sources: the mirror, a torch, another torch in the cave, and, finally, images of flame. And it is in darkness, amidst these flames, that we hear sonnet 53:

> What is your substance, whereof are you made,
> That millions of strange shadows on you tend?
> Since everyone hath, every one, one shade,
> And you, but one, can every shadow lend.
> Describe Adonis, and the counterfeit
> Is poorly imitated after you.

The Renaissance occultist in Jarman is naturally attracted to the Neoplatonic language of the first two lines, and the flickering flames around a man's face serve as an appropriate accompaniment for the first quatrain. As the Adonis lines are heard, a swath of flowers crosses the screen, appearing suddenly out of the darkness. Another small illustration, then, since the flowers make for a witty and self-conscious underlining of the reference to Adonis. The flowers also serve to complicate any oversimple structuring of the narrative. We thought that we were on some kind of underworldly descent, yet this poem seems relatively more optimistic than anything we have heard thus far. In the midst of darkness, these flowers. The flowers are, in fact, the image with which the film ends, so they, like the return back to the very first scene for the reading of sonnet 53, serve to disabuse us of an overly linear sense of narrative.

And this is a brilliantly felt and conceived underworld, conveying a unique and otherworldly atmosphere with great economy of means. Here is a Miltonic "darkness visible," indeed, construed through the outlines of flames and the suggestions of walls—an amorphous cavern that bears mentioning in the same breath as those other fabulous, dark interiors: the ruins of Cocteau's *Orpheus* and the great mysterious building at the center of Tarkovsky's *Stalker*. The visual atmospherics are overlaid with a hypnotic sound track, part medieval chant, part postmodern electronics. Just as Jarman's images in *A Finger in the Fishes Mouth* may subvert as well as substantiate the words of a poem, the music in the caverns both confirms (as archaic-sounding, as haunting, as implying ancient catacombs) and contradicts (as monklike chanting is contradicted by erotic desire) the images before us.

For the first time in the film, we see both men together in the same frame. They come together ritualistically, assembling themselves as living hieroglyphs, at the edge of legibility. They stand one behind the other, both facing forward into the camera, with the famous hieratic frontality that Paradjanov learned from Pasolini. In his notes to *The Garden*, Jarman calls these ritual poses "emblemata":

> Now a series of emblemata (improvised): Tilda holds a sword and lilies; Pete, as a haughty princeling, crowns himself; Jack does a Can-Can in a scarlet judge's robe.[8]

So, too, in *The Angelic Conversation*. Like living emblems in a Renaissance book, the man in front holds two torches, and the man in back holds the mirror. There also appears to be a third man behind both of them, although we can see only his hand holding a fan. The mirror, like the two torches, signals once more likeness and doubleness. The doubling effect is heightened by repeating most of this shot exactly a few moments later on. Doubling will be emphasized still further by the scene that follows, in which a man fights off his shadow self with a staff. The fan held by the mysterious third figure is not a very obvious symbol (in comparison with the doubling mirror and the torches of desire), and it will reappear in later scenes. Since water imagery starts now to penetrate and interrupt the fire imagery, we might take the fan as a kind of contrary to the concentrating mirror, as signaling over against the mirror a watery relaxation, a dissolution, a fanning out, a drifting away. This hovering, statuesque, beautiful, and barely readable scene of men with torches, mirror, and fan could itself be taken altogether as a momentary emblem for Jarman's lyric cinema.

We hear music of the orchestra tuning up (from Britten), which we also heard during the credits; once more we have the sense of doubling back, back to the beginning. Again we find ourselves in light, and a man blinks his eyes into that light as sonnet 148 is read. "O me! What eyes hath love put in my head, / Which have no correspondence with true sight!" We seem

106

to have emerged from the darkness for the moment, finding ourselves in a new element, now wholeheartedly the element of water. After eight lines of sonnet 148, we cut to a man kneeling formally (on one knee) and holding up a shell. He kneels on an outcropping of beach, water all around him. In a sense, the mirror held aloft has become that shell.

Then, for the first and only time in the film, we hear another sonnet immediately following on the last. This is sonnet 126, another sonnet that seems clearly addressed to a man: "O thou, my lovely boy." As this sonnet continues, we stay with the image of the man at sea's edge. The camera zooms slowly out, then cuts to a brilliant shot closer in: the sea's sparkles shifting, slide by slide, all around him. Finally, when the sonnet arrives at a time image ("May time disgrace, and wretched minute kill"), the film cuts again to the window scene of the very beginning, clock ticking. Once more we have the impression of focused, forward narrative movement with a sense of segmentation (cave, water), but also an impression of looping, of labyrinthine doubling back.

Water is the predominant image of the next several episodes. First there is an extended passage of a man swimming, or rather twisting and rotating in the water. As the film moves on, there is more and more emphasis on the body. We hear dramatically played Britten, a marked contrast to the determinedly spooky music by Coil, and we hear ocean sounds and sea gulls. The obstacles and fog seem past, replaced now by brightness, color, clarity. The beauty of the male body is celebrated as the man turns and revolves among the glittering waters. After a time, we cut to the other man on rocks overlooking the sea, and we may imagine that this man watches the swimmer.

Over the watching man's face, then, we hear the most familiar sonnet thus far, sonnet 29: "When in disgrace with fortune and men's eyes / I all alone beweep my outcast state." In this bright world, Dench's voice does not emerge from an echo chamber as before; her voice projects as clear as the image. This sonnet has no particularly exact relationship with the pictures before us, but at the middle of line 10 the music gets strange again, and a shiny metal ball appears. Images of the ball in different settings move us through a montage to three men kissing the ball and then at last settling down to the washing of the so-called tattooed man. The tattooed man is, whatever else, a regal figure, and sonnet 29 has probably been selected for the language of its final couplet:

For thy sweet love remembered such wealth brings,
That then I scorn to change my state with kings.

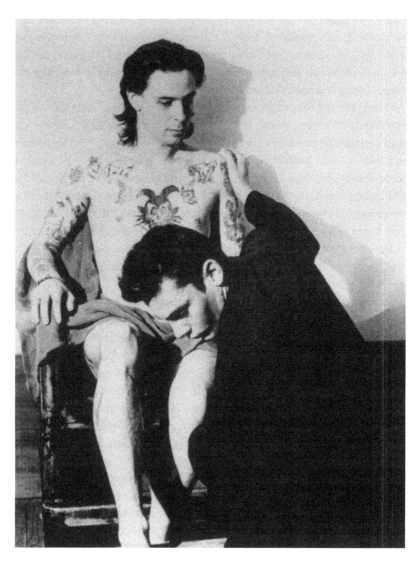

FIGURE 4.1
The ritualistic washing of
the tattooed man in THE
ANGELIC CONVERSATION

The washing of the tattooed man continues the imagery of water, now as part of the most obvious ritual in the film. Other actions and poses in the film may be characterized as ritualistic, but this scene looks concretely to enact a social custom, recorded at length, as if in anthropological detail. We first see all three men kissing the ball, which suggests a psychology of love where there are not just two men mirroring each other, but three (we seemed to see three men also in the cave,

Derek Jarman and Lyric Film

as we noted earlier). But instead of reading the third man as a third party, a third corner in some kind of triangle of desire, consider that this third man is also a trope, a further embodied metaphor for the relationship between the two men. One way of reading the third figure, therefore, is as a kind of personification of the language of aristocratic hierarchy (king, servant) that runs throughout the sonnets. Jarman, as we noted, does not wish to allow one man to dominate over the other; hence his use of a female voice. The appearance of the tattooed man rather brilliantly means that we will not see one man abasing himself in front of the other. This third figure allows the two men's desire a trajectory, where they can each, equally, bow to him.

We hear bells, to underline the sacred nature of this washing. We see repeatedly the sponge dipped into a vessel of water, again emphasizing that this is a formal, socially acknowledged ablution. One lover washes, the other holds two torches; these actions and poses give the appearance of formal, prescribed roles. The scene is the first in the film (except for the briefest moment elsewhere) to be shot in real time, without the stroboscopic effect. This visual change makes for a transcendental paradox, where the deepest, most unconscious desires suddenly become the most real. Having passed through stroboscopic darkness and then stroboscopic brightness, we emerge into a cavernous, abstract, transcendental reality. With a very visible devil (a skull with ram's horns) on his chest, the tattooed man is not an amiable prince or a boy-angel with make-believe wings. He is at the heart of a dark unconscious in a realm of time-bound desire and eternity.

The psychology of the ritual—as the two lovers interact not with each other, but around the regal figure—is partly explained by the first eight lines of sonnet 94, which we hear upon the investiture of the tattooed man (he is given a pearl necklace to hold and a large sword, which is placed in his lap):

> They that have power to hurt, and will do none,
> That do not do the thing they most do show,
> Who moving others are themselves as stone,
> Unmoved, cold, and to temptation slow—
> They right do inherit heaven's graces,
> And husband nature's riches from expense;
> They are the lords and owners of their faces,
> Others but stewards of their excellence.

Jarman himself comments on the scene as being a treatment of male dominance; in contrast to the watchful dominance of the radar screens, this scene exemplifies "service willingly given, not exacted. There is no compunction in the scene. 'He that has power to hurt and will do none.'"[9] This scene not only allows the figurations of hierarchy to dissolve in selflessness and equality, but it allows the tattooed man to mediate between the two lovers in their physical desire for each other. They arrive at each other's plainly beautiful bodies by first moving through his spetacular, regal body. One man now showers the king's body—his chest, his arms, his legs—with one careful kiss after another. The king figuratively stands for the final distance between the men, who have wandered through so much darkness and death to find each other.

In *The Angelic Conversation* as in *Sebastiane*, the element of water aligns itself with flesh and sensuousness, although the ritual ablution clearly means to keep flesh pure. After the scene with the tattooed man, there are

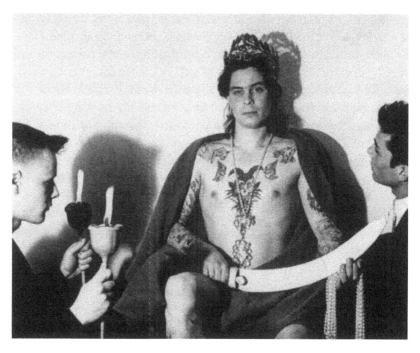

FIGURE 4.2
Through the tattooed man, toward each other

further sequences with water. Now a man kisses the shell, dips the shell in water, pours water over his face; throughout, the gleaming wetness of skin is emphasized. If the mirror's light focuses desire in the eye, water in *The Angelic Conversation* is associated with (pure) physicality, the immersion in the body, the tactile flesh as answer to the eye's calling. Sonnet 30 appears ("When to the sessions of sweet silent thought / I summon up remembrance of things past"), and at line 5, where the water

Derek Jarman and Lyric Film

imagery begins, the film cuts back to the man pouring water over himself with the shell:

Then can I drown an eye, unused to flow,
For precious friends hid in death's dateless night,
And weep afresh love's long since cancelled woe.

Then a brief pause, and we remove to a man with a torch in a cave and listen to the famous sonnet 55: "Not marble nor the gilded monument [sic, as read by Dench] of princes shall outlive this powerful rhyme." The placement of this sonnet seems entirely rhythmical, a pause between the watery episodes, which have followed one after the other, and before the fight scene to come. The audience is allowed to relax in recognition, to drift along with a familiar sonnet, and the accompanying picture is one that is shot without cutting and of relatively familiar terrain. A carefully structured breath before the climactic scenes that follow.

The fight scene is the narratively logical culmination of the spatial, and consequently emotional, relationship between the two lovers. Now they finally touch, but it is to fight and wrestle rather than in ritual or in tender embrace. The difficulty of love is once again emphasized, and the restless music underscores a relationship in tension. Their identically clad bodies (no shirts, black pants, bare feet) emphasize again the mirroring between them, and neither dominates as they twist and turn through the frame (the twisting bodies visually recall the swimmer turning through the water). The last part of the scene is, in fact, superimposed over light flashing on water, which draws a visual connection between mirror and water once again. In *The Angelic Conversation* water has also come to connote a sensuous and tender aspect, so that it makes sense to close out the fight scene with this image before moving to the love scene following and the resolution of these tensions. Although the fight scene can be read as a strong interpretation of the tumultuous nature of the Shakespearean sonnet, there is noticeably no voice-over here, just timpani and snare drums (suggesting military engage-ment) and other noises of discontent.

After the fight, the lovers sleep together, a sleep annotated by sonnet 27 ("weary with toil, I haste me to my bed, / The dear repose for limbs with travel tired"). Slowly they awaken, and we move through a montage of emblematic images collected from previous moments in the film: the torches, the shell burning, and again the blazing mirror, which precedes the two men (identically dressed in black shirts) kissing. The mirror image is interposed again, along with a man, whom we have not seen before, holding a large reflecting tablet or book. Even now, as the men's bodies

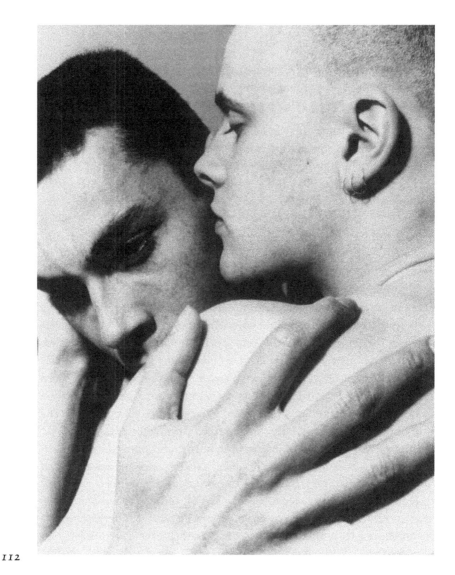

112

FIGURE 4.3
After a journey of many stages, reach their nearest approach, all distance
the two men embrace collapsed, these figurative third parties still
appear, destabilizing the isolated solitude of
the loving couple. The music played is on electronic keyboard, but is now
more ordered, "classical," based on arpeggiated chords, both minor and
major. Again the mirrored, doubled nature of their desire is highlighted.
One shot has them forehead to forehead, a pose that Jarman will use to
similar effect in *The Garden,* which here gives the exact impression of a

Derek Jarman and Lyric Film

man looking into a mirror. Indeed, this mirrored pose is held throughout the entirety of sonnet 61:

> Is it thy will thy image should keep open
> My heavy eyelids to the weary night?
> Dost thou desire my slumbers should be broken,
> While shadows like to thee do mock my sight?

At the end of the sonnet the faces pull away somewhat so that we may realize with certainty that this is not a mirror after all.

This is as close as the two men will come, and *The Angelic Conversation* now begins its ascent back to the everyday world. We cut to another picture of the men embracing, and we hear the sounds of water. Once more, the continuity between mirror and sea could not be more clearly indicated. The ocean sounds continue, but are interrupted by the turning radar arms. We are moving back to the surface, out the other side of the vision. From now on the lovers will be seen separately. The film returns to the image of the man holding the shell aloft and kneeling on the shore. As seagulls cry in the background, we hear sonnet 56, perfectly chosen:

> Sweet love, renew thy force, be it not said
> Thy edge should blunter be than appetite,
> Which but today by feeding is allayed,
> Tomorrow sharp'ned in his former might.
> So love be thou, although today thou fill
> Thy hungry eyes, ev'n till they wink with fullness,
> Tomorrow see again, and do not kill
> The spirit of love with a perpetual dullness.
> Let this sad int'rim like the ocean be
> Which parts the shore, where two contracted new
> Come daily to the banks, that when they see
> Return of love, more blest may be the view;
> > As call it winter, which being full of care,
> > Makes summer's welcome, thrice more wished, more rare.

Lines 8–12 comment particularly on the water imagery before us, but the poem as a whole serves as a moving "bon voyage" to the spirit of love, a prayer for love's renewal after such fulfillment and resolution as we have witnessed.

The lovers exist in separate realms, and we concentrate our attention on the man seen originally at the window. He is outside the house, walking along the grounds; the details confirm that we have returned to the real world. There is a new sense of openness about him; he is no longer waiting inside by the window, looking out, but rather walking outdoors beneath the clear, large sky. He also carries the fan, hiding behind it, fanning himself with it. We have the impression that he has brought it back as an artifact from the other world, like a time traveler with his visible proof. The fan is the most ambiguous symbol that we have encountered, but, again, it may connote a kind of dispersal, an airiness, a centrifugal force, aiming away from the center, away from intensity and tumult. We have returned to the everyday world, but it has changed since we began there. We began indoors, now we are outside. The lovers are separate, but our sense of the world has changed because of their meeting.

The final sequence cuts back and forth between a man's face immersed in flowers and what are presumably his memories of the other man turning in the water. Memory and distance are emphasized, although the flowers have also replaced the rocky landscape with which we began. Over these images we hear sonnet 104, the fourteenth sonnet of the film, a sonnet of sonnets.[10]

> To me, fair friend, you never can be old,
> For as you were when first your eye I eyed,
> Such seems your beauty still. Three winters cold
> Have from the forests shook three summers' pride,
> Three beauteous springs to yellow autumn turned
> In process of the seasons have I seen,
> Three April perfumes in three hot Junes burned,
> Since first I saw you fresh, which yet are green.
> Ah yet doth beauty, like a dial hand,
> Steal from his figure, and no pace perceived;
> So your sweet hue, which methinks still doth stand,
> Hath motion, and mine eye may be deceived:
>> For fear of which, hear this, thou age unbred,
>> Ere you were born was beauty's summer dead.

The film ends (with ominous help from the music) abruptly on the word "dead"; the man's face in the flowers suddenly turns from stroboscope to freeze-frame (as at the unresolved conclusion to Francois Truffaut's *The 400 Blows*).

Conventionally, cinematic sound locates a body in cinematic space; sound contributes to the illusion of three-dimensional reality. But the sound tracks in *The Angelic Conversation* and *War Requiem* do not obey cinema's conventional relationship between sound and visual space. The rights holders to Britten's *War Requiem* did not allow any sounds to be added to the music, so to an almost unprecedented degree in a film with a sound track, all the sounds are nondiegetic, emanating from a space beyond what we see on the screen. No person in *War Requiem* is given weight or dimension by a sound on the sound track; there is necessarily a ghostly or dissociated quality to each human figure and action.

The sound-space of *The Angelic Conversation* is not so extreme, but there is a similar disjunction between visual image and sound track. Sounds do not seem to emanate naturalistically from the characters, but from thoughts or some imaginary realm. When we first see a man walking over a sandy beach, the sound track provides a man walking through water. The contrast between image and sound pointedly informs us that the collage of images will themselves be collaged under layers of sound, so that sound and image will annotate one another only elliptically. Sound will not substantiate a three-dimensional real world; on the contrary, sound will lead us into unsubstantial, imaginary spaces.

In the influential terms set down by Sitney in *Visionary Film*, *The Angelic Conversation* is a "trance film" whose theme, like that of other "psycho-dramas that marked the first stage of the American avant-garde cinema" is the "quest for sexual identity."[11] Maya Deren's *Meshes of the Afternoon*, Anger's *Fireworks*, and Brakhage's short films (particularly those featuring Jane Brakhage) might be seen as avant-garde precursors to Jarman's film. Compared to longer films by Anger (*The Inauguration of the Pleasure Dome*) or Brakhage (*Dog Star Man*), Jarman's work is notably much less ecstatic, less heterogeneous, less chaotic. The imaginary world is built out of a few basic, concentrated elements. Jarman's cinematic world is layered but spare; the carnival element is relatively atypical. *The Angelic Conversation* is one of the most relentlessly focused and unwavering of all of Jarman's works, looking directly toward the remarkably spare sets with which Jarman concluded his career in *Edward II* and *Wittgenstein* and even toward the mercilessly unvarying blue screen of *Blue*. In its fierce concentration on homoerotic passion and its relentless disruption of visual naturalism (here through the stroboscopic slow motion), *The Angelic Conversation* may be seen, indeed, as an earlier form of *Blue*.

I. MONUMENTALITY AND ELEGY IN *War Requiem*

War Requiem holds a strange place in Jarman's work, and Jarman himself seemed retrospectively more than usually displeased with the film. The film received very mixed reviews on its release, and even Jarman's staunch supporters do not spend much time on this movie. Yet the project is clearly an extension not only of Jarman's political interests (themes of pacifism, masculinity, and authority studied through fellow homosexual artists Wilfred Owen and Benjamin Britten), but also of his interests in poetry. Since a recording of Britten's music provides the entirety of the sound track, the film might reasonably be thought of as a visualization of that music. Yet Jarman goes as far as to write: "The poems and the liturgical mass—the 'libretto'—are the rocks to which I am anchored. In a way the music is merely a vehicle."[12]

To focus squarely on the language and the poems makes for a very odd emphasis, no doubt, but again demonstrates the centrality of poetry for Jarman. Jarman's images do not necessarily subvert the music, as one might expect from reading the excerpt just quoted, but they do respond to the sound track in complicated and elliptical ways. Jarman does not view his project as a mere annotation of the music; the images are not background for the masterful sounds. Quite the contrary, Jarman foregrounds the poetry, and films poetic and symbolic scenes in place of secondary commentary or narrative. If we see properly what the film sets out to do, we can perhaps regard the film as more successful than it has been thought up until now.

For the purposes of narrating such a poetic film, Jarman logically focuses on the figure of Owen, the poet. He does give this figure a skeleton of narrative. Jim Ellis argues that to provide the music with such a plot might push our experience into the realm of opera. I would add to this, however, that to organize a narrative around the poet is, simultaneously, not just to create a narrative for the sake of structural coherence, but also to reconfigure our sense of what narrative is and can be.[13] This plot is only barely a plot. In his published journal on *War Requiem*, Jarman says that he has written "a loose story around Wilfred Owen, a Nurse, and the Unknown Soldier," and later on, in the epilogue, he writes, "*War Requiem* is a collage. A cut-up" (*WR*, p. 1). The images that come before us build up small regions of allegorical plot or story, but these are always performed symbolically rather than naturalistically. The film thus becomes another representative of lyric cinema: a film that proceeds contingently rather than linearly, represents figuratively rather than realistically, and once again incorporates actual poems in order to ground the viewer's expectations in poetry rather than prose.

One of the repeated objections to Jarman's approach is precisely at the level of this symbolic interpretation; this art-house manner does not seem forceful enough for the tremendous anger of the poetry and the passion of the music. One critic claimed "Owen's attempt to portray the horrors of war in all their stark reality was scarcely in tune with the 'beautiful' and symbolic visual images conjured up by the director."[14] This distrust of poetry in the face of truth goes all the way back to Plato, of course; and more to the point, it is expressed from the very outset by Owen himself. The "Preface" to Owen's poems begins with just these concerns:

> This book is not about heroes. English poetry is not yet fit to speak of them.
> Nor is it about deeds, or lands, nor anything about glory, honour, might, majesty, dominion, or power, except War.
> Above all I am not concerned with Poetry.
> My subject is War, and the pity of War.
> The Poetry is in the pity.
> Yet these elegies are to this generation in no sense consolatory. They may be to the next.
> All a poet can do today is warn. That is why the true Poets must be truthful.[15]

This is directly comparable to Jarman's preface to his script for *Queer Edward II*:

> It is difficult enough to be queer, but to be a queer in the cinema is almost impossible. Heterosexuals have fucked up the screen so completely that there's hardly room for us to kiss there. Marlowe outs the past—why don't we out the present? That's really the only message this play has. Fuck poetry. The best lines in Marlowe sound like pop songs and the worst, well, we've tried to spare you them.[16]

Poetry, for both Owen and the Jarman of *Queer Edward II*, implies a civilized artifice not up to the horrific truths of war or of AIDS. But in *War Requiem* Jarman is still willing to take a symbolic approach by implicitly using a more traditional defense of poetry, which claims that a route through the imagination and the figurative can be as accurate a way toward truth as realism and documentary.

Jarman's *War Requiem* combines found footage of bloody war with his filmed scenes, and the documentary images are, indeed, thought by critics as sometimes worthy of the powerful message of Owen's poetry and Britten's music: "Only in the 'Libera me,' where genuine archival war footage (from the bloody Cambodian conflict) accompanied the build-up to the cataclysmic climax on the G minor chord . . . (the nuclear attack on Hiroshima) did the film seem convincingly in harmony with the music."[17] Even the investors, before filming had begun, wanted Jarman's treatment

117

"to be more violent, less cosy" (*WR*, p. xii), and, we may assume, not just for purposes of commercialization. The critical consensus seems to be that the art in Owen's poetry—for those are poetic texts, not photographs—and in Britten's music as well, does not obscure their terrific antiwar messages, but that the art and the poetry in Jarman's version may well fail to match up to the music and the tremendous seriousness of what it says. In my opinion, Jarman's film is still flawed and self-defeating in certain respects, but if we will allow a visualization of Owen's poetry and Britten's music that is not based entirely documentary footage (and surely the horrors carried within Owen's poetry are conveyed through poetic structure, rhythm, and symbol), then we might allow Jarman's film some successes and not feel only lack and insufficiency.

I will try to emphasize the strengths of Jarman's adaptation in the pages that follow, and I think that the second half of the film is very powerful indeed. But it must be admitted that for most viewers this is going to be a more than usually difficult film to watch and appreciate. Audiences experienced in cinema's poetic trajectories may not necessarily go in for the classical music. Avant-garde enthusiasts might expect something more like Sally Potter's *Thriller* (1979), which appropriates in postmodern fashion Puccini's *La Bohème*. Art-house moviegoers accustomed to opera might expect a treatment more like Franco Zeffirelli's masterful productions of Verdi's *La Traviata* (1982) and *Otello* (1986). In other words, the overlap between opera buffs and experimental-movie fans is a conjunction not often visited.

It is true that there are difficulties that attend many art-house movies. How can I, for instance, continue even to look at the screen in Pasolini's *Salò* (to take an extreme example); what is going on, scene after repetitive scene, in Resnais's *L'Année dernière à Marienbad*? But the difficulties of Jarman's *War Requiem* are not just intellectual challenges or gut-wrenching disturbances, though these are there, too. These are difficulties of a rather different order. For example, although Owen's poems are sung in English, it is not easy to understand what the words are, and the Mass, of course, is sung in Latin. A viewer really needs to have studied Britten's texts already, which may be a good idea before going to the opera, but is not usually necessary when showing up for a film. What is more, Jarman produces various signals for how his film should be viewed and what kind of film this is, and these are signals that an experienced viewer ought to be able to process rewardingly. But not all the signals match up properly, and the film itself provides us with some false expectations. Most interesting films make more sense with repeated viewings, no doubt, but *War Requiem*, I think, actually

Derek Jarman and Lyric Film

makes relatively little sense the first time through. You need the first viewing to arrange your expectations and to learn how to read the film on its own terms.

The first lesson, as we might expect, has to do with poetry. The opening of the film immediately underscores the centrality of poetry amidst all the music. We first see a written paragraph on the screen: "Wilfred Owen, the soldier poet whose words inspired Benjamin Britten's music, was killed in the last week of World War I at the age of 27." Anyone who knows something about Britten or the *War Requiem* probably knows that already, but the main purpose of these lines is not so much to provide information as to place a poet at the heart of the work. As Jarman describes his spare, invented narrative: "I shall relate the life of a soldier poet, who will inevitably be identified with Wilfred Owen, although no real details of his life are possible" (*WR*, p. 1).

A scene follows where an old soldier, played by Laurence Olivier in his final film role, is wheeled across a courtyard by a nurse, played by Tilda Swinton. The scene frames the work firmly in the present and puts us in mind not just of memorials (his medals), but also of memories (he looks at an old photograph, together with what seems to be an old letter). The film's framing device is common enough in Jarman's work—Elizabeth and John Dee in *Jubilee*, the sleeping Jarman in *The Garden*—but is here presented with a disjointed effect. We learn immediately that Owen has died in the war (from the paragraph on screen), and then we see an old soldier who has survived the war and who remembers his way back into scenes of war that center not on himself but Owen. This opening frame is not very tidy, then, nor will there be a corresponding frame at the end of the film.

This prefatory scene is the only scene in the film without Britten's sound track. It partly functions as a kind of star turn for Olivier, who reads a poem while a bell tolls in the background. What the scene also performs immediately, however, is a kind of silence: Swinton's nurse and Olivier's old soldier chat animatedly throughout, although we hear not a word. Sound is strangely dislocated from image. In *The Angelic Conversation* the effect of such dislocation, I have suggested, is to further the otherworldly quality of the images; the images before us are not located or substantiated in three-dimensional space through the use of sound. A similar effect occurs in *War Requiem*, where the interior, psychological quality of sets and performances is heightened through the pictures' tenuous relationship to the sound.

So the prefatory scene moves forward, and we hear Olivier reading the Owen poem "Strange Meeting," which will also be the last of Owen's lyrics set to music in *War Requiem*. We note that the images on the screen do not have a close connection to what is conveyed through the sound; the hellishness of the poem is not emphasized in the actors' playing of the scene. What this preliminary scene teaches us about the film is fourfold: the importance that poetry will have for the film (we should not forget that the songs we are about to hear are sung poems); sound and image will not necessarily match up (the horrors and despair of the poetry will not necessarily be illustrated through the images); the images will be gestural and generalized; and narrative will be oblique and relatively fragmentary. It is worth noting, finally, that Olivier's reading of the poem ends just over halfway through. The last lines in his reading are:

> For of my glee might many men have laughed,
> And of my weeping something had been left,
> Which must die now. I mean the truth untold,
> The pity of war, the pity war distilled.
>
> ("STRANGE MEETING," WILFRED OWEN)

Now Jarman loved Olivier's voice ("Olivier's voice rings as clear as that chapel bell in Chaucer's Prologue to *The Canterbury Tales*," WR, p. 3), and would not, I imagine, have sacrificed half the poem to the audience's potential impatience. But these are appropriate final lines for Jarman's prologue, since they conclude with the pity of war, the pity that Owen linked with the poetic ("The Poetry is in the pity"). *War Requiem* is a requiem, an expression of grieving, of pity, and so the film that follows will in part be war and the images of war, but more fundamentally expressions of grief, elegy, memory, "the pity war distilled." As I will argue below, Jarman stages his own version of a requiem through a visual dialogue between monumentality and performance.

The wrong signals, as I call them, that Jarman's film transmits to the audience are in some of the more realistically filmed early scenes. These scenes are rather dull, fail to do much of anything interesting, and emphasize only the restraints of the budget. At the beginning of his *War Requiem* book, Jarman writes:

> I'm going to film the lead character's childhood with my home-movie, Super-8 camera. Other perils of low-budget film-making mean that we have to work within easy distance of London. There are some pluses: images of war, soldier and nurses, are easily understood by an audience, so they should be able to follow what's going on.
>
> (WR, P. 1)

This remark, too, is easily understood, but grounds what in my opinion is a mistaken and self-defeating set of scenes in the early going. Why do we need to see men exercising in the courtyard or digging a trench? We can follow the plot, but our expectations are misled. By the end of the courtyard scenes, we have an effective image of male tenderness, but it takes awhile to get there.[18] These scenes look rather generic and stereotyped (we have seen them in films dozens of times), not to mention a bit cheap-looking compared to those in other war movies. It may be argued that we need some foundation, some norm to deviate from later; not everything can be a dream or a symbol. But these easily understood scenes have the danger, on the one hand, of appearing clichéd or boring, or, on the other, of providing the audience with the expectation that the film will, in fact, be easily understood, whereupon the symbolic approaches elsewhere may seem opaque. Hence the first viewing of the film teaches us to discount these scenes to some degree. These sequences cannot compete with either the reality of the documentary footage or the equivalent scenes in other movies or the more imaginative approaches of the film itself. We learn that these scenes are to be regarded as structurally significant, perhaps, but not central, ultimately, to the overall effect of the film. As the film continues, these scenes become less frequent, and the film becomes more successful—more successfully effective in its response to both the music and the poems—as a consequence.

Imaginative and powerful use of limited resources is made by returning repeatedly to a set of steps in otherwise minimalist, decontextualized surroundings. This set, not the courtyard scenes or the ditchdiggers, has everything to with what the film is about. The steps in different scenes serve different purposes and provide multiple connotations, but always lead toward a meditation on the monumental. The steps and setting visually parallel the exasperated and elegiac responses to war and death that Britten's *War Requiem* images in its music.

In the first set, the body of the dead poet lies before us, "set up like Charles Sargeant Jagger's Hyde Park Memorial" (WR, p. 3). Jagger's Artillery Memorial is one of the most famous works of public sculpture in Great Britain, and perhaps the most well-known sculptural response to World War I in England. Jagger's War Memorial is not used haphazardly by Jarman as a model. Although Jagger's Memorial is "clothed in academic style," as David Lee writes, "it is yet, enclosed, compact, and inward looking."[19]

The still figures look pensively down. This is no celebration of victory, like the immodest, bombastic war monuments of Eastern Europe and the old Soviet Union, but, instead, a reminder of deeds and sacrifices by individuals. It is precisely what a war monument should be, an object which invites still, silent contemplation.[20]

Jarman's *War Requiem* imagery tests out precisely similar tensions between academicism and experiment, public ostentation and private mourning, heroic leader and common man. Like Jagger's memorial, Jarman's *War Requiem* is a public artifact that aims the viewer toward the private and the ordinary. Jarman's film provides literal, realistic scenes from war (marching, digging trenches) and documentary footage that provides "war as it is." The film also provides responses to that war through the requiem, which involves selective retellings and reconfigurations of war (retellings that are in themselves elegiac responses) in addition to cinematic meditations on the fixing of grief in the monumental. In *War Requiem*, Jarman's representations of elegy are usually much more original, convincing, and powerful than his representations of war.

This observation leads us to notice a clear gender division in *War Requiem*. Men fight the war, and are seen fighting; the elegiac response to war is concentrated for the most part in women, in particular women played over the course of the film in different guises by Swinton. In the filmmakers' express intention, Swinton's roles were added to correspond to the voice of the soprano in Britten's music. As Don Boyd, the producer, writes, "there are no women in Wilfred Owen's poems, but there is a very powerful female voice in the Britten score" (WR, p. viii).[21] Yet Boyd puts the case too strongly, since even in "Strange Meeting" one of Owen's speakers already evokes a feminine presence.

> Whatever hope is yours,
> Was my life also; I went hunting wild
> After the wildest beauty in the world,
> Which lies not calm in eyes, or braided hair,
> But mocks the steady running of the hour,
> And if it grieves, grieves richlier than here.

Here amidst this Keatsian lushness is the only moment when the images in the film's prologue really illustrate the poem, and at this moment emerges a female figure. Olivier's old soldier looks at an old photograph of a nurse, and archival footage then shows us a number of nurses. In a way, Jarman's illustration and Olivier's photograph may actually deflect the idea that those braids belong to the soldier's heterosexual lover, by pointing the memory and attachment instead toward a female caregiver. That the female voice comes into visual life as a nurse may strike us as a rather stereo-typical invention, but one could more generously regard that role as clas-sical—archetypal rather than stereotypical. Such a female mourning figure follows in the footsteps of the Trojan women wailing elegiacally at the close of Homer's *Iliad* after their great warrior Hector is killed in war. Swinton thus does not appear specifically in the character of a nurse as much as she performs and embodies different versions of requiem.

The bravest and most brilliant contribution by Swinton occurs in the first section of the "Sanctus." The script reads: "The nurse sits at the base of the altar, responding to the mood of the music, a static seven-minute shot" (WR, p. 35). The difficulties attending the editing of this scene come out in Jarman's later commentary:

> The poem 'The End,' and the *Sanctus*, which precedes it, have been particularly fraught. For two months now a debate has gone on whether we leave Tilda's seven-minute take intact, and then how we follow it. It's not just a problem of performance, it's a problem of scale. The *Sanctus* fits into our scheme of concentrating on the actors, but this poem gives us the only moment in the film where we pull away from the individual into images that are boundless.
>
> (WR, PP. 36–38)

Jarman here worries about the scene in sequence with what follows; he also worries simply about seven uninterrupted minutes of performance.

The extended performance is, however, a well-established element of Jarman's poetic repertoire. "Jordan's Dance" in *Jubilee* is a similar excur-sion, and Swinton herself performs a comparable role when she cuts up her own wedding dress at the end of *The Last of England*. Ellis again reads this extended scene in *War Requiem* as operatic in nature:

> The scene consists of one extraordinary seven-minute take of Tilda Swinton braiding her hair (which continues the images of bodily care) and weeping in an obviously theatrical yet oddly affecting way. The scene is operatic in the extravagance of the emotions portrayed, and in this scene Swinton is very much the diva, a role for which she is especially suited, given her reputation in the rarefied world of art house cinema.[22]

Instead of reading the scene as grounding us firmly in the world of opera and thereby expanding the generic confines of the music, however, I would prefer to see the scene as linked with the more heterogeneous genre of "per-

123

formance piece," which plays more ambiguously and less melodramatically with our responses. As Ellis notes, Swinton also covers her ears to the music, only one of a number of actions that, I would argue, keep her undoubtedly elegiac response from freezing into either monument or opera.

What happens in this scene? The script always calls Swinton "a nurse," but there is no indication of that here. On the contrary, her dress slips off one shoulder, emphasizing a role more like that of a lover than a nurse. She wears many tightly curled braids, and she braids her hair at the beginning, reminding us inevitably of the "braided hair" in "Strange Meeting." The opening scenes have already told us that Swinton will appear in different roles: she is the nurse to Olivier's old soldier in the present; she is also a nurse contemporary with World War I. So when Swinton sits again on the steps of the memorial (which is itself absent), dressed in a different costume, her role and character are open. To a degree she is on the side of the music, perhaps, emoting and performing like an opera diva, but she is also clearly listening to the music. Is she not, indeed, more like a member of the audience than a character in an opera?

In general, performance pieces tend toward a heterogeneity of character, genre, and effect, and surely such is the case here. Swinton holds perfectly still, as still as the stone steps on which she sits. The music builds, and she brushes her hands over her face and bare shoulder, on the edge of a sensuous response. The music clearly impacts the body: she rocks back and forth. Her hands conduct, quietly dance, are held close to her sides. Swinton seems to alternate between unselfconscious absorption in the music and recollections of sadness and nightmare. She is frequently at the edge of weeping, but the performance is far from melodramatic, since Swinton projects so many different emotions, no sooner occupying the hysterical than calming to a dreamlike swoon.

This extended sequence is only the most remarkable of several scenes that take place on those steps and explore versions of elegy and monumentality. After Olivier's prologue, we cut to the body of Owen laid out on the altar, a candle burning beside him and a crumpled piece of paper centrally visible in his hand. Olivier's voice, as it concludes his excerpt of "Strange Meeting" ("The pity of war, the pity war distilled"), forms a sound-bridge from the prologue to this scene, which serves to focus our attention on poetry, on poetic responses to war and death. Each in their turn: the poet responds by poetry, the nurse by weeping, the composer by music, society by building monuments. All of these responses are immediately before us at once, in our eyes and ears. The poet, it would seem, is given pride of place, since he is also the dead soldier for whom we mourn. Yet compared to music and monument, his poem looks, perhaps, most fragile of all. None-theless, Swinton takes that poem away with her, saving it for posterity. She screams at the war helmet but treasures the poetry, as much for memory's sake, no doubt, as for art's.

The crumpled poem placed surreally in the dead Owen's hand is later readable in the scene as "Anthem for Doomed Youth." This is the first poem in Britten's sequence of lyrics, and Britten, too, must have thought of his *Requiem*'s response to war in light of Owen's imagination of no response whatsoever:

What passing bells for these who die as cattle?
Only the monstrous anger of the guns.
Only the stuttering rifles' rapid rattle
Can patter out their hasty orisons
No mockeries for them from prayers or bells,
Nor any voice of mourning save the choirs,—
The shrill, demented choirs of wailing shells;
And bugles calling for them from sad shires.
What candles may be held to speed them at all?
Not in the hands of boys, but in their eyes
Shall shine the holy glimmers of good-byes.
The pallor of girls' brows shall be their pall;
Their flowers the tenderness of silent minds,
And each slow dusk a drawing-down of blinds.

Britten's music and Jarman's images—burning candle and mourning nurse—answer Owen's self-elegy as best they can, filling the void with sight and sound. The shiny bright steps of the monument—lit and arranged as theater, not reality—stage the perplexities and variety of emotional response ("anthem," "requiem") that centers above all on a poem. In its handwrit-ten, eyewitness, personal perspective, the poem connotes authenticity but also fragility.

The "Requiem Aeternam"—the first of the six sections of *War Requiem*—returns once more to the monument's stairs for the brief conclud-ing chorus, following the tenor solo. Now Owen himself sits on the steps, reading a book. The set is lit differently: instead of the slick, theatrical black of the opening scene, now the lighting is softer, more natural; this seems to be the real world in the afternoon. The altar table is the focus during the *kyrie eleison* of the chorus, but the camera zooms in slowly on Owen, cut-ting away from the table, and finally zooms in on the book, which we can see to be a volume of Keats's poems. The contrast between the ornamental cover of the poetry book and Owen's shiny boot is marked, and the image of a soldier reading a book of poems is self-divided unto itself. Yet the poetry, not the altar table, seems to be at the foundation of reality, and the film cuts from the book to show a home movie of bread being broken at a table. Surely the figurative logic here is that poetry is not an otherworldly or exotic response to war's suffering, but a living, experiential response, as necessary as bread or breathing.

Like section I ("Requiem Aeternam") and section IV ("Sanctus"), then, the third section ("Offertorium") begins at the monument's steps. In place of the female figure of Swinton, however, now we find four old military men, not as aged and decrepit as Olivier's old soldier, but much closer to him in years than to Owen. Generational drama is at the center of this section of *War Requiem*, which focuses on the story of Abraham and Isaac. Owen's poem bitterly and shockingly rewrites the Biblical story by depicting a modern Abraham, who does, after all, kill his son:

Behold,
A ram, caught in a thicket by its horns;
Offer the Ram of Pride instead of him.
But the old man would not so, but slew his son,—
And half the seed of Europe, one by one.

("THE PARABLE OF THE OLD MAN AND THE YOUNG")

Jarman illustrates this poem quite literally by showing us an Abraham (played by Nigel Terry) who ignores a child angel and a ram (each of which recall scenes out of *Caravaggio*) and who, to the delight of buffoonish, cigar-smoking grotesques, cuts Owen's throat. The old men that we see at the beginning of this section are therefore implicated in this parable, in which one generation offers up another to slaughter.

Instead of Swinton's "operatic" performances on these same steps, the four men now respond more stoically—the male palette more limited than the female in this case. Their expressiveness is muted in comparison with the nurse's, but their roles remain multiple, since they respond partly as colleagues, as fellow soldiers, but also as patriarchs, as seniors responsible for the welfare of the young. Instead of another table rising above the steps, this set has a coffin-shaped hole cut into the stairs, and the four men lower the body down into this emptiness. This grave is more anonymous, less elaborate; earlier, the poet, dressed in his uniform, rested on the altar with his poem. Now, however, this is an unknown soldier, nearly naked, and his grave is correspondingly spare. The old soldiers turn and sit on the steps

Derek Jarman and Lyric Film

simultaneously; they all assume exactly the same pose. The wrinkled faces are human and sympathetic, but the identical poses underscore the uniformity and impersonality of military sensibility.

The steps return for their final appearance in the concluding scene of *War Requiem*. This set is lit a bit differently once again, now in between, perhaps, the slick, artificial black with which we began and the more naturalistic lighting of the scene with Owen on the steps. This set is more open: lumber is visibly strewn about outside the doors, whereas we could not see outside the room in earlier versions. Figures come and go through the doors; what is outside seems to be a wreck; what is inside seems once more to be an attempt to organize a response to that ruin and wreck beyond.

The scene above the steps changes three times. Each scene change might be said to perform a different version of requiem. First we see the unknown soldier, St. George flag in hand, costumed in halo and orange robe. Below him sleep four soldiers: this is a stage re-creation of Piero della Francesca's *Resurrection*. Whereas such posed quotations in *Caravaggio* are always tinged with postmodern wit (Caravaggio is outfitted in a stylish blue suit, even at his death), this grouping seems essentially without irony, straightforwardly implying a traditional response to war's suffering through Christianity and art.

These posed figures watch over most of the scene, but when we look again in a moment, we see only the kneeling unknown soldier, bereft of accouterments, dressed as he was when buried by the four old men. The figure of the unknown soldier, naked expect for a kind of diaper, stages now a requiem without "art"; this is the unadorned truth. Finally, in the last phase, all the figures vanish; only a candle burns on the table. Clearly the changes in this sequence perform alternatives of emotional response: first, an elegy, either patriotic or Christian; second, the naked truth; third, a candle's light amidst nothingness. The film as a whole may be said to embody and work out these alternatives, scene by scene, over its wandering yet carefully structured course.

The various stagings in the final scene and the repeated use of the stone stairs throughout create a dialogue between monumental and performative responses. An image is used repeatedly—the stairs—but in various circumstances and with multiple effect. If anything in *War Requiem* may be considered to have the resonant force of poetry or symbol, these scenes do. Jarman himself likes to keep track of repetitions. He does not mention the repeated use of the memorial set, but he does point out other repetitions, both within the film and beyond:

127

The film has its feet on the ground: in the first scene the Nurse ties the bootlaces of the poet (the foot soldier); a rose thorn sticks into the foot of the Unknown Soldier; in the parade we see feet stamping, marking time. Later, the Unknown Soldier's feet are washed by his mate in the trenches, an echo of the washing of Christ's feet. In the final sequence, the wounded foot is revealed with the marks of the stigmata. These connections are clearly woven throughout the work like a spider's web. This morning, in the middle of filming, the largest wolf spider I have ever seen flew out of the dark, and remained suspended a few feet above the crew. Everyone jumped. Spiders have arrived in three of my films in this way. Two of them became extras: a bright yellow one in *Sebastiane*; another delicate one runs over Prospero's staff in *The Tempest*. It was rather a thrill when this happened, as it wove the films together for me.

(WR, pp. 15–16)

The repeated image of the foot is readily noticed, but not necessarily easy to assimilate. "The film has its feet on the ground" is a tactful joke, and it properly avoids a reductive interpretation. The repeated images of feet, like the images of the spiders, do not appear too obvious or forced; the connections just happen.

But not all of Jarman's imagery is so fortuitous. The snowball scene (in section III, "Dies Irae") is an obviously symbolic scene, and the kind of invention, which, in its premeditation, might give poetic narrative and symbolism a bad name. In a reading of Buñuel's *Belle de Jour*, a film that dissolves back and forth between reality and fantasy, for example, Michael Wood discusses at length the appearance of a wheelchair to Pierre midway through the film, a wheelchair that foreshadows that Pierre will end up in a wheelchair.[23] Foreshadow, yes, but only in a clunky, heavy-handed way, so much so that Pauline Kael wrote, "[Buñuel] leaves in miscalculation, and fragments that don't work—like the wheelchair on the sidewalk in *Belle de Jour*."[24] But Wood defends this moment in Buñuel ("this is a fragment that couldn't work") by suggesting that the sheer transparency of this symbol is a kind of ironic commentary on the unsubtleties of interpretation. There is another layer, then, Wood argues, beyond the felt weight of the image, a weight which otherwise would threaten to drag the light web of connections awkwardly to the ground. I bring forward this example from Buñuel by way of saying that the snowball scene seems also to involve miscalculations, but without the saving self-consciousness or randomness that Wood attributes to Buñuel.

Derek Jarman and Lyric Film

The snowball scene allegorizes the confusions of war by focusing on three men: a German soldier, Owen, and an unknown soldier (whom the four old soldiers bury later). "The Unknown Soldier is playing a piano alone in empty, snow-filled room" according to the script (WR, p. 23). The piano, according to anecdote, was discovered in this room by accident, but the scene seems nonetheless to aspire toward a cliché of surrealism. Jarman notes the origins of these ideas:

> The whole sequence is built around snowballs, and the legendary Christmas Day when the English and German soldiers exchanged greetings and played football in no man's land. Tilda's grandfather led the British team. Other sources are the snowball that Dargelos throws in the Bal de Conte [sic] Orgel—The Bloody Snowball. I also saw just such a room in Moscow in 1984 in a student film (surely one of the most magical ever made), where a musician walks through an old palace in which the snow is falling silently through the rafters.
>
> (WR, p. 24)

Falling snow (both inside buildings and out) is used in many films to lyrical effect; for instance, there is snow falling memorably through a ceiling toward the end of Carol Reed's generically heterogeneous Odd Man Out (1947). But is there not something forced or obvious here in War Requiem, especially compared with the boundary crossing of interior and exterior, of snow and sculpture, in Cocteau's The Blood of a Poet? The German soldier tries to fend off Owen's blow with an old battered trumpet. "What could be more poignant," Jarman asks, "than his attempt to ward off the fatal bayonet thrust with this battered instrument, green with age and verdigris?" (WR, p. 27). Jarman barely comments on Swinton's splendid performance, but openly melts at his manufactured poem: "Everything is pretence, but when the music of the Lacrimosa fills the room, everyone's transported; tears fall from the crew's eyes" (WR, p. 27). The bloody snowball itself stands as a sentimental emblem of the symbolically reduced warfare. Jarman is "certain that Britten would have been happy with this sequence— piano, trumpet, and fatal snowball" (WR, p. 27). Jarman is often happy to celebrate his own efforts, especially in the moment of production, but there is something pushy about how good this symbolism is, which might make us consider that even Jarman sees its faults. This sequence falls into the category of poem that Cocteau and Tarkovsky always railed against, the film that tries so hard to be poetic and beautiful that it isn't any more.[25]

The snowball scene labors under a difficulty that I think may be stated

129

130

FIGURE 4.4
The shining pool in
WAR REQUIEM

as this: we are more open to poetic responses to war than to poetic retellings of war, the requiem more than the war. The bitterness and horror of war that come through in Owen's poems are captured powerfully by documentary footage. The most brutal footage—from recent conflicts in Cambodia and Afghanistan—is reserved for the final section of the film and edited to the severe rhythms of the music. Jarman's re-creations of World War I, either straightforward (digging ditches) or symbolic (the

Derek Jarman and Lyric Film

snowball scene), have a hard time competing with the documentary footage. The elegiac response to war, however, takes place in a complex and amorphous interior world and asks necessarily for multiple representations and embodiments. This then becomes a way of arguing more explicitly for why I think the scenes on the monument's steps, as well as the Super-8-filmed memories, are more convincing than some of the earlier war scenes.

The final section of *War Requiem*, "Libera me," is probably the most uninterruptedly effective piece of the film. The opening chorus is matched with documentary footage, and the final chorus is set around the monument's steps, which we have earlier discussed. "Strange Meeting," the poem on which this final section centers, is a hellish dream from beginning to end and so is more readily conducive, perhaps, to cinematic reimaginings. Jarman films the poem rather literally for a while: Owen walks "down some profound dull tunnel," a narrow corridor in the hospital, and he comes upon "unencumbered sleepers," bodies plastered into the ground like so many grim sculptures. When the baritone takes over to read (sing) the lines of the "other" ("'None,' said that other, 'save the undone years. . .'"), the German soldier appears and signals what the script calls a kind of "blessing" to Owen, but the gesture seems to us ambiguous rather than clear. So that when we now return to those lines—"the wildest beauty in the world"—we see an image from childhood, child and mother, which, like the images from Olivier's opening prologue, again deflects heterosexual romantic love.

Then the poem begins to rain.

Then, when much blood had clogged their chariot-wheels,
I would go up and wash them from sweet wells,
Even from wells we sunk too deep for war,
Even the sweetest wells that ever were.

This provides Jarman the opportunity for his signature watery passage: no desert oasis this time, but instead a muddy pool in hell, though still surrounded by men, who slowly wash themselves and drink. The rain falls, the tears drop, the blood flows; the pool sparkles and shimmers, even in hell. When the scene changes, the men around the shining pool turn into a meditation on monuments and stone.

CARAVAGGIO

and

the

Mirror

of

Gold

Caravaggio (1986) is probably Jarman's most well-known film. It is the Jarman film chosen for the British Film Institute's "Modern Film Classics" series and written about so brilliantly by Leo Bersani and Ulysse Dutoit. Shot in 35mm with at least a little more than Jarman's usual threadbare budget, the film looks more like what a mainstream audience might expect and unfolds in something approaching a narrative. "This film is the first in which I have developed acting parts and bowed to narrative: a necessity imposed by the situation and a reflection of Caravaggio's style."[1]

As we shall see, many of Jarman's cinematic choices in this film reflect his situation (as a director with finite economic resources), and reflect Caravaggio's paintings, too, as if Jarman were as much the receiver as the creator.[2] Yet *Caravaggio* is all about the mammon-fingered economics of art—its filthy lucre—and so the film everywhere complicates this metaphor of reflection. Reflecting mirrors and glittering gold are always interrelated in this film, and we have not seen these golden mirrors before in Jarman's work.

In its relatively mainstream look, *Caravaggio* may seem the least obviously poetic of Jarman's films, yet I suggest that it still fits well into the set of problems and motifs that I have described up to this point. Although Caravaggio is a painter, and though he clutches no Keats and quotes no Blake, the film can be rewardingly placed in the context of other lyric films, films that not only proceed in a "lyrical" manner, but also include poems. An early script did, in fact, contain an outwardly recognizable poem, as Jarman writes:

> The one major loss in the new script is at the final moment when I
> stretch hands across the centuries with Mayakovsky's wonderful final
> poem—'Love's boat has smashed against the daily grind now you and
> I are quits'—but perhaps that is now implicit in the script and doesn't
> need to be realized as a tangible image.[3]

As far as I am aware, this is the only reference to Mayakovsky in Jarman's writings, but it makes for a fascinating reference. Mayakovsky's poetry often manifests both his original desire to work as a painter and his ongoing interest in cinema (he wrote thirteen film scenarios). His poetry is both revolutionary and surreal, originating, as he says, in "the silly fish of imagination." The poem to which Jarman refers was included as part of Mayakovsky's suicide note:

> And, as they say, the incident is closed.
> Love's boat has smashed against the daily grind.
> Now you and I are quits. Why bother then
> to balance mutual sorrows, pains, and hurts.[4]

The inclusion of Mayakovsky's last poem would have generated an image of a solitary, suicidal love, but one caught up in all the political sloganeering and social consciousness that one associates with the Russian poet. These tensions and contradictions may now well be "implicit in the script" and in the film, as Jarman suggests.

Another poem is printed as a poem in the script, but does not appear in the film:

> The painter restrains the burning action of light;
> he separates the sky from the earth,

the ash from the sublimate,
the outside from the inside;
and when the hour of happiness is over, carefully
gathers the heaped-up ashes.

(C, P. 101)

And in the film Caravaggio reads lines of poetry aloud from a book—lines from the Song of Solomon from the Bible (and printed as follows in the text of the script):

Upon my bed at night
I sought him whom my soul loves
I sought him but found him not
I called him but he gave no answer.
I will rise now and go about the city.
In the streets and the squares
I will seek him whom my soul loves.
I sought him but found him not.

(C, P. 54)

These examples show that Jarman's impulse to mark *Caravaggio* through poetry still exists. In much of the film, however, poetry remains tangible not through texts, but rather in the sensibility of expression that finds kinship with a tradition of poetic cinema. Indeed, we can best begin this discussion by bringing forward three directors from our "pantheon" of lyric cinema—Pasolini, Tarkovsky, and Paradjanov—who will help us organize the chapter as a whole according to voice-over, painting, and temporality.

As students of Jarman's *Caravaggio* know, Pasolini is the director whom Jarman brings forward himself. *Dancing Ledge* is the first of Jarman's many autobiographical texts, and it moves through scenes from childhood, school years, adolescence, art school, and so on toward the first films. But *Dancing Ledge* originated as a defense of Jarman's filmmaking in general and as a description of the making of *Caravaggio* in particular (the first illustration in the text is Caravaggio's painting *David and Goliath*). The journal entries begin on December 26, 1982, in Monteverde, Tuscany, and it is not long before Jarman's thoughts turn to Pasolini. Earlier in Rome, during March 1973, Jarman had worked on the set design for Ken Russell's *Gargantua* (which was never filmed), and had been "thrilled to discover the production office for *Gargantua* was adjacent to that of Pasolini's *The Arabian Nights*."[5]

Derek Jarman and Lyric Film

And so Jarman tells us in the first sentence about Caravaggio: "Had Caravaggio been reincarnated in this century it would have been as a film-maker, Pasolini."[6] The entry continues:

> There is a remarkable lack of emotional force in modern painting.
> Who could shed a tear for it now? But you can weep at Pasolini's
> *Gospel According to Matthew* and *Ricotta* can make you laugh. In
> 1600, who knows, painting might have evoked the same immediate
> response. Of course Pasolini painted very badly.[7]

The Pasolini films that Jarman mentions here are refractions of the Bible: on the one hand an extended depiction of the gospel story, and on the other a short, comic treatment in which Orson Welles plays a director who is reshooting the crucifixion as a set of still lifes. Since *Caravaggio* is built out of the re-creation of famous paintings, *La Ricotta* is perhaps more to the cinematic point in this reference, and a still from the film is reproduced in *Dancing Ledge*. But clearly Jarman invokes Pasolini not so much for their overlapping cinematic interests, which are many, but in view of his sexuality: "[Caravaggio] became the most homosexual of painters, in the way that Pasolini is the most homosexual of film-makers."[8]

Bersani and Dutoit set down these same quotes about Pasolini, with the accumulating focus on homosexuality, but only to turn around the quotes entirely:

> More interesting than this, however . . . is Jarman's total indifference,
> in the film *Caravaggio*, to the oppositional politics he seemed so ready
> to embrace. Unlike *Edward II* and *The Garden*, *Caravaggio* neither
> victimizes nor exalts gay love. You would never guess from the film
> that during a long period in its preparation Jarman seriously thought
> he was making a film about 'the most homosexual of painters,' one
> who 'took on the Church as his true and deadly enemy' since it had
> outlawed 'the center of his life.' Probably more faithful to early sev-
> enteenth-century politics than the comparison of Caravaggio's fate
> to Pasolini's, Jarman's film represents a notable indifference to sexual
> orientation.[9]

In this early section of their book, Bersani and Dutoit assure us that Jarman's film is better than what Jarman says about it, and it might be argued in general that artists are not always the clearest guides to their own work. But the importance of Pasolini for Jarman should still be pursued and developed.

We will modify Jarman's equation of Pasolini and Caravaggio, then, by saying that Jarman is attracted to Pasolini as a heroic figure not only because of his homosexuality, but also because of the ways his films proceed. If Pasolini was the "most homosexual" of filmmakers, it did not come through in the content of the films so much as through their style. Neither *The Gospel According to Matthew* nor *La Ricotta*—the films that Jarman chooses to name—represent homosexuality in any direct way, but they do propose an alternative manner of proceeding in cinematic terms, a manner of proceeding that Pasolini associated with "the cinema of poetry." Jarman's strong-felt attraction to Pasolini has certainly been noted by critics, and his references to Pasolini often depend on matters of content—Pasolini's "vita violenta," his biography, the young, wandering boys in the films.[10] Yet these matters of content and oppositional politics might not be enough by themselves, were it not that Pasolini is as relentlessly oppositional in his formal relationship to cinematic narrative, an opposition that he always calls poetry.

What is this "cinema of poetry" in Pasolini? There is no evidence that Jarman read Pasolini's theoretical prose, although Jarman's practice of turning out almost as many journals and scripts as films is very much in the Pasolini mode (and it is hard to think of other directors comparably prolific in both cinematic and textual media). Thus Jarman makes no mention of any of the essays in *Heretical Empiricism* (*Empirismo eretico*) such as "The 'Cinema of Poetry,'" where Pasolini most explicitly theorizes a sense of poetry that runs throughout his critical works. Pasolini's general terms for the poetic could be gleaned from the films themselves: "irrational, oneiric, elementary, and barbaric"—language that explains why Pasolini continually returned to archaic myths and third-world settings.[11]

But it is important to note that Pasolini grounds his poetic cinema in a grammatical or narratological device: "free indirect discourse." Free indirect discourse characterizes the cinema of poetry for Pasolini and forms a join between the subjective and the objective, the lyric poet and the social
136 collective. The cinema of poetry is not just lyric (subjective), in this view, but also political (objective), and the technique of free indirect discourse is the most representative expression in its arsenal. Pasolini explains that free indirect discourse is more than an "interior monologue" spoken by a character; it is, by contrast, speech by a character where you hear the author's voice come through.[12] These definitions and formulations have been criticized by Metz and extended by Deleuze, and Pasolini did not specify how this technique applied to his own films.[13]

But the dynamic that Pasolini sets down in this essay—one probably unread by Jarman—is exactly pertinent to Jarman's *Caravaggio*, since it is obvious to every student of the film that Jarman's subjective immersion in the historical Caravaggio is at the center of everything one wants to say about the film. The relationship between a lyric, subjective point of view and a historical, social worldview is being worked out in every frame of the film. The blatant anachronisms immediately evidence the director's imposition of himself on history and are only the most obvious visual signs of the tension between subjective desire and objective reality. With Pasolini's essays in mind, we may note, too, that a further embodiment of this tension resides in the interior monologues that Jarman writes for Caravaggio. These monologues are spoken from Caravaggio's point of view, but are clearly overwhelmed by Jarman. In a moment, we shall look further at these monologues and call them what they are—namely, poems.

Another figure from the tradition of lyric cinema who will help organize the discussion of *Caravaggio* is Tarkovsky. Tarkovsky's *Andrei Rublev* seems much more distant from *Caravaggio* than films by Pasolini, and so is less obviously kin, but I suggest that Tarkovsky's historical film about a painter of religious themes can nonetheless help point us toward the way that Jarman works with painting in his own film. Tarkovsky's spiritual, sacralizing sensibilities seem at first quite alien to Jarman's satiric, political impulses. Yet each director is drawn to historical painters for similar reasons; each director finds that the cultural power formerly bequeathed to the visual art known as painting is now held by the visual art known as cinema. Jarman's comparison of Pasolini with Caravaggio cited above explicitly says that painting's power continues in the form of cinema; in *Cinema and Painting*, Angela Dalle Vacche similarly argues that Tarkovsky reenacts in *Andrei Rublev* the aesthetic ideology of icons: "the experience of time pulsating through the filmic image is the best modern equivalent for the transfiguring force icons were supposed to possess in ancient times."[14]

Although Tarkovsky is clearly interested in the paintings as such—the glorious visual conclusion of *Andrei Rublev* consists of an extended series of pans over religious murals—he does not seem to be interested much in technique. Thus we see the painter, Andrei Rublev, actually painting only once.[15] It might be argued that this, in effect, keeps the paintings even more sacred; we do not see Rublev physically interact with the images, and the paintings simply appear at the end, accompanied by beautiful music. Yet I would argue the opposite: instead of enforcing a clear boundary between art and life, the effect is to make painting seem to be one aspect of a multifaceted religious life. Le Fanu notes the interrelatedness of death and life, painting and water, in *Andrei Rublev*: "As one of the workmen in the ambush episode falls dying, the stream mingles with his paints, covering its surface with a milky pale translucence."[16] Yet in addition to reading this interrelatedness as a sign of God's or nature's omnipresence, I would read it as a phenomenological indication: painting does not stop with the frame, but rather flows outward, beyond itself, refusing the duality of subject and object.

Human creativity and expression are connected to nature in Tarkovsky, to earth and to water, connections most memorably visualized in the episode of the casting of the bell at the end of *Andrei Rublev*. The continuity between the muddy clay of the hillside and the splendid bell in conclusion is rendered for us in exquisite detail. Yet the physical effect of this creation, of this desire to express (in sound), is measured in this episode, as everywhere else in the film, through the body. Boriska, the bell-maker's son, is physically and emotionally wrecked by the pressure of making this bell for the prince (since if the bell fails to ring, he will be flayed or decapitated).

When we look at those beautiful paintings by Rublev at the end, then, it is only after traveling through a landscape of violence and sexuality, through the bodies left behind by the raiding Tartars and past the temptations proffered by the naked women in episode 3, "The Passion of Andrei." In *Andrei Rublev*, Tarkovsky wants us to rethink what painting is, where it begins, what physical space it passes through, and where it ends. Jarman's approach to painting, in his turn, will be more overtly self-conscious and postmodernist, but he too, with different ends in mind, will complicate the fixed image of the framed painting, as well as emphasize the equally complex boundaries of the human body and human expression.

In the third section of this chapter, I will look at the way that cinematic time is organized in *Caravaggio*. Here I am compelled by a small but powerful image at the end of both *The Color of Pomegranates* and *Caravaggio*: the boy angel. As both films aim toward death—of the poet, of the painter—an angel appears, and in both cases, it appears as the childhood self of the character, dressed up in an angel costume. In Paradjanov, Sayat Nova looks up to see his boy-self floating over his head, holding one angel wing in each hand. After the killing of Ranuccio, Caravaggio flashes back to an Easter parade, where he, too, is a little boy dressed as an angel. He then goes inside a room, where he sees the posed tableau of *The Entombment of Christ*—and the adult Caravaggio is discovered as Christ in that representation. Causal temporality is obviously much loosened in both *Caravaggio* and *The Color of Pomegranates*, but we need to describe the temporal elements with even more precision in these films in which our angelic, childhood selves are seen to look directly upon our dying, older selves.

138

I. POETRY AND THE VOICE-OVER:
GOLD OCEAN AND DEADLY MIRROR

Nigel Terry contributes to the mainstream appeal (if such it may be called) of *Caravaggio*, as much of a star as we are ever going to see in Jarman's films (Terry earlier played King Arthur in John Boorman's *Excalibur* [1981]).[17] Yet Terry becomes a central figure in Jarman's work, not just because of his star quality and his remarkable face (Jarman thought he looked just like Caravaggio), but because of his voice. Terry is the voice of *The Last of England* and by far the predominant voice of *Blue*. His elegant, patient voice reads the poems in all of these works. Whatever poetry is in Jarman, Terry's voice is aligned with it; his is the voice of Jarman's poetry. It is impossible to listen to *Caravaggio*'s voice-over, which is so crucial to its auditory space, without thinking of the voice tracks in *The Last of England* and *Blue*. The voice-over in *Caravaggio*, spoken in the mind of the dying artist, is composed in an obviously noncolloquial, noncontemporary idiom. In Terry's careful inflection, Jarman's prose takes on a literary resonance closer to that of Shakespeare or Marlowe. Indeed, with some specificity, we can responsibly say that Nigel Terry's voice-over in *Caravaggio* is poetic.

"Poetry" appears in various ways in Jarman's films. In each film, poetry has different attributes, resonances, and associations. In *Caravaggio* poetry represents a conscious artifice, a difference from prose, a formalism. It represents these differences as deriving from alienation and homelessness. This is made clear at once in the opening lines of the film:

> Malta, Syracuse, Messina, Naples . . . four years on the run, so many labels on the luggage and hardly a friendly face, always on the move, running into the poisonous blue sea, running under the July sun, July 18th of 1610, adrift. Salt water drips from my fingers leaving a trail of tiny tears in the burning sand. The fishermen carry me high on their shoulders. I can hear you sobbing, Jerusaleme. Rough hands warm my dying body, snatched from the cold blue sea.

(C, P. 9)

Caravaggio thus begins by carrying over the imagery of water and homelessness from *A Finger in the Fishes Mouth* and *The Tempest*. On the soundtrack we can hear slowly falling waves, and the sea will be heard throughout the film in all the scenes set in "Porto Ercole. Hospital Interior": "The silence is broken only by the rhythm of the sea" (C, p. 17). The historical exactitude of "July 18th of 1610" in this passage is immediately subverted by both the anachronistic idiom ("so many labels on my luggage") as well as by the clearly poetic tone ("salt water drips from my fingers leaving a trail of tiny tears in the burning sand"). If we want at the outset to term *Caravaggio* a biopic or historical film, then the opening voice-over insists that we qualify our generic choice, by asking us to account for something once again that emerges in something more like ethereal poetry than fact-based prose. What is more, this opening soliloquy is spoken over an overtly emblematic image—the head of Caravaggio, one eye closed and one eye open. At the end of the film, he will be buried with shiny, reflecting gold coins in his eyes (which give the effect of sunglasses); for now, he's half in the world, half out. Poetic monologue thus emerges in a liminal space of death, and the sea drifts all around.

The deathbed perspective flows into everything in the film, so that every scene should be considered subjective memory as much as objective history. Jarman himself compares the framework of *Caravaggio* to his shaping of *The Tempest*, where he interpreted everything in the play as part of Prospero's dream. *Caravaggio*, too, proceeds with a dreamlike logic. When Caravaggio falls asleep next to a painting of Medusa, we see his dream of the serpent. But Caravaggio is not asleep at all when, in a bar, he mentions the Colosseum, and we suddenly hear an outburst of applause in the soundtrack ("It's the most successful disaster in Rome. I should have set my easel up in the Colosseum," C, p. 38). The combination of such a sound, the anachronistic settings (Caravaggio is wearing a 1940s-type fedora in this scene), and the minimalist sets (small because of budget, but contributing to the surreal effect nonetheless) gives a dreamlike quality to the film, a quality that Pasolini would associate with the poetic side of cinema.

Now Pasolini in "The Cinema of Poetry" is not interested so much in dramatic monologues as such—monologues that might call to mind a soliloquy by Hamlet or a poem spoken by Robert Browning's Duke of Ferrara—as in the idea that an entire film is a dramatic monologue. Here is Pasolini's key example from Antonioni:

> In *Red Desert* Antonioni no longer superimposes his own formalistic vision of the world on a generally committed content (the problem of the neuroses caused by alienation), as he had done in his earlier films in a somewhat clumsy blending. Instead, he looks at the world by immersing himself in his neurotic protagonist, re-animating the facts through her eyes (she, not by accident, clearly needs professional care, having already tried to commit suicide). By means of this stylistic device, Antonioni has freed his most deeply felt moment: he has finally been able to represent the world seen through his eyes, because

he has substituted in toto for the world-view of a neurotic his own delirious view of aesthetics, a wholesale substitution which is justified by the possible analogy of the two views.[18]

The interior monologues or voice-overs in *Caravaggio* signal the degree to which the whole film is in some sense from Caravaggio's point of view. Instead of a neurotic protagonist, as in Antonioni, we have a dying protagonist, whose situation *in extremis* similarly allows the narrative to take on what Pasolini would call a poetic freedom. *Caravaggio*, therefore, may be said to work as poetic cinema in Pasolini's terms, in that the entire film is essentially a monologue.

In our own more conventional terms, then, if not in Pasolini's, we may also understand that each of the voice-over monologues in *Caravaggio* is a poem. I have already enumerated the reasons: each passage has the same relationship to ordinary language as the characters' speeches do in plays by Shakespeare and Marlowe; spoken by Nigel Terry, the monologues share the relationship of voice-over to image in *The Last of England* and *Blue*; the monologues are written in the same figurative manner as Jarman's poems throughout his career. Where, then, does the voice-over originate? Where does this metaphorical language come from?

First, it comes from the world of death. The primary source of the voice-over is Caravaggio's deathbed. Poetry and poetic language emerge from a place outside of time. So these monologues are, indeed, comparable to the deathlike spaces of many Browning monologues, which, for all their famous vitality, often emanate from the end of a life or from a similarly extreme circumstance. Second, this amorphous space of Caravaggio's voice might be identified as the classically transcendental place of poetic lyric, a place of prophecy and truth, although cloaked in darkness. As Bersani and Dutoit point out, however, this "transcendence is downward; it is identical to drowning."[19] Thus we note how so many of the images in these monologues are watery; "I am rowing to you on the great dark ocean" (*C*, p. 124). As Bersani and Dutoit observe, Jarman has changed the historical circumstances of Caravaggio's death so that now he dies by drowning; "rough hands warm my dying body, snatched from the cold blue sea" (*C*, p. 9). As in *A Finger in the Fishes Mouth*, poetry originates in a subjective space of displacement and fluidity.

Bersani and Dutoit note that Jarman links this fluidity with ejaculation, so that "sexuality is the self-lacerating passage from life to death."[20] This linkage is clearest in the passage they cite, in which Caravaggio embraces the dead, drowned Lena.

Look! Look! Alone again. Down into the back of the skull. Imagining and dreaming and beyond the edge of the frame—darkness. The black night invading. The soot from the candles darkening the varnish, creeping round the empty studio, wreathing the wounded paintings, smudging out in the twilight—sharp knife-wounds that stab you in the groin, so you gasp and gulp the air, tearing your last breath from the stars as the seed runs into parched sheets and you fall into the night. I float on the glassy surface of the still dark lake, lamp-black in the night, silent as an echo; a mote in your eyes, you blink and send me spinning, swallowed in the vortex. I shoot through the violet depths. The unutterable silence of these waters. A tear forms and drops. The ripples spread out beyond the furthest horizon. Beyond matter, scintilla, star. I love you more than my eyes.

(C, p. 113)

Death is inextricably linked to sexuality in these monologues, as Bersani and Dutoit convincingly observe. For example, the second monologue is spoken over the naked form of Jerusaleme. And a further monologue remembers an occasion where Michele masturbated Pasqualone (C, p. 97). Eros and thanatos are truly turned together, in what Bersani and Dutoit call a "drowning love."[21] Yet we may take the examination of this watery motif still further.

As in key passages in A Finger in the Fishes Mouth or as in Ariel's shining presence at the seaside when Jubilee concludes, the oceanic realm may be associated with a realm of glass, with a mirror. The ocean may be a wild vortex, where one loses oneself and drowns, yet the ocean may also be the mirror of identity: "I float on the glassy surface of the still dark lake." The line is powerful and appropriate, since Caravaggio now holds the drowned Lena in his arms. The image of the glassy surface reinforces what we see, the unbounded, intersubjective relationship between Caravaggio and Lena, a relationship both narcissistic and overwhelming, both mirror and flood. The mirror of identity and the ocean of vortex are at the double center, not just of this monologue, but of the structure of Caravaggio. When Lena drowns, the script tell us, "Lena's body floats in the golden waters" (C, p. 102). Golden water, abysmal death; echo upon echo. Now she resembles a Victorian painting, "like Ophelia" says the script (C, p. 102), and she will be painted into another, Caravaggio's Death of the Virgin. Why is the water golden? As Michele tells us in another voice-over: "She dyed her hair with lemon juice and pure lime, so that it reflected the gold her protector so much admired" (C, p. 42).[22]

142

Caravaggio's determined focus on golden death may also be seen as an emphasis drawn from Pasolini. Up to this point in his films, Jarman has not foregrounded money this much, nor will he again. Almost all of Pasolini's films may be regarded as analyses of our responses to the unequal distribution of capital in society. Pasolini's films do not just repeatedly meditate on money in their content; they embody a response to capital and capitalism in their very form. His poetic (archaic, oneiric, discontinuous) manner of filmmaking is a direct response to mainstream film, which is made precisely to be easily consumed. Thus Pasolini so often aims to provoke or offend bourgeois sensibility and to implicitly or explicitly comment on the way that the owners of wealth cherish or spend their cultural capital.

Film is light-writing, and the way that Pasolini uses light is crucial to our reading of his "countercinema." It is important to notice that a film like *Porcile* (1969) is shot absolutely without glamour. Exterior light in the moonscape desert is dull—no postcard sunsets here—and the lighting of the great palazzo is equally utilitarian. This difficult, grotesque film collects light anticinematically, as it were, refusing us the pleasures of good photography. Pasolini's *Oedipus Rex* makes thematic the figurative blindness of its protagonist; in the desert world the light is bright, but now overbright, hard to look at, again in defiance of conventional visual expectations. *Teorema* most deliberately and fabulously works out the destruction of the bourgeois family; and interestingly it does, in fact, glamorize Terence Stamp, "The Visitor." Pasolini shoots Stamp backlit and in haloes, underscoring his otherworldly aspect, his divinity. In Pasolini's very various but also relentlessly countercinematic oeuvre, *Teorema* is one of the few films to consciously adopt the techniques of cinematic glamour.

This overly brief survey of light in Pasolini will nonetheless help us realize to what degree Jarman's films continually analyze glamour. Jarman is fascinated by the aesthetic opportunities afforded by light and the human figure. Compared to Pasolini, he shoots the male figure much more attractively, or, one might say, more conventionally, to the point that Bersani and Dutoit complain about the "cover boys" in *The Garden*.[23] I would try, however, to render his light-writing and photography more ambiguous than not. So that instead of placing Jarman in the context of supermarket magazines, we might set him next to Andy Warhol, who once and for all revealed the art museum to be a glamour factory and who cooperated in complex ways with those operations.[24] Or we might compare Jarman's use of photography to that of Cindy Sherman, who also often shoots her subjects glamorously, but also with enormous ambivalence—the effects can be called neither entirely conventional nor entirely parodic.

Jarman's cinema is always self-conscious, and so is continually investigating its own primal relationship to light and its necessary relationship to money. A film like Bresson's *L'Argent* is much more obviously countercinematic as it watches with preternatural rigor the destruction of human lives by money. *Caravaggio* is a self-conscious examination of cinema, art, and money, but is not pitched in as extreme a mode as Bresson or Pasolini. This need not be explained by the notion that Jarman is more cooperative or less pure, but rather by the fact that Jarman's films usually do retain a positive program of representation, no matter how apocalyptic the surroundings, and by the fact that he still wants to celebrate male homoerotic desire.

We know that Jarman and his cinematographer attempted to re-create the very light of Caravaggio's paintings.[25] The darkness of the film is therefore an attempt on Jarman's part to revisit Caravaggio's chiaroscuro and to represent the literal darkness of Caravaggio's physical appearance. "Caravaggio's style corresponded to his physiognomy and appearance; he had a dark complexion and dark eyes, and his eyebrows and hair were black; this colouring was naturally reflected in his paintings" (Bellori, as quoted in C, p. 7).[26] Yet the light not only reflects Caravaggio's paintings, it reflects Jarman's elemental cinematic eye. *Caravaggio* is always as much a re-presentation of Caravaggio's life and history as it is a projection of Jarman's life and cinematic concerns.

Even as the sea rolls in the soundtrack of the hospital interior in the first scene—a Jarman sea more than a historical, Caravaggio sea—the soup that Jerusaleme ponders is filmed in close-up as a bowl of light, all reflection. In the second scene, when Caravaggio goes to purchase Jerusaleme in "a shepherd's hut in the Abruzzi hills" (C, p. 10), the inhabitants of the hut are filmed in dark spaces, but Caravaggio's money is thrown down in a glitter of light, and his wallet noticeably sparkles when he brings it forward. These glitterings and reflections take their place in our collection of mirrorings and mirror images from throughout Jarman's works. Yet these mirrors, as we have observed, will also look different, and sometimes very different, from film to film. How do these mirrors of gold relate to the mirrors of identity that we have seen in earlier films?

Money and mirroring form the pivot of a scene early on in the film ("Selling Art on the Streets of Rome," C, p. 18), where we see the young version of Caravaggio—looking more than a bit like Mick Jagger—painting outside on the steps. The young Caravaggio is not only selling art, but also selling himself; as the voice-over in the script tells us: "The best way for a boy to get on in life is to sell his arse along with his art, pad out his crotch, split his trousers in the right places" (C, p. 18). These lines do not appear in the film, but the situation is perfectly clear; at one side the restless pimp chomps an apple. Over his shoulder we can see that Caravaggio is painting a figure, which may be a self-portrait. But the mirroring effect is overt in the sequence that follows: Caravaggio and the Englishman he's brought with him spin around in a circle, and the camera shows each from the other's point of view, cutting back and forth between them. Finally Michele says, "Ogetto d'arte! Ed io sono molto caro," which he even translates thus, "In plain English, I'm an art object and very very expensive" (C, p. 21). The repetition through translation is still another kind of mirroring, and we will see a similar repetition of lines at the beginning of *Edward II*.

The spinning around performed by the camera shows us the circulation of subject and object and demonstrates that Caravaggio himself is both painter and (explicitly named) object. The mirroring of art is caught up in these movements of doubling and reflection, and all in the midst of monetary exchange and consumption. At the close of the scene, Caravaggio counts out his money, takes a swig from a wine bottle, and crowns himself to look just like a Caravaggio painting called *Bacchus*. "I painted myself as Bacchus and took on his fate," says the voice-over here, and the film cuts first to his imagination of himself as a fully decked-out model for the painting and then to the painting itself, his "art object" status fully realized, and for the sake of his own art. "There he is," writes Jarman in *Dancing Ledge*, "as the pretty vain boy of the early genre paintings, painting himself in the mirror as Bacchus."[27] Awash in money, this is vain narcissism, the Narcissus of Ovid, not Cocteau.

The mirror that doubles and reflects both light and gold is shown in another scene as well, the boxing scene. When we first see the boxers, we see them as shadows; the two men cannot be distinguished from each other. Ranuccio and Davide are tied together at the waist by a rope—joined at the hip, as it were. From the editing back and forth of point-of-view shots, it is clear that Caravaggio, sitting in the audience, looks at Ranuccio, who is winning. So his gaze distinguishes between the two men, but also doubles them, since they are both objects of his desire (two scenes ago we saw Davide in his bed). As in *The Angelic Conversation*, identical dress emphasizes the mirroring of the men. When Davide is finally defeated, Tilda Swinton steps in as Lena ("Ranuccio's girl", C, p. 46) and cuts the rope between them. When she kisses Ranuccio, the homosocial doubling is visually broken apart. But in a few moments Caravaggio is there to congratulate the winner, and he offers him a coin, which noticeably glitters in the light.

A sudden cut then works to punctuate and recapitulate the mirroring images. The scene now abruptly shifts to an image of Jerusaleme holding a large orange rectangle, which he uses to reflect light at a posing model. Essentially, this image is that of a man holding a large golden mirror. The mirror works precisely to annotate the boxing scene, just as mirrors worked in *The Angelic Conversation* to signal the focus of homoerotic doubling. Here the mirror further signifies the exchange being transacted as a shiny coin passes from Caravaggio to Ranuccio. When we cut away from Jerusaleme and his reflecting device, we find that the model is, in fact, Ranuccio.

In an extended passage on "Gold" in *Caravaggio*, Jarman makes apparent how self-consciously thought-through are these various connections between mirror and money, gold and light:

> Incorruptible metal. The philosophic gold. The gilded canvases on the wall of my room catch the late afternoon sunlight, throwing shafts of warm light across the walls. Gold to translate into light has been a constant topic of conversation in the seven years it has taken to raise money for the film. . . . For Caravaggio I gilded my teeth and spent an evening out watching the reaction of the boys in the pub. Caravaggio hands Ranuccio a golden ducat; gold is the prize. He poses him for *The Martyrdom*. High above Jerusaleme lights him with a gold reflector, with the light from a two-kilowatt source. As the coins were thrown to pay Ranuccio for the pose, his mouth filled until it was contorted into a golden scream. Everything conspired to mirror the painting.
> Caravaggio kissed him with a kiss of gold. Gold flowed through the film. Lena caressed Ranuccio with it. Later, when she drowned, we took the camera to the riverbank and waited for the tide. We rigged up the lights and then the sun came out and turned the Thames into a sea of liquid gold.
>
> (C, P. 52)

In this view, golden imagery is neither obviously positive nor negative; it is related to the filthy lucre of finance, but it is also warm, autumnal. The flowing trails of light and gold in this passage conclude with a "golden scream" or a golden drowning, but these violences and deaths are not the only associations that remain.

In a discussion of his use of anachronism, where Jarman argues that anachronism does not distort history but instead allows us a "true perspective" on it, Jarman deploys, indeed, the archetypal figure of the mirror:

> This should allow us to make a genuine exploration of this painter and his impact on the culture. The film will dig and excavate and

make no attempt to hold the mirror up to reality. When Caravaggio paints the reflection of Narcissus it is no true reflection but a comment on all vanity and our film should treat his life in a similar way, penetrate the surface.[28]

This is one of the few places in Jarman's works where the superficial aspect of that mirrored surface is emphasized, where the mirror clearly does take its position in a tradition of *vanitas*, where the idea of self-love is perceived as waste and sin. Mirrors and surface reflections in *The Art of Mirrors* or *The Angelic Conversation* speak complicatedly about the focused light of a camera or the repetition of homoerotic desire, but do not, it would

FIGURE 5.1
The narcissistic mirror
in CARAVAGGIO

seem, connote vanity. Yet the light in Caravaggio's chiaroscuro must necessarily be a peculiar element if he himself is dark and his life is a dark, violent life. The reflections of light in *Caravaggio* take on unique resonances and associations with respect to Jarman's other films, insofar as they are now linked immediately with the glittering purse and the shining coin.

Another sequence in the center of the film emphasizes this mirror of narcissism, which happens now also to connote heterosexual relations, in

CARAVAGGIO *and the Mirror of Gold*

contrast to the mirror of homosexuality that we find in *The Angelic Conversation*. After posing playfully for Caravaggio, the boy Pipo (played by a woman) visits Lena and Ranuccio at their house. As the script has it: "Lena sits at the window. Pipo breaks her dreaming by focusing the last rays of sunshine onto her with a mirror" (C, p. 78). This is playing, a "gentle mocking" (C, p. 78), but a broken dream at the same time. And why does Pipo have a mirror? It must be that she has become interested in herself as an object to be viewed. Indeed, she is there to invite Lena and Ranuccio to a costume ball; desire and greed are in the air. "What more do you want?" asks Ranuccio. "Much more than you could imagine," says Lena, sternly (C, p. 78).

Thus Pipo's mirror prepares us for two more self-absorbed mirrors, one after the other, in quick succession. First, Giovanni Baglione, the art critic in a bath, "leans forward, an angry peacock admiring himself in the mirror" (C, p. 84). After the party, writhing with anger and egotism, Baglione will close off his review of Caravaggio by appropriating the language of mirroring: "A SAD REFLECTION OF OUR TIME" (C, p. 94). And in a second example, "Lena, dressed in her glittering gown, admires herself in a hand mirror" (C, p. 84). Another egoistic mirror, then, and Lena is off to the party, with as classical a sense of narcissism and doom as could possibly be imagined.

Mirrors and mirroring make frequent appearances in *Caravaggio*, although their golden light is often dark with death and drowning. Mirrors appear in *Caravaggio* more conventionally than elsewhere in Jarman, which is to say that they often connote vanity and narcissism. Yet we know that the construction of a self in Jarman is always various and layered, such that this self-regarding self will necessarily be difficult to reduce to type or convention too quickly. What this cinematic self looks like needs to be further characterized, therefore, and we can do so by examining how the self interacts with the materials of self-expression and by focusing, in particular, on paint.

II. READING PAINTING:
JARMAN, TARKOVSKY, AND BACON

These poetic monologues with which we began implicitly allegorize the power of creativity, the power of the artistic voice. In Tarkovsky's *Mirror*, the creative voice is powerful ("I can speak!"), but also associated with death and dissolution, since the narrator apparently dies of strep throat by the end. One can read *Caravaggio* as we read Tarkovsky. In Caravaggio's first monologue, in his "imagining and dreaming," he gasps for air and is "swallowed in the vortex." When Caravaggio takes back his knife from Cardinal Del Monte, he draws the knife across his mouth—an emblematic gesture if ever there was one. Most of Caravaggio's voice-overs are silently directed toward his manservant Jerusaleme, who is a mute. The self-contradictory nature of poetic and artistic power—both imaginative and destructive—is thus figured in *Caravaggio* through mouths and voices.

For example, when Caravaggio returns to his studio with Jerusaleme for the first time, the round, shieldlike painting of Medusa is placed on an easel in the center of the room. It is noticeably shiny, and little Jerusaleme makes a silent face at it, imitating its open mouth and sticking his tongue out. This is the first of many mouth gestures for the mute Jerusaleme. When the little boy playfully tries to frighten Caravaggio, the painter pretends to be afraid, but responds without language (offering only silence, and finally a little, generic roar). Yet what is this picture, this round shield of Medusa? This is, in fact, the first painting we see that has been authored by Cara-vaggio, and it is a mirror. After all, it is the reflection of her own face in Perseus's shield that petrifies the monstrous Medusa.

Paintings themselves are like reflections, in this metaphor, and we will see throughout the film paintings that mirror life and lives that mir-ror paintings. When Caravaggio recalls bringing home Jerusaleme for the first time, he says, "You looked a true St John brought from the wilder-ness" (*C*, p. 13). The very first painting we see suggests that paintings do in fact hold a mirror up to life, even though that life be extreme and even though that life be monstrous. A Medusa on a shield shows clearly that mirrors are both powerful and dangerous. When Lena's body "floats in the golden waters" (*C*, p. 102), in waters shimmering like a golden mirror, the voice-over begins, "Your hair streams out dark as the Medusa weed in these golden waters" (*C*, p.102). The mirror's dangerous connotations are carried through with Caravaggio's knife, which itself is often shot reflecting back a blaze of light, a kind of mirror in itself ("[The Cardinal] puts on his spectacles to examine the prize [the knife], holding it in the light," *C*, p. 27). Knife mirror, shield mirror: as noted in the first section of this chapter, these mirrors are unusually dangerous mirrors in *Caravaggio*.

Poetry in Jarman's films means not only the enunciation of figurative language, but the avoidance of prose discourse and dialogue. *The Garden* has no dialogue, just voice-overs and a sound track filled with music, ambi-ent noises, screams, or random chatter. *Caravaggio*, as the extensive script attests, has a good deal more conventional dialogue, but it also continu-ally goes out of its way to compose scenes without dialogue and to make strange those scenes that do have dialogue. Jerusaleme, as we noted, is an invention of Jarman's, and, since he is mute, can necessarily have no part in any dialogue. He plays a one-note whistle, a degraded version of a Pan figure, perhaps, which we will see more clearly with Spring in *The Last of England*. Jerusaleme can at most pantomime, and from time to time, as noted earlier, he makes strange gestures with his mouth.

The Last of England also shows most clearly of all the films Jarman's strong affinities with traditions of performance art, yet there are similar scenes in *Caravaggio*, too. There is the extended set piece where Caravaggio watches as Pipo "performs a series of languid gymnastics" (C, p. 75). The audience makes connections between the painting *Profane Love* (on the left of the studio) and the model Pipo as he (although played by a woman) spins a blue globe with stars on it and stands before the wings in which he posed. With wings, globe, and painting, the scene asks quietly to be read, and the scene once again works more like an associative poem than one that caus-

FIGURE 5.2
Performing the languorous elaboration of time

ally motivates the narrative. A similar scene, without dialogue but full of expressiveness, occurs when Ranuccio poses as the executioner in *The Martyrdom of St. Matthew* and Michele throws Ranuccio one piece of gold after another, which he then "sticks greedily in his mouth" (C, p. 51). This is yet another performance piece and another visual meditation on orality. The mouth does not speak, but it consumes with as much significance as any poem.

Derek Jarman and Lyric Film

Caravaggio is organized around paintings by Caravaggio; the shape of the biographical film is based on Jarman's interpretations of paintings by Caravaggio. "When I left Rome in July," writes Jarman, "I had completed the first script which was based on a reading of the paintings rather than the biographies of Baglione or Mancini."[29] Jarman is often overtly interested in secrets and codes and, consequently, in the problems associated with reading and interpretation. How is painting "read" in *Caravaggio*? How does interpretation play into the staged scenes of painting? How should we read the act of painting itself?

The first visual image we see in the film, beneath the opening credits, is in fact an act of painting. Or, we see first a black screen, which then changes to a screen painted black; we can see streaks of white and texture in the black field. As the credits continue, a painting hand fills in the canvas with more and more black paint, stroke after stroke, until the perfect black with which we began is regained. An entirely black painting is already anachronistic and ominous to say the least (if we wish to make sense of it, we can assume that he is painting in background), and the film will begin with the corpselike head of Caravaggio. Already, therefore, painting is figuratively related to life. The blackness of this (impossible) painting is the infinite void, the empty sea into which Caravaggio has fallen.

The sound track is interesting as well, and is close to an exact allusion to the credit sequence of Pasolini's *Oedipus Rex*. In the Pasolini film, we first hear the sound of crickets, then classical music; the tension between nature and culture that stands at the center of the Oedipus myth is sonically before us in the first instants. Similarly in *Caravaggio*, the first sounds we hear are the ocean waves, the lapping of the surf. Then we hear voices organized into chants, songs. Beneath the sounds of the ocean, beneath the chants, we see a hand painting black. The relationship between nature and culture, between life and art, is brought before us in this carefully conceived title sequence. It is worth pointing out, too, that just when the frame becomes entirely black, we pause, and the hand comes through for one more set of strokes down the canvas. This pass, perpendicular to the last, has the effect of reintroducing light to the image. The strokes of paint at this angle reflect light so that scintillating white shines in among the black before the film begins. Even the black reflects.

Paintings often occur at the beginnings and ends of films because these are places of stillness. But in directors like Tarkovsky or Jarman, the credit sequences are not just there to convey information, to tell us what set of people made the movie, but rather to comment implicitly on the nature of cinematic origin and movement. The opening credits of Tarkovsky's *The*

Sacrifice, for example, begins with a detail of Leonardo's unfinished *Adoration of the Magi* in which we see a man giving a vase, or more generally, a gift, into female hands. The camera is motionless as the sound track plays Bach and we contemplate the image before us. As we meditate, perhaps, on gifts and sacrifices, the music is augmented by the cries of seagulls, and then the music stops. The seagulls continue to cry, and the camera, absolutely still until now, begins to move toward the top of the painting. The camera passes several figures and comes finally to a tree at the very top of the painting's frame.

The credit sequence then cuts, and we find ourselves beside a shore where a man is planting a tree. Again the contrast between nature and culture is projected before us. Nature (the seagulls) seems more vital, perhaps, than the old painting or the classical music, since the moment we hear the gulls is exactly when the camera begins to move. On the other hand, the film proper begins with the image of a man working in nature, expressing himself through nature, as he begins the story by planting a tree. In *The Sacrifice* civilization will appear as a disaster; culture has built itself into a self-destroying apocalypse. But people can also save the world by what might be thought of as the ultimate act of civilization, a faithful sacrifice. And so Tarkovsky's camera moves away from the center of the painting, but it does not entirely leave behind its stillness.

A similar sonic annotation occurs in a later scene in Jarman, where Caravaggio broods on his first version of St. Matthew. The studio is dark, "deep in the night," and he "traces the arc of the executioner's sword across the canvas" (*C*, p. 40). When we first cut to the studio, we hear a low roar, as if the ocean from Caravaggio's hospital deathbed has returned. But the roar increases, divides, and grows more regular as the single shot continues. Now it is clear that we are hearing a train. Eventually we even hear a train whistle, just to assure us that we did not dream it. This sonic reference again is as anachronistic as some of the hats that Caravaggio wears, but it is more than that. Why the sound of a train here? The night goes on, the train runs on through the night. The soundtrack suggests that the painter is like a machine, which is an obviously complicated analogy. The naturalistic approach, or an approach to painting that wanted to foreground nature, could easily give us the sounds of night: silence, an owl, a branch creaking in the wind. The train aligns Caravaggio with technology and culture, but also with a sense of Hardyesque foreboding rather than assuredness.

In Jarman's *Caravaggio*, what, then, is painting? What is paint? In such a relentlessly deconstructed film, where the life of Caravaggio is based on the paintings and then shot like the paintings, and where Caravaggio himself is both artist and art object, where does the painting end and the life begin? Caravaggio himself speaks in a language infiltrated by paint, as if his eyes and thought were all oils and frames and canvas. The poem— "Thought without image / lost in the pigment / trapped in the formless umber wastes" (C, p. 40)—is characteristic of the way that color and paint flow over everything in the flowing consciousness of Caravaggio, and thus over everything in the film as well, since it is all to some degree his dream, his thoughts, his painting. Scenes are shot like paintings, but not only that; people themselves are treated like sculptures and paintings. Is this a pose or is this life? That the scene with the journalist Baglione in his bath is set up like Jacques-Louis David's *Death of Marat* is only the most extreme and most parodic version of these self-consciously framed and allusive poses.

Take the scene where Ranuccio and Caravaggio fight. Caravaggio is hurt; as the script says, "he puts his hand to his wounded side, and taking the blood, wipes it on Ranuccio's face" (C, p. 58). In scenes just previous we have seen Caravaggio working with the paints and colors of *The Martyrdom of St. Matthew*; we have slowly panned over his studio table to reveal "the colours, the flasks of oil, the porphyry slab for grinding the paints, mortars, brushes, [and] spatulas" (C, p. 54). When Caravaggio, the great artist, wipes blood on Ranuccio's face here—saying, as he does it, "blood brothers"—he is, therefore, painting him. Ranuccio the model becomes Ranuccio the canvas, even as Caravaggio announces that their doubled relationship (the distinctions between artist and model dissolved now into the sameness of identically clad fighters) has been ritually confirmed. In this scene, paint is blood, a metaphor verified again when Caravaggio is tended by Davide shortly thereafter:

In the wound the question is answered.
All art is against lived experience.
How can you compare flesh and blood with oil and ground pigment?

(C, p. 60)

Yet this is just the comparison that is made throughout the film; art and life, flesh and blood, are always circulating around in relationship to each other—there is no resolved hierarchy or permanent evaluation. Even as Caravaggio makes this statement, arguing for life over art, he is posed exactly like Christ in a painting of St. Thomas the Apostle doubtfully inspecting Christ's wounded side. Thus we, too, may doubt Caravaggio's statement, refusing to take it for a conclusive summary or facile motto.

In a fascinating interview that *Sight and Sound* published in 1997,

153

French director Olivier Assayas talked about his immersion in Tarkovsky's *Mirror* and of the importance that film had for him. He is especially interested in the winter sequence that "reproduces" the painting *Hunters in the Snow* by Pieter Brueghel the elder. Assayas describes a cinema that is constructed out of multiple points of view or a "circulation of the gaze":

> With Brueghel appears the idea that a painting has a point of entry, that one circulates within the painting from gaze to gaze, and the whole dramatic structure of this painting lies in that circulation. This is something that I use almost literally in my films, based on the idea that the global picture is gradually constructed within the circulation of the gaze.[30]

We do not ordinarily think of Tarkovsky as self-consciously referencing painting in the manner of Jarman's *Caravaggio* or Godard's *Passion*, but his *Mirror* is every bit as self-reflexive as theirs in working through the multiplicity of forms that attend his autobiographical excursion. Such a deliberate and recollective camera will necessarily be haunted by painting, even when the subject is himself rather than a painter.

Tarkovsky's *Nostalghia*, for example, is in some ways as obsessed with painting as *Andrei Rublev*. This film is set in Italy, and every frame plays with our memories of Italian Renaissance painting. Our attentions and expectations are framed from the very beginning when Eugenia gets out of the car and calls the landscape a "fantastic painting." When she goes into the isolated cathedral to look at the painting of the Madonna (Piero della Francesca's *Madonna del Parto* [*Madonna of Childbirth*]), the camera follows her moving slowly among rows and rows of columns, and so provides pictures that take their own part among all those exercises in Renaissance perspective. The enormously extended shots, the slow camera, and the carefully framed interiors all ask to be read against the history of painting, as much as any postmodern reference in *Caravaggio* does. "Nostalghia" here is nostalgia for the Russian homeland as imagined through Italy and Italian painting. The film is a beautiful, melancholy contradiction, since it is a film both lost in painting and aware that its own painting, and its poetry, is a temporary projection.

In *Nostalghia*, Tarkovsky investigates not just the framing symmetries and historical allusions of painting, but the very materiality and texture of paint. In a remarkable sequence halfway into the film, Gorgachov leans against the corner of two brown, peeling walls. He is reflected in a mirror to our right; surrounded by the thickness of paint all around him, the mirror's image becomes a framed painting. The camera then pans left across a terrain of leaflike peels and veins of paint to continue toward a still life of a gourd, bottle, and leaves. By cinematic magic, Gorgachov appears at the other end of that same camera movement. His magic reappearance prepares us for an utterly remarkable moment. For out of the darkness a picture—a painting, apparently, although close to a photograph—now appears. In colors and tones that blend in precisely with the peeling wall, this strange picture is of a baby with grim, blackened circles for eyes. This seems to be a baby who was born into a world of night. Such a picture is the painterly opposite to Piero della Francesca's *Madonna of Childbirth*; it is, indeed, an antipainting, anonymous and without followers. Yet this baby looks like it belongs to this film, to the texture of its burning poems and burning prophets, made out of ash and bad dreams. Existing out of time and place, this is the very picture of "nostalgia."

Let me suggest one more cinematic context for the paint and painting in Jarman's *Caravaggio*. Very relevant to the intense world of paint and representation into which *Caravaggio* is flung is the recent film *Love Is the Devil: Study for a Portrait of Francis Bacon* (1999). John Maybury, the director, designed costumes for *Jubilee*, edited video on Jarman's *War Requiem*, assisted with music videos by The Smiths, and was an editor on *The Last of England*. Maybury's film is his own, no doubt, but it is worked together with a strong sense of Jarman's posthumous spirit. In its radical claustrophobia, *Love Is the Devil* certainly looks like a good deal of Jarman. A film made almost entirely out of a few rooms is a conscious choice on the director's part, only partially related to minuscule budgets.

Bacon himself is an important artistic figure for Jarman, and we shall expand on this significance during our description of the butchery in *Edward II*. For now, it is important to note that Maybury's life of Bacon is also determined by the paintings of Bacon. Just as Jarman makes no effort to tell Caravaggio's life based on biographical detail, but, rather, invents situations that move us from painting to painting, so too does *Love Is the Devil* reenact painting after painting by Bacon. What the anamorphic distortions, endless mirrorings, and reframings must mean to a viewer not familiar with Bacon's works is unclear; one might surmise, perhaps, that the weird visual effects stem from Bacon's madness and melancholy.

With the paintings in mind, however, we can view the film as an obsessive exhibit or gallery—more than a biography, more than a psychology. It is the paintings that determine how the screen looks and how the narrative, such as it is, proceeds. That Bacon paints beneath that single, dangling lightbulb or that George Dyer (Bacon's lover) collapses into the toilet does not carry reality along, but rather turn these actors, these figures, back into

155

paintings. This is less a psychology of madness than a self-conscious analysis of the texture of cinematic visuality—its possibilities, its conventions, its overdeterminations. Although apparently a complete metaphysical opposite to Tarkovsky, for whom art exists to help humans in their spiritual progress, *Love Is the Devil* is, as much as works by Tarkovsky or Jarman, an examination of the relationship of cinema to painting.

III. PARADJANOV, RHYTHM, AND TEMPORALITY

The mysticism and magic of Paradjanov may seem to be an utter contrast to the postmodern ironies of Jarman. It is impossible to imagine Paradjanov placing a man in a bathtub and having him first write anachronistically on a typewriter and then slump into the recognizable pose from David's *Death of Marat*. Yet Paradjanov poses and collects as much as Jarman. He does not pose his figures after paintings by David or Caravaggio, but that is because he is collecting and redistributing images and iconography from an Armenian tradition.

In *The Geopolitical Aesthetic*, Fredric Jameson describes both men as working in the field of "magic realism": Paradjanov (as well as Tarkovsky) is one of the most important influences on that aspect of contemporary Soviet cinema, and Derek Jarman (along with Raul Ruiz) exemplifies the "new magic realism" (and *Caravaggio* is the Jarman film that Jameson chooses to name).[31] "Magic realism" is a particular and complex Jamesonian term that originates in his work on romance in *The Political Unconscious*.[32] For our purposes, Jameson helps us see once again the confluence in artistic impulse that joins Jarman and Paradjanov, a confluence I have termed lyric film.

Interestingly, Tarkovsky and Paradjanov constitute two of the outright failures among Jameson's worldwide survey of cinematic expression. Of Tarkovsky's *Stalker*, Jameson writes:

This novel [the Strugatsky brothers' *Roadside Picnic*] Tarkovsky made over into the most lugubrious religious fable, his camera and his actors moving if anything more slowly than real time itself, with a solemnity quite intolerable to any but the truest believers (in Tarkovsky, I mean, and I speak as one who has a great deal of tolerance for the longueurs of this auteur). . . . The objection is not so much to the religious content (although see note 4 below [to Paradjanov]) as it is to artistic pretentiousness. The operation consists in trying to block our resistance in a two-fold way: to forestall aesthetic qualms with religious gravity, while afterthoughts about the religious content are to be chastened by the reminder that this is, after all, high art.[33]

Jameson also severely criticizes Tarkovsky's vaunted representation of nature for its lack of self-consciousness:

> The deepest contradiction in Tarkovsky is then that offered by the highest technology of the photographic apparatus itself. No reflexivity acknowledges this second hidden presence, thus threatening to transform Tarkovskian nature-mysticism into the sheerest ideology.[34]

Paradjanov is similarly taken to task for *The Color of Pomegranates*:

> Perhaps we might minimally agree that stories about priests are in whatever form intolerable, whatever religion they purport to serve; in that sense Paradjanov's *Color of Pomegranates* is as detestable as Bernanos, despite the naif folk-art splendor of its images.[35]

In Jameson's terms, Jarman's films—which are always more complex than Jarman's statements about them—are dialectical, self-conscious, self-reflexive, and mediated. Jarman's "magic" constantly tells us how it is produced: through camera framing, through obsessive lighting, through anachronism and generic heterogeneity. From the early films onward, Jarman maintains his interest in the visionary, but unlike Kenneth Anger, where the camera seems to be a vehicle in itself to worlds beyond, Jarman's camera is self-aware, as much obstacle as assistant, as much a tool of demystification and irony as mystical celebrant. Jameson sees Tarkovsky and Paradjanov in the way that we have described Anger, as naively magical, where the visual splendor of the images obscures that which has not been thought through ideologically.

Yet every instant of *The Color of Pomegranates* bespeaks its artifice, from the painterly boundaries of the frame to the fluid movements of the figures and materials inside. This film is as self-conscious as any opera or painting or film can be. If it exalts nature or nation or poetry, it does so in a relentlessly mediated way, through extremes of formalism, both in visual and in structural terms. The mobility of the camera in Wenders's *Wings of Desire* may appear more self-conscious, but does not Wenders idealize the camera by aligning it with the angels? Paradjanov's camera never moves, and his angels have obviously pretend wings. If narrative and temporality are transcended, it is not through willful prophecy or poetry, but through self-conscious artifice that thus demystifies its magic with every collection of traditional objects and every premeditated rhythm of poses.

CARAVAGGIO *and the Mirror of Gold*

If Paradjanov dislocates naturalistic representation through artificial framings and posings, he dislocates continuous temporality through assertions of rhythm. Through music, dance, and rhythmic gesture, the film establishes its own countertemporality, an angelic sphere of time, as it were, that runs outside our own and is itself an obvious construction. Henri Bergson, influentially, recognized a subjective, private time, which he called *dureé* (duration); modern art finds itself often in such regions of subjectivity. As cultural historian Stephen Kern writes: "Three major developments can be marked in the shift away from the traditional narrative framework: the affirmation of subjective time, the subversion of narrative, and the recognition of simultaneity."[36] Although a celebration of Armenian heritage, *The Color of Pomegranates* exemplifies clearly all of these modern dislocations of time. But more than this embodiment of modern temporality, subjective time in Paradjanov is reorganized through rhythm.

Rosalind Krauss finds a "rhythm, or beat, or pulse" in the art of Max Ernst and Marcel Duchamp, and thus foregrounds an alternative aesthetics to that celebrated by Clement Greenberg in modernist abstraction, with its immediacy and instantaneity.[37] For Krauss this rhythm is more than formal, it is corporeal; these artists "corporealize the visual, restoring to the eye (against the disembodied opticality of modernist painting) that eye's condition as bodily organ, available like any other physical zone to the force of eroticization."[38] Rhythmic division and punctuation is sometimes overtly erotic in Paradjanov—in dances, in the episodes whose subject is love—but it is certainly always sensuous, material, more than a formalism, and working in concert with the sensuousness of the visual imagery. This return of the body is not a return to naturalism, since the body itself is such an invariably mediated construction (consider, for example, that the same woman plays not only the poet's love and the angel of death, but also the poet himself in one of his youthful stages).

Rhythm is equally important and equally eroticized in *Caravaggio*, though not necessarily emanating from an individual body (such as Caravaggio himself). The rhythms and gestures associated with social ritual or akin to performance art are more readily apparent in *The Last of England* or *The Garden*, but are apparent throughout *Caravaggio* as well. *Caravaggio* begins with the rhythmic sweep of waves and then the repetitive chant of men: both rhythms wider than the breathing of an individual man. The paintbrush adds a third rhythm; and *Caravaggio* as a whole is characterized by layered rhythms, rhythms that imply context and relationship. "I'm dying in time to the plash of the oars," says Caravaggio in his opening monologue (*C*, p. 9), and the waves wash back and forth in the sound track.

The acting in *Caravaggio* is more conventional, more naturalistic, than in *The Garden*, but it is still organized around poses, gestures, silent movements: Jerusaleme carving a piece of straw with Caravaggio's knife and blowing it into pieces; Jerusaleme standing before a window (colored like an abstract painting) and making strange movements with his mouth; the young Caravaggio drawing his knife across his mouth. And the whole film is organized around still moments, those re-created pictures of Caravaggio.

Unlike *The Color of Pomegranates*, *Caravaggio* is not organized rhythmically by music. *Caravaggio* uses different kinds of music, usually to substantiate or annotate in a relatively straightforward manner (the jazz music played at Giustiniani's party is surprising only in its unabashed anachronism). The sequences are shaped rhythmically, nonetheless, but by silence instead of music. Many scenes in *Caravaggio* start off with a repetitive action, a kind of beat that measures the silence, a rhythmic count. Just to take a few examples: in the first scene, "Jerusaleme nervously carves a piece of straw with Michele's knife" (C, p. 9); each knife cut is a kind of beat. Caravaggio goes to buy little Jerusaleme, and the exchange is measured out carefully, the woman picking up each coin, one by one. When Caravaggio brings little Jerusaleme home to the studio, the sequence starts with Caravaggio opening one window after another. Jerusaleme begins a later scene (C, p. 54) by spitting out lemon seeds, one after the other. A cardinal taps on his calculator (C, p. 74); Baglione types and opens his magazine three times (C, p. 84). Scenes tend to begin with silence or a rhythmic action rather than speech.

The few scenes that begin outright with dialogue (C, p. 101), are all the more striking for their noise and abruptness. Although there are a few fiercely violent scenes, in general this film teaches us to wait. It is not painterly in the way that Tarkovsky's *Nostalghia* is, with its extraordinarily extended shots; nor is it painterly à la Paradjanov, with his unmoving frame. *Caravaggio* is painterly not like a painting so much as like the act of painting. In a way, all of these repetitions are versions of the repetitive stroke of the paintbrush, which measures out the hour one daub of paint at a time.

Caravaggio teaches us to endure the painting, the act of painting, even if sometimes it seems as boring as watching paint dry. There are numerous scenes in *Caravaggio* that stage the scene of painting as mind-numbingly dull for everyone who is not the painter. While Caravaggio paints, spectators yawn, make unwelcome remarks, or fall asleep; his models pose until they are not only sleeping but actually dead. Caravaggio returns one night to find Jerusaleme asleep in his pose as John the Baptist; this scene may prepare us to some degree for Caravaggio's grotesque decision (in the mad tradition of Browning's "Porphyria's Lover") to pose the recently dead Lena as the deceased Virgin Mary. The rhythm of the sequences of *Caravaggio* asks us first to inhabit the empty time of repetition and silence, which may well be boring, akin to falling asleep ("Now I'm counting the sheep").[39]

But eventually we come to see that this empty time is the silent time of death. When silence surrounds Lena and then finally Caravaggio, no one is bored; on the contrary, everyone looks upon the dead Caravaggio with absolute absorption. The time that had seemed so empty, measured out by generic acts of repetition, now seems absolutely full and captivating at the moment of death.[40] Caravaggio twice quotes Pasqualone's commonplace, "Time stops for no man," but art and cinema at least reroute time's flow into different paths and eddies. When *Caravaggio* is just ten minutes underway, we have passed through six or seven sheets of time: we see the dying Caravaggio, Caravaggio buying the little Jerusaleme, Caravaggio's brief memory of the adult Jerusaleme, and the young Caravaggio. Later, we will even see the little Michele as he seems to look upon his adult self. Linear time is reorganized and redrawn, yet there is also a sense of time's inevitability, since the waves of memory and dream will eventually crash against the beachhead, with a fateful cadence.

Caravaggio rings in the New Year waving his scythe; he is a figure of mortal time itself. Yet what is time?

> Long live the 1600s
> Uncertainty and Doubt
> Long live Doubt
> Through Doubt comes Insight.
>
> (C, p. 42)

The anachronisms and temporal circlings in Jarman do not seem to signify transcendental control so much as analytical experimentation. Jarman unsettles time, asking us to think again (to doubt), but without claiming victory over time. Little Michele, with his angel wings, is out celebrating Easter, the day of resurrection, but the plash of oars we hear as the final credits roll indicate the "distant sound of Charon's boat taking Michele to Hades" (C, p. 131). As time moves forward, we may properly either ask questions or just sit back and look, but time will eventually eat the questioners (*tempus edax rerum*).

The still lifes in *Caravaggio* are postmodern quotations where we see how cleverly reproduced are these images or how surprisingly the invented narrative runs us into these framed allusions. The still lifes are also allegories of time; apropos of a photograph in Ozu, Deleuze writes:

> The still life is time, for everything that changes is in time, but time itself does not change, it could itself change only in another time, indefinitely.[41]

The still lifes in *Caravaggio* vampirically absorb the people into the paintings, like another version of Wilde's *The Picture of Dorian Gray*. The last two paintings are inhabited by dead people, Lena and Caravaggio, as if the stillness of painting were the same as the stillness of death.

Caravaggio does not pray for Wildean youth, but he does pray for the present. On his deathbed, Caravaggio pushes away the crucifix and mouths his knife's motto: "No hope! No fear!" (C, p. 117). *Caravaggio*'s lyric, languorous time is, in this view, more like that of *The Picture of Dorian Gray* than that of *The Color of Pomegranates*. Time in Wilde's novel exists not in poetic transcendence but in a languorous and sometimes violent present. And is not Caravaggio laid out resplendently in his blue suit?

> When they entered, they found hanging upon the wall a splendid portrait of their master as they had last seen him, in all the wonder of his exquisite youth and beauty. Lying on the floor was a dead man, in evening dress, with a knife in his heart.[42]

Reading Pictures: Emblem and Gesture in THE LAST OF ENGLAND and THE GARDEN

The Last of England and *The Garden* are perhaps Jarman's most original and lasting contributions to lyric cinema. Both foreground poetry through the use of poems read out in voice-overs, but for the most part it is non-verbal sounds and gestures that express the "poetry" in these films. The sequences that make up these nonnarrative but deliberately structured films will need to be discussed in some detail. As usual, Jarman is first in line to emphasize the hermeneutic potentiality of his own films, and he constructs his own readings in script notes, journals, and autobiographical commentary. Hence this is, apparently, not a modernist poetry that seeks merely to present images, a poetry that attempts to ward off academic midrash (as William Carlos Williams intends when he writes, "T. S. Eliot's *Waste-land* gave poetry back to the academics"). Instead this is poetry layered in contexts and interpretations—part medieval allegory, part postmodern col-lage—which in every scene demand critical redescription and reevaluation.

I. THE INSISTENCE OF TIME:
PROPHETIC DOCUMENTARY AND *The Last of England*

The Last of England returns to the apocalyptic and visionary realms of *Jubilee*, but with significant alterations in purpose and effect. The fires of end times and apocalypse allow for a surreal and transcendental approach, and *The Last of England* makes the most of this opportunity, proceeding unashamedly by means of allegorical signs and emblematic performances. *Jubilee* located its power in the traditional magus figure of John Dee, along with his Shakespearean sidekick Ariel; *Jubilee* conjured, as a contrast to this wreck of contemporary England, a hopeful world of Elizabethan idyll. *The Last of England*, in its turn, emerges now from the director's perhaps magi-cal, but more obviously mortal, brain, yet with no consoling frame what-soever. Although apocalyptic in its chaotic imagery and anarchic violence, *Jubilee* remains grounded in the identifiable gestures of both documentary (these are scraps of contemporary punk culture) and science fiction. *The Last of England*, however, is splendidly pitched beyond our recognizable world and certainly beyond recognizable genre. Original, unforgiving, and otherworldly, *The Last of England* aims for and achieves a truly visionary cinema.

The film is structured as a series of set pieces with no dialogue, but unlike in *The Angelic Conversation* or *War Requiem*, here there is a nearer relationship of sound space to screen space. As Jarman writes, "*The Last of England* works with image and sound, a language which is nearer to poetry than prose."[1] Both the extended performances and the contributions of sound will loom large in our discussion. Of all Jarman's works, *The Last of England* is most readily seen as made out of performance art, and it is brought forth with one of his most sophisticated sound tracks. Jarman fur-thermore terms *The Last of England* a "dream allegory," where the film's images correspond to the dream of a poet: "In dream allegory, the poet encounters personifications of psychic states."[2] We might add that in this dream allegory the poet encounters psychic nation-states, since the film is a visionary response to the contemporary state of England. Those whirling arms of the radar, which desire and intimacy managed to move away from in *The Angelic Conversation*, are felt implicitly throughout *The Last of*

England. There is no idyllic retreat to the past; there is no refuge in desire and love.

And then there are the poems, the first really original poetic texts in the films thus far. *Sebastiane*'s lyrics are imitations, and of course the poetry in *The Tempest* and *The Angelic Conversation* is by Shakespeare. As Jarman writes in *Kicking the Pricks*: "I've written four 'voice-overs': my reaction to the view from the window of a culture riddled with death-watch beetle. Nigel Terry delivers them in a BBC monotone."[3] In the text of *Kicking the Pricks*, these voice-overs are treated like poems; they are given their own individual titles and printed as either prose poems or verse. They also sound poetic, and thus, like the poems by Arseny Tarkovsky in his son's *Mirror*, they signal once more that the film is structured "poetically." In Jarman's view, the poetry emerges as an interior and imaginative response to a dying culture.

The Last of England is more overtly autobiographical than any Jarman film to this point, since Jarman presides over the film from the very beginning. Until now, Jarman has appeared only as a cardinal in *Caravaggio*. But that was a cameo walk-on, with only a bit more point and satire than Hitchcock's signature appearances. Yet now we see him and his camera, along with home movies from his childhood, which were taken by his father. As in the equally autobiographical *The Garden*, however, Jarman significantly complicates the meaning of his authorial presence. Remember how ethereal and ungrounded was that "I" in his early book of poems. Although by now as political and outrageous as any Beat poet ever was, his poetic "I" is still remarkably self-effacing and difficult to locate.

At the very beginning of *The Last of England*, Jarman appears in his studio, working at his books. When the voice-over begins, then, the impression we have is that these are his words. Jarman's poet-dreamer is another Prospero or John Dee figure, yet now much more isolated: a Prospero without an island, a John Dee without a queen. Yet although he is solitary, this creator still seems powerful, purposeful, industrious. In contrast to *The Garden*, where Jarman appears glazed over and half-asleep, *The Last of England* shows him alert and thoughtful. What is more, this creator figure seems to be working in every possible medium. We see him writing during the voice-over (although the words, noticeably, do not match), suggesting that the creator is a kind of a poet, and he is surrounded by books. Yet he is also surrounded by paint, and he paints in the book, as well. At one point he puts a leaf between the pages of the book. Altogether these gestures accumulate to form the composite character of the multifaceted artist that Jarman himself is: poet, painter, and gardener.

This is, then, a dreamer who is not asleep, a visionary who is not mad.

He works at night, darkness all around him, but his studio is brightly lit and looks productive. The impression Jarman wants to convey is that if what follows seems melancholy, despairing, exhausting, and doomed, then let us not attribute that to the "mad" subjectivity of a drunken poet. This toiling, inventing magus figure before us makes stronger claims for his vision than that. *The Last of England* is a true dream, an objective vision, a documentary—rather than a fantasy—of the imagination.

One of the ways that Jarman continually undercuts his own association with magic and poetry in his journals is to call his inventions documentaries instead of poems:

> My own feeling at the moment is as if some mega production were going on off-screen, perhaps life itself, and I'm travelling through, documenting it. The film is a documentary. I've come back with a document from somewhere far away.[4]

Just as he signals the poetic by including poems, he signals the documentary by including stock footage and home movies. The Super 8 camera paradoxically stands for both a personal, autobiographical point of view (man-sized, home movies) and a more objective, documentary perspective (linked to hand-held journalism). What Jarman might mean by "documentary" has been touched on in several important critical articles.

In "Autobiography, Home Movies, and Derek Jarman's History Lesson," Justin Wyatt argues that the home movie footage grounds *The Last of England* in a real world: "without the home footage, the rest of the film could be construed as fantasy."[5] Wyatt also observes how open these home movie scenes are to interpretation. Since there is a "lack of explicit documentation and identification, Jarman encourages a defamiliarization of the home movie."[6] As Wyatt observes, we might read the home movie in straightforwardly personal terms. That is, bolstered by Jarman's journals, we may see this ideal family as being treated with irony and suspicion, and thus read the footage as linked to Jarman's personal history of sexual identity and now illness (he was diagnosed as HIV-positive in December 1986).

But compared to *The Garden* or *Blue*, *The Last of England* is really rather abstract about its personal and even political concerns. Thus Wyatt's important conclusion is that "*The Last of England* multiplies the possible meanings of the home footage";[7] this footage does not merely mean that this movie is "my" autobiography or that these images are "my" dreams. It is much more compelling to read *The Garden* or *Blue* in that strongly personal way, but *The Last of England* is more generalized, despite the appearance of its creator at regular intervals throughout the film.

This generic combination of narrative discontinuity with documentary subjects and techniques (urban wasteland, home movies, handheld camera) has lead some critics to consider the form of *The Last of England* as "poetic documentary." With his usual acuity, Michael O'Pray writes: "The carnivalesque air of *Jubilee*, with its black humor and theatrical excess, is replaced by the unrelieved anger of a poetic documentarist who uses the wasteland of London's docklands to create an atmosphere of hysteria, paranoia, and pessimism."[8] This juxtaposition of poetry and documentary necessarily brings to mind the films of Humphrey Jennings. As John Hill observes: "[*The Last of England*] may also be linked to a British tradition of 'poetic documentary,' and to the work of Humphrey Jennings, with its mix of realism, surrealism, and national allegory, in particular."[9] In a splendid inspiration, Annette Kuhn compares in some detail *The Last of England* to Jennings's *Listen to Britain*.[10]

My only addition to these very useful critical descriptions is to underline the prophecy in the poetry. Kuhn's emphasis on the poetic and metaphorical aspects of *The Last of England*, its "constructionist aesthetic" and "modernist sensibility," leads her to the following conclusions:

> Their [Jarman's and Jennings's films'] *bricolage* of visual and auditory fragments also confers a sense of timelessness on both films—which perhaps prompts the question: is there some inherent connection between poetry, memory, and a feeling of timelessness?[11]

The film is indeed timeless, in that it contains no deliberately contextualized analysis of history and very few references to contemporary England. But there is, nonetheless, an enormous sense of urgency, of the shortness of time. Although *The Last of England* and *The Garden* seem to be very similar poetic compositions, they may, in the end, give entirely contrasting impressions in this regard. *The Garden*, although politically insistent, is, as I will argue, rather like a garden in that it leaves one time to contemplate; there time expands. Contrastingly, *The Last of England*, in its often hyperfast editing and cutting, in its music (which verges on rock video), and in its relentlessly doomed atmosphere, may not historicize, yet it still forces upon us the pressure of time. *The Last of England* is, no doubt, "out of time" insofar as it takes place somewhere else, somewhere out of our world, but insofar as we feel that we are "out of time," that time has run out, is over and done with, this prophetic work draws us down, like gravity. It does not release us from conscience or from our past.

We might see, furthermore, that these varied activities of Jarman's

166

creator figure coalesce into something more specific than a poet; namely, this is the poet as archeologist. During the fourth voice-over or poem, for example, we see Jarman painting with such thick paint that the whole work becomes three-dimensional, sculptural. Into this dark goop he embeds a bullet; overall, the thing seems to be a kind of scrapbook made out of mud. Jarman's activities here are intercut with footage from an archeological dig; we see a man uniformed in white coat and gloves dig up a large light bulb and then some film. Toward the end of the sequence, Jarman neatly paints around an embedded image of the sphinx, which reclines in front of a pyramid. Jarman's creator figure, therefore, does not just deploy ambiguous images, such as a sphinx, which also appeared in a postcard in *A Finger in the Fishes Mouth*. He collects and documents with the understanding that his work, too, is part of the historical record.

Let us begin to work our way through the film by examining the four poems as well as the set-piece sequences and performances. The first voice-over substantiates our characterization of the poet as a distanced archeologist, a poet whose voice is as public as it is private and whose sense of time is vast rather than local. The text of the voice-over is constructed out of two prose poems printed in *Kicking the Pricks*, which there have the titles "4 AM" and "Imperial Embers." That Jarman takes the first title in some degree literally is evident when we hear, before the poem begins, four tolls of the bell:

Imprisoned memories prowl thro' the dark. Fuck it. They scatter like rats. Dead souls . . . rat a patta patta into the silence. Ashes drift in the back of the skull. A goblin parts the curtains with a slant-eyed chuckle. Panic. I blink as he vanishes into the shadows, hint of prophetic cats-eyes. The dust settles thick, so by five when I stagger to the freezing bathroom I leave footprints for other to excavate. They say the Ice Age is coming, the weather's changed. The air stutters tic tic tic tic, rattle of death-watch beetle on sad slate roofs. The ice in your glass is radioactive, Johnny. Outside in the leaden hail, the swan of Avon dies a syncopated death. We pull the curtains tight over the dawn, and shiver by empty grates. The household gods have departed, no one remembers quite when. Poppies and corncockle have long been forgotten here, like the boys who died in Flanders, their names erased by a late frost that clipped the village cross. Spring lapped the fields in arsenic green, the oaks died this year. On every green hill mourners stand, and weep for *The Last of England*.[12]

But if the bells literally provide us with information, by telling us "it is 4 o'clock," or "the artist works at night," then they simultaneously ring with more figurative implications; these clock chimes ring also as funeral bells. Time, as we have suggested, is a pressure in this prophetic documentary, and, like the ticking clock at the beginning of *The Angelic Conversation*, is not something easily left behind or passed beyond. And note how the poem moves away from relatively personal comments, the memories of a self who says "I" ("I blink"), and toward more general histories and observations. The speaker explicitly situates himself as archeologist ("I leave footprints for others to excavate"), while he observes from a distance, from out of a capacious stretch of time ("they say the Ice Age is coming"). The remarkably absent or ungrounded "I" of the early poems here becomes absent for the sake of generalization; that is, the "I" becomes "we" ("we pass the curtains tight over the dawn"), whereupon large pronouncements descend ("on every green hill mourners stand"—a purely Blakean figure).

With *War Requiem* in mind—although, once again, that film is to follow—we may also see here to what degree *The Last of England* is, indeed, a requiem, an elegy, a meditation on monumentality through performance:

> Poppies and corncockle have long been forgotten here, like the boys who died in Flanders, their names erased by a late frost that clipped the village cross.

Surely this dialogue between monumentality and performance names just what is at stake in the performance pieces of the film. These performances have been linked by other critics to methods and practices from Eisenstein or Brecht, but Gilbert and George seem to be a nearer context.

In this first sequence, Spring first stomps on the Caravaggio painting, punk barbarian, but then he tries to fuck it. This surreal and transgressive representation of violence and sexuality is relatively common in performance art contemporary with Jarman. In Vito Acconci's *Seedbed* (1971), for example, the artist notoriously "masturbated under a ramp built into the gallery over which the visitor walked."[13] Spring performs, whatever else one might say, a love-hate relationship with this painting and represents in himself a figure of both sexual desire and destruction.

In Jarman's view, Caravaggio's *Profane Love* already shows the destruction of art through its wicked, grinning angel, and according to Jarman, Spring is equally destructive, this Cupid's mirror.[14] But the painting also stands in as a "masterpiece," as "art," as a monument amidst these ruins. This is why the interviewer in *Kicking the Pricks* twice asks Jarman if the trampling of the Caravaggio painting parallels the later sex scene on the flag. "It could be seen that way," says Jarman.[15] But the parallel is transparent: each scene performs—excessively, transgressively—a response to cultural monumentality, painting and flag.

The way poetry and documentary coalesce in *The Last of England* is made apparent in the figure of Spring. On the one hand, he is potentially a stereotypical subject of documentary, the down-and-out young man, whom we see wandering through urban rubble, kicking out windows, and shooting up in an abandoned building. Some of these scenes would not be out of place or found surprising in any run-of-the-mill urban documentary. Spring takes a few puffs on a cigarette and coughs, heaving; he falls asleep. The content here is realistic, the images relatively unadorned in themselves; but the editing and montage give these scenes a different reading. For Spring has also a more active, magical role. Now, in slow notion, he carries a lit torch through dark, cavernous rooms. The created space here recalls the otherworldly chambers in *The Angelic Conversation*. His performances with the Caravaggio painting have already told us that he is not just an unconscious subject of the documentary camera, but rather a complex agent—an actor—whose actions are multilayered and deserving of critical interpretation.

After the second poem (which we shall come to in a moment), the camera looks down at Spring's boot from his point of view. This shot once again stresses that he looks and acts, that he is not only looked at and acted upon. When the boot stamps on water, the sound track suddenly reinforces his stomping by sounding loud metallic bangs. The point-of-view shot and the sound track combine to give Spring substance and authority. Although in *Kicking the Pricks* Jarman himself reads Spring merely as a figure of destruction, Spring is more than that; he is a poetic, creating figure in this first part of the film, not a mere example of urban decay.

This idea is furthered when we see Spring sitting on a pile of rubble and playing a panpipe. Here he is a Pan figure, a poet figure, however aimless and confused, and is directly comparable to Oedipus at the end of Pasolini's *Oedipus Rex*. Read as a picture from a realistic documentary, the image is unlikely, to say the least; but as a visual summary of the role of Spring, the image could not be clearer. Although sound has not reinforced visual space very often to this point, the sound track now plays his melancholy pipes. He is the spirit of this place, the *genius loci*, and these are the songs of Spring.

Unlike any of the other poems, the second voice-over is not reproduced in *Kicking the Pricks*:

My teacher said, there are more walls in England than in Berlin, Johnny. What were we to do in those crumbling acres, die of boredom?—or recreate ourselves, emerging from the chrysalis all scarlet and turquoise, as deathsheads from gyp plants, moths of the night, not your clean-limbed cannon fodder for the drudgy nine-to-five, sniffing glue instead of your masonic brandies. We fell off the cogs of misfortune, out to lunch in 50IS, notching up the pricks in the disco, we heard prophetic voices. I saw the best minds of my generation destroyed by madness, starving, hysterical, naked, not with a bang, but a whimper. And gathered everything you threw out of your dream houses, treasured your trashcans, picking through the tatters of your lives, we jumble the lot and squat in your burnt out hearths. Your world, beavering away at its own destruction, serviced the profit machine, and creaked to a halt, not with a bang. Even our protests were hopeless, neat little marches, down blind alley, all around malevolent bureaucracies mutated large as dinosaurs, a [thin] yellow pus drained through exhausted institutions. Citizens stood mute, watching children devoured in their prams, and all you did in the desperation was celebrate the Windsors yet again, old cows staggered to the slaughterhouse to emerge as roast oxen.

This second voice-over is equally abstract in its description of culture and society and pauses only for a moment to indicate sexual identity ("notching up the pricks in the disco"). As a whole, it is a belated Beat poem that rejects the squares ("the drudgy nine-to-five") and embraces margins, madness, and trash. To dwell in the margins allows the speaker prophetic insight ("we heard prophetic voices"), and the poem closes with a stark, violent vision of the apocalyptic present ("old cows staggered to the slaughterhouse to emerge as roast oxen"). The poem explicitly attaches itself to prophetic utterances by T. S. Eliot ("The Hollow Men") and Allen Ginsberg ("Howl"), yet feels no special need to update, transfigure, or particularize those canonical outbursts. The images on the screen underscore the poem's depiction of ruin: when a moment of color appears in the voice-over ("emerging from the chrysalis all scarlet and turquoise"), the matching picture is Spring hacking and retching, barely able to stick a cigarette in his mouth. Later in the sequence we are shown a few frames of a yellow-tinted butterfly, but the voice-over is saying "yellow pus." The image of Spring rutting against the Caravaggio picture is now matched against the close of the poem, and then, after a few beats, the Bach violin sonata is heard, making for a dramatic and portentous conclusion.

The third voice-over is reproduced with very few changes in *Kicking the Pricks*, where it is titled "Evasion" and this time formatted as a poem:

What do you see in those heavy waters? I ask.
Nothing but a bureaucrat from the ministry poisoning the buttercups
    with a new defoliant.
What's that I hear?
The sound of Gershwin on his ghetto blaster.
What else?
The atom splitting.
And the whispering?
Half-truths spilling from the minister's case.
Wriggling in the sunlight.
What are they saying?
All's well, no comment. Some of them are silent.
Ah here's the guard.
What's the password?
EVASION.
What else do you see?
Lies flowing through the national grid, and bribery.
All's normal then?
Yes.
Where's hope?
The little white lies have carried her off beyond the cabbage patch.
They've murdered her?
Yes.
And Tomorrow?
Tomorrow's been cancelled owing to lack of interest.
You saw the graffiti years ago on the Euston Road, and didn't believe it;
What proof do you need the world's curling up like an autumn leaf?
The storm's coming to blow it into the final winter.
Can't you feel the days are getting shorter?[16]

This passage is antiauthoritarian and apocalyptic once again, but more original and striking than the previous Beat diatribe. A quiet piano in the sound track emphasizes the poem's distant, less obvious approach. The "world's curling up like an autumn leaf" verges on euphemism, a Tennysonian response to crisis. The words "buttercups," "sunlight," and "cabbage patch" show us something like country idyll, leaving it to the pictures to show us urban wasteland. Why does the bureaucrat play "Gershwin on his ghetto blaster"? Because he is blasting the ghetto, inappropriately, with

Gershwin? Or because he is misusing art, blind to his own art, too dull to be touched by beauty? There is still a distance projected by the lines, but one with piercing points and, again, the insistence of time at the end ("Can't you feel the days are getting shorter?").

This first section of *The Last of England* contains all four of the voice-overs, and is characterized by its poetry and by its meditation on art. Spring is the spirit of the place, its poet and muse, not just its documentary denizen. Spring continues to occupy the focus of the film's attention until the fourth and final poem, solidifying the connection between Spring and poetry that has been established so far. But in this last section, between the third and fourth poems, he seems to be more a ghostly reference, a transitional figure, not quite as much at the center of our attention. Home movies of playing children are spliced together with stroboscopic images of Spring climbing about on piles of rubble; the implication is that this idyllically happy child has grown into a down-and-out punk. We follow behind Spring, jerky and speeded up, as he walks down New York City streets. The film cuts back to an earlier image of Spring hacking and coughing on his cigarette, and then there is the fourth poem. Between the third and fourth poems Spring is no longer the active and destructive force we saw at the beginning, but a comparatively empty form. He is still our poetry guide—and no poem can take place without him—but he is leading us into another cinematic landscape where no articulate words can follow. After the fourth poem, he will be seen for only a few moments and in an entirely different guise.

The fourth and last poem in *The Last of England* is printed in *Kicking the Pricks* as "The Winds of Change":

> The sad old Emperor bent beneath his black top hat smiles in the deathly sunlit silence. The Lady next door to me says "There he is! There's Hirohito and his Empress Nagasake." Look! Johnny look! They're playing the funeral march for the Royal Doulton. He stole the patterns way back when you were a little boy, no one cared much. They were busy squandering our threadbare patrimony on the atom. Now you see it, now you don't. England had it years back, us kiddies weaned on food parcels from uncle Randy in the wild west, choc-full o' comix and bubble gum. I grew up in the wind of change ma'am! Quite! Quite blew away my reason. His father's father's father's presentation clock, a black marble mausoleum ticked out my childhood. 101 years of middle class assurance. The bomb dropped with regular monotony, leaving us waiting—the frosty heart of England blighted each spring leaf, all aspiration withered in the blood.

In the silence of an English suburb power and secrecy dwell in the same house, while far away in the big city the A to Z clamped a grid on despair.[17]

Again time ticks and ticks; we hear raps like rats scurrying and knocks like bombs dropping. The rhythm of these prophetic poems finds its cadence in the clicking of the deathwatch beetle, calling all to alarm. Here the archeological images that we noted earlier appear, arrayed against these words linking middle-class power to bombs and nuclear destruction. Once again, the self is scarcely able to assemble itself into consecutive, logical sentences; a passage like this stands in for the structure of the whole film. So fierce and effective has been the surrounding oppression that the victims, it seems, can register only outbursts and slogans, brief poems and weird performances, before falling once again into silence.

What does it mean to go from Spring to Spencer Leigh? Earlier we saw Leigh throwing bricks while Spring played his panpipe. Now Spring vanishes, and Leigh is at the center of the collage. Leigh is a less mythological figure than Spring, not just in name but in appearance. He, too, wanders through the ruins, but crying from time to time rather than wrecking. Not labeled specifically as anything like bourgeois or working-class, Leigh's character nonetheless looks more normal and less like the glue sniffers in Jarman's Beat poem or the drug-taking, window-smashing Spring. Leigh is an everyman, an average Johnny who is likewise caught in a world of rubble. And it is Leigh who will shortly be executed by a firing squad.

This execution stands at the heart of this next section of the film and arguably at the very center of *The Last of England*. Yet there is, so far, scarcely any attempt by critics to describe what this firing squad actually is, what it means. Who are these soldiers in balaclavas? Terrorists? Government representatives? Government terrorists? Hill writes that "the second part [of *The Last of England*] is organized around scenes of people being rounded up by soldiers/terrorists who ambiguously represent state authority."[18] O'Pray describes the scenes similarly: "Refugees huddle in the cold escorted by sullen soldiers in balaclavas who could be a new form of military or terrorists—it is hard to tell which, and that is, perhaps, Jarman's point."[19]

Considering the intensity and mercilessness of these scenes, it is surprising not only that critics have not commented in greater detail on these scenes, but also that Jarman himself does not give us more specific indications of what is going on here. The closest Jarman comes to identifying these fearsome militants in *Kicking the Pricks* is when he describes the plot of *Neutron*, a script whose apocalyptic atmosphere overlaps with *The Last of England*: "It was a very strange script. Based on the Revelation of St. John. The angels were a paramilitary group called the Outriders engaged in mopping up the remains of a world, our world, that had passed away; they relocated it in a bunker where the saved, 'The Saints,' cannibalized their captives."[20] But even this description reminds us once again of to what degree *Jubilee* and *Neutron* are recognizable science fiction and to what degree, by contrast, *The Last of England* does not allow its soldiers or its apocalypse to inhabit conventional cinematic genre. These soldiers are all the more terrifying for their lack of context.

I would read this whole section, from the central execution to all the rays of militaristic imagery that shoot out from this center, as a foreshadowing of the critiques of patriotism and war in *War Requiem*. Owen, in fact, springs readily to Jarman's mind at this point in *Kicking the Pricks*:

FIGURE 6.1
Art and expression
at the end of time in
THE LAST OF ENGLAND

Would you describe yourself as a patriot?
Yes, I think of Wilfred Owen's parable of the old men and the young saying: 'Abraham slew his son. . . . And half the seed of Europe one by one.[21]

Owen's sensibility—"like the boys who died in Flanders, their names erased by a late frost which clipped the village cross"—is probably more important in *The Last of England* than that of T. S. Eliot or Allen Ginsberg, the poets whom Jarman specifically invokes. Annette Kuhn has given the most useful

Derek Jarman and Lyric Film

description along these lines: "[this is] a contemporary England in which militarism now frankly figures as chaotic and destructive, and patriotism (flag waving) seems to be synonymous with pointless death."[22]

The terrorists are formally introduced with a sequence of machine gun-like drum bursts; we see them leading a group of people out of a glowing red interior. The apocalyptic world is now, to a remarkable extent, an elemental world, a world of fire and water. They walk through pools of water, bonfires all around, an effect familiar to us from Tarkovsky. Conventionally beautiful images of sunsets accompany the terrorists, but now these sunsets connote the withdrawing of the light, the end of things, the last of England. The world was ruined in the first section of the film, no doubt, and we still find ourselves amidst abandoned buildings and warehouses, but the film suggests a strong link between the primal landscape and the terrorists.

The "elemental," "natural" surroundings suggest that society has descended to its most brutal components and that there is nothing left but cruelty and power. We have little indication of who the terrorists are or how we might identify their victims. There is some sense that the victims are what we might think of as marginalized or displaced people: a man with a mohawk is thrown to the ground to dramatic music. There is a vaguely punk aspect about some of the victims, but Jarman does not press this identification too hard. The terrorists themselves are purely oppressive, threatening with their guns, arranging firing squads. And even though they seem to be absolutely in control, all-powerful, they still wear those masks. Jarman is not just playing back frightening pictures from our contemporary visual repertoire. He intends these masks to mean.

They mean because they tell us that even though we have entered a world that is structured as sheer power and that is much closer to nature than to art, there is still artifice. The soldiers create themselves, create their own impressions. Although horrific and brutal, they also perform. And so we are able to see what passes for art in a world that has respect only for power and where even the rays of the sun seem to suggest only blood and *175* fiery nightmare.

And so the soldiers, indeed, begin to perform. They circle their prisoners with torches, weirdly taking their place next to other torchbearers in Jarman's films, from the men in *The Angelic Conversation* to Spring earlier in *The Last of England*. That even the terrorists start to blend in with what otherwise would seem to be Jarman's figures of illumination (recall ahead of time, too, the figures circling Jarman's floating bed in *The Garden*) suggests to what extent these horrific creatures are being dreamt by Jarman. Or to put it another way: the terrorists come first to us as horrific dreams of apocalyptic television, and yet we can see the poet trying to wrench the figures back over to his side, to dream their power away from them, to make them dance.

The terrorists' dancing around their bonfire transitions directly into the disco sequence, which is a kind of dance video from hell. The disco sequence has some affinities with the performance pieces later (eating the cauliflower, cutting up the wedding dress), except that those performances emphasize the extension of a single act in something like real time, whereas the disco sequence is so obviously centered on editing. To employ a tenuous distinction, this sequence should be read as a kind of video rather than a kind of theater. This "performance video," then, the most extended set piece so far, is an entirely self-reflexive enterprise, since the genre into which many viewers would most readily situate *The Last of England* is, in fact, that of the rock video. Thus Janet Maslin says in her *New York Times* review of September 28, 1988: "Surely Derek Jarman's *Last of England* is the longest and gloomiest rock video ever made."[23] In 1987 or 1988, what other visual experiences would be comparable to *The Last of England*, a film that has no dialogue, that has music that is not just classical but also rock, and whose images include punks walking up and down city streets?

The disco sequence itself is a kind of hallucinatory antivideo played to dance music that seems to arise out of machine-gun fire. After all, who can dance in such a world? What would a painting look like at the end of time? This male ballerina has a horn on his head and dances as if amidst flames. We cut in overly fast and distorted splices to naked terrorists who wear only their masks, dancing in red light. Again there is the impression that this video is being dreamt, insofar as images from other parts of the film creep in, from both earlier passages as well as later ones. The sequence, with its remarkably "synchronous" sound (the sound for once linked closely to the pictures), seems to be its own self-sufficient artifact, but at the same time, it is not, since other images find their way into the mix.

176 As the sequence proceeds, an almost subliminal series of images shows us the flowery tutu floating in the water. We cut back and forth rapidly between the dancer in his tutu, who turns about, as gracefully as he is able, and the tutu itself, floating in the water like a wreath of flowers that someone has dropped and left behind. The sequence pauses on that wreath, holding it before us for a moment, then turns to a sound track filled with Hitlerian shouting and other military commands. The wreath of flowers pauses before us, a quiet dream of beauty amidst this hellfire and noise, a lyrical passage, before giving way to more shouts and coercion. The ballerina is the hallucinatory embodiment of what art remains, at the end, in *The Last of England*.

Imagination has been confined; the music is repetitive and loud; the images are distorted; there are only the slightest remnants of civilization.

The next set piece is that of the two soldiers fucking on a Union Jack. From the retrospective view of *War Requiem*, we can read the Union Jack scene as a further response to the madness of patriotism. The scene begins with a terrorist figure in uniform lying prostrate on a raised platform covered by a huge Union Jack. The platform is a kind of altar, certainly not a bed, and thus far the body is unmoving. Empty bottles are strewn everywhere in place of candles. The whole scene goes back to an idea that Jarman expressed in reference to *Imagining October*:

> Q: It is a very complex film. The other theme, of course, is the connection between sex and the heroic monumentalism.
> J: Monumentalism is always erotic: look at the Albert Memorial. Monumental sculptures search for the first Adam, the original, the ideal before the fall; they are pre-conscious. Because nothing can be wrong with them, they're dangerous.[24]

The Union Jack sequence makes literal a nightmarish inversion of the erotic monument, as a man quickly disrobes and climbs onto the collapsed body. As Bach plays, the two bodies very slowly roll over, but the impression is one of utter exhaustion, both figures at the edge of consciousness, where sexuality has become only an expression of a lust for power. Instead of an erotic, ideal, preconscious monumental space, we find ourselves in an utterly fallen, almost unconscious place, one essentially devoid of eroticism. We hear a couple of grunts or moans on the sound track, which round the figures into a sexual sound-space for a moment, but the scene is surely anything but erotic, since these characters seem far more dead than alive. This scene continues the satirical eroticism staged in *Jubilee*'s "Rule, Britannia," and it inverts the authentically erotic wrestling of the identically clad figures in *The Angelic Conversation*.

The Union Jack sequence concludes with a kind of coda: the film turns to black and white, and a man throws bottles against the wall, echoing similar images from earlier in the film. Then a robed man slowly carries a torch through a dark warehouse littered with tires. Another moment of lyricism, then, which parallels the abandoned tutu in the disco sequence. When the man exits the back of the cavernous room, the music neatly stops, and we cut to the well-lit precincts of a clearly new scene.

The terrorists now emerge from a building, taking Spencer Leigh with them. Although the execution sequence is one of the most brutal scenes in the film, there is also a tranquility about the whole sequence. Bird noises in the sound track; none of the omnipresent bonfires; the film is not speeded up or cut superfast. In fact, one might read the sequence in a dialectical manner: namely, that precisely at this nadir, in this valley of death, there is hope to be found, a light that is not just a searing or a blinding. For the first time, one of the terrorists is unmasked; he has a face. It is a stern, military face (later he will become an officer leading exercises in *War Requiem*), but it is still a visible face, maskless in a world of masks. The openness goes along with the weather; the band of terrorists no longer seems so entirely alien or monstrous. Indeed, we are even invited to consider ourselves as one of them through a point-of-view shot in which the audience, in essence, offers a matchbox to the condemned prisoner. That we are implicated in this murder—there is no similar point of view from Leigh's perspective—is disturbing, no doubt, but would have been unimaginable in previous parts of the film where masks drew down absolute divisions.

Along with this newly felt openness comes a female presence, a presence that has been hidden until now (the masked soldier in the Union Jack sequence was, in fact, actually a woman), but that will become an important element for the remainder of the film. As Leigh lights the cigarette before he is shot, images from the Spring section appear; we naturally read these images as his memories. These earlier images of wandering about among ruins, of wandering over the wrecked landscape, are harshly confirmed through his execution. Everything is indeed over, his life is a ruin, there is nothing left. Yet still, not quite; for even as he dreams these ruined memories in his last moments, there appear new images, memories that we have not seen before, of Tilda Swinton in flowery fields (although the restless sound track and speeded-up film undermine the idyllic nostalgia of these memories).

The execution occurs, but then it begins to start over again, and we realize that narrative time is unraveling. Is the repetition a sign of fatality and doom? Or perhaps a sign of hope? Notice that the second time we aim for the execution the sound track is suddenly entirely ambient. Again we hear the birds, but there is more: now every boot and step is deeply etched in sound-space. Maybe the earlier version, with only the birds, was a kind of dream, whereas this is the thing itself. Yet above the sounds—the clips falling to the ground, the heard commands now of "aim" and "fire"—we hear a briefest voice from nowhere—"Don't be sad"—a female voice. We cannot help but attach this voice to the memory of Swinton. Amidst all the violence, this voice is the wreath of flowers, the distraught figure on the memorial steps; this voice from the air is the requiem in the war.

The scene switches again. Now this female response, parallel to the female roles in *War Requiem*, is made even more substantially present when the voice of Marianne Faithfull sings over a huddled group of refugees. Her unaccompanied voice is more lyrical, more beautiful than any human voice we have heard in the film so far. Although she describes their cold weather, their wintry situation ("loud the waves roar, thunderclouds bend before"), it seems inarguably, nonetheless, to be a voice of consolation, in contrast to a commanding voice of torment or a poet's voice of prophetic despair. This song is the elaboration of the female voice from the air that we've just heard ("don't be sad").

The sailing images in the song are matched by seabirds' cries and ocean noises in the sound track, and the people are gathered next to the water. They are preparing, it appears, to assemble in the boat of the title painting, *The Last of England* by Ford Madox Brown. Like *War Requiem*, this is another of Jarman's films that aims for the water, water that once again is freeing and salvific. The tranquil associations of water are then underscored in the transition to the next sequence. A very peaceful guitar, surely the quietest and most relaxed music we have heard so far, plays over a speeded-up time-lapse photography of the water beyond the bonfires. The water keeps moving, its sheer speed expressing an underlying restlessness, no doubt, but the fire in the foreground slowly burns out. This is the most substantially optimistic moment that we have experienced to this point, and it has us reflecting on the water.

But the mood is short-lived, to say the least, since we find ourselves abruptly into a sequence where for several minutes we watch a naked man eating a cauliflower. This is another performance that would not surprise us in the least if found in a small, downtown, underground theater. The sound track here is brutally satiric, giving us doses of religion ("we need prayer for everything") and, more than that, repeated appeals to consumerism ("You want to make money? We all do"). The radio slogans stand in stark and inadequate juxtaposition to the embodiment of homelessness and poverty who stands before us. The radio voices mark this sequence as contemporary (in contrast to the voices of Hitler and Churchill elsewhere), with the consequence that we are not allowed to relegate the film's apocalypse to the nowhere realm of science fiction or prophetic dream. This apocalypse, implies the radio collage, is right now. Hence there is present a kind of reality effect, which assures us that these symbolic actions still correspond to current reality. Yet at the same time, the cutting of the sequence is also self-consciously theatrical, a tacit acknowledgment that this sequence is also a performance.

The episode of the cauliflower eater drops us out of the clear reach of the terrorists for a time (it takes place obviously in their ruined world, but they appear in only a couple of brief, nearly subliminal cuts during the sequence), thereby again disrupting a too linear or too transparent sense of narrative. We cannot easily say that here is the section with Spring and here is the section with the terrorists. But at the end of the cauliflower sequence the terrorists immediately return, and are now annotated once and for all through the montage. Although Jarman has kept us in some suspense as to who they are, the terrorists are now clearly aligned with imperial power. We see images of the terrorists ducking around corners, images that are juxtaposed with footage of statues and soldiers. The stock footage emphasizes especially British India, and satire attains its greatest clarity when "Pomp and Circumstance" plays over this montage. The juxtapositions work reciprocally: on the one hand, as identifications—the terrorists are imperial stormtroopers—and on the other hand, as accusations—namely, that in spite of its public displays, the government is empowered, in effect, by masked terrorists.

The red wreath that was born out of the floating tutu earlier now reemerges from this montage to encircle a peephole through which we enter the next sequence. A funeral sequence commences that will provide a stark contrast to the wedding sequence that concludes the film. Three women, dressed as mourners, emerge from a fiery red interior, carrying the red wreath before them. They are attended by terrorists and are clearly in league with them; perhaps their husbands are fallen terrorists or soldiers. Cut to more home movies, bombs exploding in the sound track. Back to the funeral and the only dialogue in the entire film.

An aristocratic lady mourner asks, "Is it loaded?" "Yes, ma'am," replies the masked terrorist. "Did you enjoy the Falklands?" "Yes, ma'am." "Preparing for the next one?" "Yes, ma'am." "Its going to be a big one, isn't it?" "I hope so, ma'am." "Keep up the good work." The dialogue echoes a little, like Judi Dench's voice in *The Angelic Conversation*, but its synchronization between sound and space is unique in the film and rounds an obviously emblematic scene into reality, just as the reference to the Falklands particularizes this abstract dreamscape into a specific, contemporary place. Once again, out of this apocalypse, the insistence of time.

A younger female mourner smiles as she holds a gun aloft. The elegiac response is on this occasion in league with violence and terror, dressed in black and looking forward to a future of more violence. As in *War Requiem*, female figures inhabit a site of mourning, but here they are complicit with power: their funeral garb is only a costume, and there are smiles at the end. This funeral that ends with a muted celebration should be directly contrasted with the next sequence, the wedding that ends with a funereal dance of death.

How are we to take this wedding procession? Jarman plays the funeral relatively straight, although with a piercingly satirical conclusion; here the wedding is immediately grotesque, carnivalesque. Presumably this is not only to subvert the straight ceremony of marriage. Swinton plays the bride and Spring returns as the groom; they are attended by three men in drag— the three bridesmaids—two of them conspicuously absurd with beards and huge wigs. They are also surrounded by wedding photographers who verge on being paparazzi; a baby in a pram covered by newspapers with terrible headlines; and a chimney sweep straight out of Dickens. That men appear in the women's roles emphasizes what a man's world this is, and not necessarily for the better. It also underscores the fact that everyone is so obviously costumed; Spring is manifestly un-Springlike in his gentleman's coat and hat.

A wedding is a social ritual where private affection is publicly acknowledged. This sequence exaggerates the ritual and the public elements by emphasizing the artificiality of the costumes and the prurience of the photographers and the newspapers. In the end, a scene like this leaves us no alternatives and little hope: the public realm is artificial, propagandistic, of a piece with power, but the private realm, as suggested by earlier naked bodies, is adrift, despairing, or terrorized. And this sequence turns us once again toward a solitary figure, this time toward the figure of Swinton, as she cuts off that wedding dress, piece by piece, with shears.

Swinton's scene, which is the climax and conclusion of *The Last of England*, is one of the most memorable and powerful scenes in all of Jarman's works. At the most literal level, we are to see this performance as a response to the death of Spencer Leigh, whose images and whose execution is collaged into the later portions of the sequence. We need not worry too much about whether Spring is her husband or whether she is Spencer Leigh's girlfriend; the scenes need not be parsed that reductively. We need only know that they think of each other, that the man is shot, that the woman's voice speaks out of the air. The woman tears off her wedding dress in an expression of anger and remorse. Swinton's performance on the steps in *War Requiem* will be more conventionally figured, but there is considerable continuity between the two scenes. Each is equally the performance of an elegy. Now, next to a flaming bonfire, which we have come to associate with the terrorists, wind whipping through the sound track, Swinton cuts pieces of her dress off with shears. She bites pieces off with her teeth, chewing them.

In an earlier performance piece, the cauliflower eater banged his flaming garbage can with a sword, and the camera closed in on bits of cauliflower on his lips. These thus become parallel scenes that ask us to meditate on the relationship between his solitary poverty and her stripping away of cultural artifice. The cauliflower eater seems absolutely hopeless, however, whereas the vigor of Swinton's performance seems to convey some hope, however dark the skies appear around her.

The femininity of that hope, which seemed to accompany Swinton on her appearance in Spencer Leigh's memories and which was present in Marianne Faithfull's voice as she sang over the refugees, appears here in the female voice that hums and cries over Swinton's cutting. A conventionally optimistic melody this certainly is not; if anything, this voice performs the storm itself, shrieking along with the cold winds. But these cries and shrill shrieks are also a response to the violence, a moan, a yell that emerges from a female figure rather than a man. Swinton, in synch with the sound track,

FIGURE 6.2
*The marriage of
fire and water*

weeps, and her crying continues through the rest of the montage. She whirls against the sunset and flames; the only adequate response, perhaps, to this violent world.

The final pictures draw on images of water that we have seen earlier, those few images that seemed momentarily calming, undisturbed. In a double exposure, the reflection of light on water streaks the screen from top to bottom, and moving through that watery space is a boat, peopled by half a dozen men in robes, one carrying a torch over head.

In another film, we might take this for a boat traveling through the under-world, but in the context of this already altogether hellish world, it seems rather to connote some kind of escape. At first the music is grating and hyperactive, but then silence falls upon the drifting boat as it steals away into its dream. Perhaps these men have escaped their terrible world, though they may have had to become spirits in order to do so.

II. A TIME FOR CONTEMPLATION: VISUALITY AND DRIFT IN *The Garden*

Many films in the tradition of lyric cinema self-consciously announce their genre, their mode, their manner of proceeding. Some, of course, do not. Pasolini seems to assume that just the title—*Teorema* (the Italian word for "theorem")—combined with our knowledge of his lifework up to that point (1967) is enough for the viewer to understand that everything in the film is meant to be taken symbolically, including the Stranger (Terence Stamp) and presumably even the strange sexual powers that emanate from the stranger's volume of Rimbaud. Cocteau's *The Blood of a Poet* provides us—more helpfully—with at least some sort of introductory context when it tells us that the following "*bande d'allégories*" is dedicated to painters such as Pisanello, Uccello, and Piero della Francesca—"*peintres de blasons et d'énigmas*" ("painters of blazons and enigmas"). Paradjanov's *The Color of Pomegranates* informs us right away that this biography of the poet will be told poetically or symbolically rather than realistically.

Jarman's *The Garden*, in its turn, also makes evident the structure and approach of the film. Even before the opening credits have run their course, another "BBC" voiceover, now provided by Michael Gough instead of Nigel Terry, intones the following lines:

I want to share this emptiness with you
Not fill the silence with false notes or put tracks through the void
I want to share this wilderness of failure
The others have built you a highway—fastlanes in both directions
I offer you a journey without direction
uncertainty and no sweet conclusion
When the light faded I went in search of myself
There were many paths and many destinations.

183

This authorial "I" claims control over the film, but on the side of wilderness and emptiness rather than civilization and success. The "I" is generous but contingent, authoritative but divided. An "I" searching for itself in darkness necessarily amounts to a divided, interior quest.

After the opening credits and a blurring, flashing mock rehearsal, we hear the command "Quiet!" as if spoken by a director, and cut on sound to black-and-white stock and the interior of a studio. We see water dripping on sculptures, then dripping on an image of a crucified Christ. Jarman himself now appears, sleeping at his desk among his creations. Once again, he is a Prospero figure, running the show, but less controlling, now less authoritative. The sculptures here, along with the images earlier, display his creativity, yet his roof leaks and he looks haggard. This is the dreaming poet once again, as seen in *The Last of England*, but a confused-looking power this, in pointed contrast to his businesslike demeanor in the earlier film.

When Jarman awakes he looks goggle-eyed, and he blinks at one of the sculptures—a round rock on dozens of spikes or nails. We cut to an extreme close-up of this sculpture; it goes out of focus, then into focus. Clearly we are to sense that this is Jarman's point of view, even if it takes him time to focus, even if he's half-asleep. And finally, by sheer association, the nails change to waving blades of grass, and the black-and-white film changes to color.

These opening segments all work together to name Jarman as the creator-poet-magus. He is in charge whether sleeping, dreaming, or waking, working by association as much as inspiration. The dripping water seems strongly to invoke the poetic school of Tarkovsky and Paradjanov, each famous for their many scenes with flowing and dripping water. As we described in the first chapter, flowing water in each of these lyric directors signals the poetic accident—the vitality and truth of what is beautiful but not under the director's complete control. Specifically, one might compare these opening scenes of Jarman's studio, where creativity is of utmost importance, with the opening scenes of *The Color of Pomegranates*, where the young poet hears about biblical creation in a cave dripping with water.

184   A lyric film important for Jarman's *The Garden* is Pasolini's *La Ricotta* (1963).[25] *La Ricotta* is significant in Pasolini's career in that it signals a clear shift from the neorealism of his first two films, *Accattone* (1961) and *Mamma Roma* (1962), to a self-consciously autobiographical, parable mode in *La Ricotta*.[26] In *La Ricotta* Pasolini casts Orson Welles as the director of a religious film; during an interview with a foolish journalist, the director reads a poem from Pasolini's published script of *Mamma Roma*. The director thus becomes an autobiographical figure for Pasolini himself, yet, again, he is not idealized. Since *Citizen Kane*, Orson Welles has become virtually the type for directorial power and genius, yet the film

subtly satirizes his godlike influence. Several scenes show us live figures made into painterly still lifes, and we feel the contrast, as in *Caravaggio*, between painted religious figures and the people holding still. The director's power is immense and comic, as when the director's command "Action!" ("*Azzione!*") is repeated by one assistant after another and then even by a (speaking) dog. When the director attempts to re-create the crucifixion scene, however, a poor man dies on his cross. At the end we see the director, blind to the class differences and death around him, mingling with upper-class socialites who are visiting the set.

Jarman's director is similarly deidealized, a creator figure who is simultaneously implicated in what he attacks. Several extended set pieces in the film link Jarman, as a camera-wielding director, to hyperbolically aggressive paparazzi. Taking pictures, making pictures, and representing subjects are not simple or innocent projects, but rather invasive and distorting procedures. In the first such set piece, three men take photographs of a Madonna—Tilda Swinton made up to look like the Virgin Mary in a Renaissance painting—and child. The three men are dressed in black leather jackets and black ski masks; using imagery from *The Last of England*, these cameramen are essentially terrorists. Jarman is probably saying something local and satirical about tabloid morality. But the satire is not simple; it is not just directed at bothersome interviewers or sensationalist headlines. For Jarman is on the side of the cameramen as well: he represents; he brings those images home; he wants to make the private public.

We see Swinton run past movie equipment to get away; we see what seems to be footage from one of the pursuing cameras. As Swinton and the cameramen finally wrestle on the ground, the sound track combines the loud clicking of cameras snapping pictures with the sound of her screams. Through representation, the static, smiling Virgin has been deprived of her royal vestments and chased across the grounds. Even as the viewer must sympathize with Swinton's character rather than the masked men, Jarman surely intends us to realize that his cinema is more like that of the disrespectful, invasive, and self-divided paparazzi than that of a worshipful Renaissance painter.

Having associated his directorial eye with figures of aggression and distaste, Jarman unleashes satirical effects that are never entirely self-righteous or simple in their targeting. In the next section of the film, for example, an angel reads the biblical story of the wise men while projected behind him we see the casino-like lights of malls and shopping centers. The young angel's pronunciation carries a working-class—in contrast to a BBC—accent, and the projected images connote a carnival of middle-class consumerism. The

185

overheard biblical story of the three kings following the star stages a blunt contrast to the images of the Christmas shopping lights.

Our stereotypical response to the arcade lights tells us "Bad consumers! Superficial glitz!" and we know from frequent remarks in Jarman's journals how disgusting he finds the whole Christmas shopping spree. But the satire is not so obvious as we might expect or, one might even say, not so obvious as our response to it. The images are presented, in actuality, rather subtly and quietly. The speeded-up night images are not so chaotic and frenzied as they might be; what is more, the lights amidst the darkness overlap with the look of the credit sequence, which showed the process of filming (this film) in darkness. We know that the shop lights connote superficiality and consumerism, yet there is an aesthetic quality to them as well, which is reinforced by shots of reflections and the creation of interesting, nonhallucinatory distortions.

Jarman further complicates his satire by now showing his gay couple digging up a crown and smiling at the sparkling jewels. The jewels scintillate in the firelight, and the couple polishes the crown with their fingers. The two men seem to like the lights on the crown more for their sparkling than for what the crown might stand for. Jarman's small-scale, low-budget films reject the seductiveness of large-scale cinema in their very appearance (absence of stars, spare sets, frequently shot in video), but in this case Jarman again does not entirely separate the seductiveness and aggressiveness of his cinematic light from the desecrating lights of the shopping malls.

The Garden appropriates narrative elements and iconographic elements of the story of Christ with the general political intent of focusing on the persecution and martyrdom of gay men. Jarman's approach, however, is along many paths, as he warned at the outset, and the transposition of Christian narrative and imagery is not always used for clear statement or unequivocal political purpose. The unique figure of Christ is split in *The Garden* several times over again: first between two identical-looking gay men and then onto a more traditional Christ figure who roams around showing his stigmata. The subject of Christ is thus shattered and pluralized, but to what effect? In her review of *The Garden* in the *New York Times*, Janet Maslin focused on the hermeneutic difficulties of watching the film:

The passion with which Mr. Jarman attempts this [turning his thoughts to AIDS, Christianity, and intolerance] is not accompanied by any fondness for clarity, and so *The Garden* is as mystifying as it is intense. While its larger ideas emerge broadly and unmistakably, there is much to ponder—in, for instance, an image of the Twelve Apostles as 12 women in babushkas, sitting at a table by the seaside as they solemnly run their fingers around the edges of wine glasses to create an ominous hum.[27]

Although the general political import is often clear, Maslin wonders how we are supposed to read many of the more local images in the film. How should we understand the sequence, for example, where the gay couple's "bliss is intercut with the cries of a Madonna-like figure whose motivation, like everything else here, is rather too widely open to interpretation."[28]

The *New York Times* is not necessarily a place to go for celebrations of alternative film, and Maslin perhaps does not have room to recall how often rather more canonical films by Antonioni or Fellini are also "too open to interpretation." But she does describe *The Garden* in the poetic terms in which the film itself began: that is, for all the clear political messages, there are still many scenes that have "no sweet conclusion" (in the poem's words) or are "too widely open to interpretation" (in the reviewer's words). Poetry once again is both a preliminary description of signification and structure, but also a critical problem, and not just for Maslin.

As we have before, let us turn this critical question to particular cases. Who are these female figures that Maslin wonders about? What is their purpose? Why does the Madonna-like figure cry out, and why do the wine-glasses solemnly hum? Female figures were of crucial significance in *The Last of England* and *War Requiem*, so we may try to account somewhat more systematically for these scenes.

To start, then, with the twelve women at the table. The scene begins with a master shot of the women, who are immediately recognizable as related to the iconography of the Last Supper (by Leonardo or otherwise); behind them is an obviously unrealistic back projection of a paper boat on an ocean. We hear the ominous hum of which Maslin speaks. How did we get here? Although conventional plot is radically diminished in *The Garden*, continuity from segment to segment is provided by many other means. Here, for instance, before we get to the women, we see the turning arm of what looks like a radar scanner, slowly revolving like a long rectangular helicopter blade. This image of omnipresent surveillance is carried over from *The Angelic Conversation*, but now deployed with a different visual rhythm, as part of a differently assembled collage. We see this image twice, and this circling—these circles—is carried over when the women run their fingers around the tops of the wineglasses. Continuity between scenes, as here, can be largely formal, picking up and collecting shapes or gestures— the continuity of form. But the composition of the women at the table is clearly of more than formal interest; the iconography is archetypal in its scope and crying out for explanation. What is the effect here of Jarman's revision of Christian imagery?

The women themselves embody an obvious gender critique of patriarchal Christianity. Instead of twelve men—all but one of whom were glorified by history, painting, and religion—twelve women. Their silence and their actions also implicitly critique a verbally discursive Christianity, a religion made out of words and laws. They do not speak; only the glasses hum. The wineglasses are borrowed from the ritual of communion, but there is only natural magic here—ordinary women, silent amidst the hum. In a way, Jarman may be naturalizing Christianity, bringing it down to the everyday; but Jarman almost always renders the natural artificial. The back projec-

FIGURE 6.3
Mirrored selves by the sea in THE GARDEN

tion is so obviously there, the background noticeably shaking up and down and the ship so clearly a model, that the constructedness of the scene is once more glaringly apparent. As so often in Jarman's films, the creation of mood and atmosphere is primary, and here, to a greater degree than in many of Jarman's films, the audience has time to think, to consider. A garden itself is an artificial space in which we have time to reflect, and *The Garden* is probably the most contemplative of all his films.

Derek Jarman and Lyric Film

The wineglasses in the foreground and the ocean in the background also recover a repeated image in Jarman's work: the mirroring ocean. The wineglasses shine and sparkle, and the ocean is impossibly bright beneath an overcast sky. The fact that three of the women wear spectacles—all the more noticeable for being in conflict with Biblical and painterly references—also foregrounds the glassy, reflecting nature of both ocean and goblets.

After a time the scene cuts to a man pointing to the horizon of the sparkling ocean. Then in long shot we see this silhouetted man approach the camera, as if walking on the water. The boundaries of shore and beach have dissolved beneath reflecting waves. And finally, then, circled by two men and two women carrying torches, we see Jarman himself in bed, in the water.

FIGURE 6.4   The water serves as a kind of origin—for the ship, for
Love at ocean's edge   the garden—but it is a dreamt ocean, a mirror. Jarman
            sleeps and dreams in the ocean; he sits bleary-eyed in
his leaky studio. The image of reflecting water runs throughout *The Garden*, often figuring originality and creativity, but it is never merely naturalistic. Water may nourish the garden, but at the center, as in *Le Roman de la Rose*, it is a mirror.

The gay couple at the center of *The Garden* appears as another mirroring relationship in Jarman's films. Their resemblance is stressed to the point of surrealism; they have similar haircuts, they dress like twins, they are physically similar. They are perfect, and handsome, mirrors. In comparison to the women at the table, most of whom are older, seemingly average-looking people (the kind not seen in movies), Jarman's pair is obviously photogenic, born and groomed for the camera—and a rather conventional camera at that. This couple is therefore clearly not an average couple, or a typical couple, but is as glamorized in appearance as Christ is in his. Once again, as in the dance of the sailors in *The Tempest*, Jarman has not chosen his gay alternative self-righteously, but complicatedly. A very traditional looking Christ marches through this film, and the gay couple is thus an equally idealistic, rather than a contrastingly realistic, alternative to Christ. They themselves constitute a kind of visual theory in and of themselves, and should thus be treated more like a theory than as a practice, as ideas rather than actual facts.

The main substance of the severe critique of *The Garden* by Bersani and Dutoit comes, indeed, from the film's excessive visuality. The following passage appears at the conclusion to their book on Jarman's *Caravaggio*, and is worth citing at some length:

> From this perspective, the final scenes of *Caravaggio* are celebratory rather than scenes of mourning. They give us Michele, Caravaggio, and Jarman continuing beyond the limits of their particular forms. The replicability of being gives rise to an expansive rather than a self-enclosing narcissism, one far removed from the victimized narcissism of much of Jarman's other work. We can now see one of the most disastrous consequences of his queer victim-pride; it plays into the hands of his (of our) oppressors by making him (us) eminently iden-tifiable, imprisoning us within a persecuted identity. Giving in to a temptation perhaps common to all victims—that of making their vic-timization the ground of their proclaimed superiority—the cover-boy martyrs of *The Garden* become especially visible in their proud and damaged prettiness. *Caravaggio* emphasizes the ontological dignity of an uncertain or fleeting visibility, of pushing beyond our form in order to circulate within universal similitudes. It is a dignity to which, as *Caravaggio* also emphasizes, art gives us access.[29]

Bersani and Dutoit object to the intense visualization of martyrdom in *The Garden* (we see the gay couple flayed and crucified) because that image freezes identity. They mock the photogenic appearance of these "cover-boy martyrs" (elsewhere calling them "two male beauties"), while at the same time objecting to the "visibility" of their martyrdom. These points reach to the very heart of Jarman's cinema, and there are no simple retorts or rebuttals. I would argue, in my turn, that the prettiness of these men and the visibility of their sacrifice are not two different mistakes, but rather related aspects of Jarman's visual self-consciousness. My ideal is also that of Bersani and Dutoit—where the image is mobile rather than frozen—but I see Jarman's use of visual images in *The Garden* and elsewhere as being much more complicated than Bersani and Dutoit will allow. *Caravaggio* is less of a complex singularity among Jarman's films, in my view, than a more typical expression by Jarman of both sexuality and visual mobility.

The self-consciousness that Jarman demonstrated from the very beginning of the film on behalf of his own participation is equally present in the visual thematics that surround these "cover-boy martyrs." A martyr is literally, after all, one who bears witness, and *The Garden* is, in part, an interrogation of the visuality and iconography associated with Christian representation. Martyrs demand to be looked at, as do "cover boys," and the fact that one can describe the couple in this way shows already how self-conscious Jarman's representation is. That these are "cover boys"—cute, photogenic—who are put at the stake shows that Jarman is not just creating victim figures that will further limit queer identity politics, but rather seeking out the problematics of such representations. A film that begins with a blurry, roaming camera at night and that shows its director groggy in a leaky house does not, to my mind, exude confidence in visual representation or the fixing of images. *Caravaggio* explodes fixed images, whereas *Blue* refuses all images, and *The Garden* needs to be seen as working in a similarly open manner.

As the film moves toward images of greater violence and an eventual crucifixion, what do we see, then, of these two men? About ten minutes into the film we see them dressed in identical white shirts and black pants, throwing rocks into the ocean. The film here is shot on video, so that it appears that we are watching home movies, and on the sound track we can even hear the clicking of a movie projector. This is an idealized scene, anachronistically projected into the past (1950s) and staged as a home movie. These men have been filmed; they are being watched, says *The Garden*, from the very beginning. It is sentimental, nostalgic imagery, no doubt, but at the same time it approaches an obviously constructed impossibility, since when was this nostalgic time anyway? The 1950s probably were not the good old days for this couple.

The scene is directly followed by the terrorist cameramen chasing around the Renaissance Madonna, and it would be overly idealized for us, would it not, to think that there are two kinds of cameras: on the one hand, high-tech cameras whose pictures distort and rape, and on the other hand, home-movie cameras whose whirring clicks convey only life as it is actually lived. Through the juxtaposition of the sequences, Jarman shows us that his gay couple is, in crucial respects, as idealized as the Madonna, and that our desire to look at the men, and his desire to show them, is as problematic as the representation of the Virgin.

The next time we see the couple—in a scene noted earlier—they are digging up a sparkling crown. This bit of treasure hunting or archeology is not as obviously innocent as throwing stones on the beach, and so they too become implicated in the swirl of neon lights and consumerism that turns through this section. The next sequence that features the couple shows them bathing each other in a tub. This is another scene that shows their tenderness toward each other, but it is not shot like home-video footage, but rather in the manner of the twelve women at the table, in front of an

FIGURE 6.5
Jarman dreams in
the shining water

obviously artificial back projection. This utopian scene of happiness and caring is thus also set in a surrealistic nowhere.

Intercut, and therefore critically intertwined, with these images are scenes of a young man (in his 20s) bathing a boy (maybe 12). This scene is more realistically filmed, documentary-style (no back projections or home-video effect), and the two are as happy as their counterparts in the parallel bathing scene. As the sequence of the man and the

Derek Jarman and Lyric Film

boy continues, however, the boy suddenly points toward the camera, and it is clear that the cameraman is now an intrusion rather than a neutral invisibility. Camera lights become apparent around them. Later in the sequence, the pursuing, obnoxious cameraman is revealed to be Jarman himself.

No camera interrupts the scene of the couple's bathing, but the boy, now in a suit that matches the couple's suits in other scenes, pops up in their bathtub, confirming with splendid literal-mindedness that the two sequences do in fact rhyme together. While Jarman as cameraman intrudes upon the first pair, the clouds over the second pair redden, and their scene ends up shot through a red filter. Clearly the way that Jarman has filmed these scenes shows how concerned he is with the difficulties of representing intimacy, tenderness, and sexuality in public, cinematic terms. That he is the cameraman does not help us to fix a clear, bounded sense of who are the victims and who the oppressors.

So far the pair has been seen only as a private, affectionate couple, in a bath or by the beach; they dig up the crown by themselves. But now, about a third of the way through the film, they become public figures. While they are seated high on raised double thrones, a young woman from the table of twelve women gives them bunches of leaves. What exactly the gestures mean, it is not necessary to specify; the ritualistic gift clearly conveys that they are being publicly recognized with a sense of their social elevation. They then make their first "public appearance" by serving as the exemplary couple for the musical number "Think Pink." In the background we see footage of marches for gay rights, while in the foreground they stand quietly by, dressed in pink suits, holding a baby. Earlier, they more or less embodied intimacy, tenderness, and privacy; now they are public figures. In no place in the film are they intended to be realistic in any great degree. By juxtaposition, too, Jarman asks us to compare the grotesque advertisement for credit (with the hanging Judas) to "Think Pink" (each as a kind of atmosphere-disrupting skit); although one is gruesome satire and the other campy activism, they each compel us to look and to interrogate our desires. 193

After a clear break in the film that registers a new day (fade to black after "Think Pink," then morning music with Jarman watering the garden, bird noises, a butterfly, Swinton taking a deep breath in a field), the film abruptly shifts gears when a Spanish guitar plays flamenco music. Another musical number is in store. We see a female flamenco dancer on the long table, surrounded by not only the twelve women but also twelve men, with the protagonist couple in the center. Clearly this is another public festivity of some sort, and the couple are honored guests. The table now becomes not only an image of communal gathering, but also a stage for performance. The scene is both public meeting and theater. The Spanish interlude, more or less out of nowhere, is perhaps a reference to a similar moment in Cocteau's *The Testament of Orpheus*. There Cocteau follows a handsome horse-man into a mysterious cave where he finds gypsies playing Spanish music. The Spanish music in both Cocteau and Jarman signals a folk alternative to high culture; one might regard either scene as a problematic dalliance with third-world exoticism. The young boy from the bathing scene dances on the table, too, and he will continue to appear on the table-stage as the film progresses.

At the same time that the gay couple is taking part in social festivities and receiving public recognition, the singular, classical Christ figure is coming into contact with society. In contrast to the couple, the Christ figure—straight from a painting, in white robe and dark beard—seems isolated, alien. When he appears at this point in the film, he stands on the top of a hill, holding his arms apart as if to acknowledge a public gaze. Here the public, however, appears as naked men crawling up and down the hill, curious about the new apparition, but also afraid. Christ's public recognition, his interaction with a community, is apparently not as auspicious as the recognition received by the couple. The mystery and awe of Christian religion are emphasized in this encounter. It is clear that Jarman, like Blake, criticizes Christian mystery—the unnecessary obfuscation for the sake of power—even as he treasures the ambiguity of ritual gesture and the ambivalence of poetic symbolism that allow an audience a multiplicity of responses. Christian mystery is associated with fear, oppression, and hierarchy, whereas poetic ambiguity, in a generous reading, is associated with vitality, complexity, and something like democracy.

Immediately after this ominous confrontation of the classical Christ with the naked men on the hill, we move to a scene with the boy on the long table again, but this time surrounded only by men, not women. Although there is a meandering from episode to episode, as the prologue voice foresaw, and no "conventional narrative" (as Jarman repeatedly terms it in his books), there is certainly shape and structure to the film.[30] It is no coincidence that when the ominous Christ appears in public, the film becomes more and more violent thereafter. His ominous power is thus related to the power of the men around the table. These men are dons, schoolmasters of some sort, and they were previously present at the flamenco dance. But now they become the first obvious persecutors, and the boy becomes the first obvious victim. The dons rap their sticks on the table, sticks that will later become flails and whips. What is Jarman saying about the link between this scene of persecution and the oppression in later scenes? How does the relatively generic oppression of childhood relate to the later sexual oppressions of adulthood? Jarman is drawing on the traditional idea that childhood is a repository of poetic emotion, a childhood that in this film is nurtured (untraditionally) by male figures such as the gay couple and that is oppressed by (traditional to the point of archaism) male figures such as these rod-wielding dons.

The film moves toward climactic images of martyrdom by passing through these several scenes of persecution, first of the child, then of a fleeing transvestite. Here a man in a dress is pursued alongside an emblematic wall covered with homo-hating graffiti. At the beginning of the sequence we see the man somewhat ridiculously smoking a cigarette as he runs away, which once again does not cast him in the most obvious martyr role. The attack itself is emblematic rather than realistic: women in brightly colored dresses try to tear off his dress and wig. The women seem to be under the direction of a cruel-looking gentleman in dinner dress who watches from nearby. And cooperating with the assault are once more those paparazzi terrorists, who seem to be part of the attack rather than standing away from it.

The scene, again, does not claim to present a concrete, sociological analysis of the persecution of transvestism, yet we might still wonder what sort of political comments are legible within its symbolic shorthand. It does not seem that the scene means, reductively, that women envy and compete with male transvestites. Rather, both men and women cooperate with each other in the persecution of social deviance; men and women can dress up in fancy clothes (which is what the attackers wear), but only in the proper fancy clothes. The women are noticeably pretty, decked out in earrings, heels, and scarves. They obviously want to compel looking; they desire to be looked at. With its beautiful women and its paparazzi, the scene again seems to underline the idea that no looking is innocent, nor are the various ways that men and women compel others to look at them.

Now, while standing in front of barbed wire and those paparazzi, the Christ figure is kissed by a man. The kiss ought to be a kiss of betrayal ("Judas, betrayest thou the Son of man with a kiss?" [Luke 22:48]), but the sound track immediately gives a cockcrow, suggesting that this man is Peter ("And immediately, while he yet spake, the cock crew" [Luke 22:60]). The Christ figure has not to this point been very sympathetically portrayed—he is very grim and ominous—but here he is surrounded by terrorist cameras and shown kissing a man. The kiss draws the same furious attention upon him that the gay couple will receive in a moment, and it makes him seem less like the patriarchal, isolated bringer of law and more like one who, at the risk of social stigmatization, openly expresses his solidarity and love for other men.

Into this sequence of persecution scenes (boy, transvestite, Christ)—none of which are entirely obvious or demonizing in their import—now appears the gay couple, but in a scene that is probably the least easy to interpret of anything we have seen so far. They are headed toward martyrdom, yes, but along an elliptical, strangely resonating route. Here they are sleeping together in bed, a moment that recalls the intimate, private moments of earlier parts of the film (beach, bath), but now they are assaulted by three Santa Clauses. One Santa Claus talks on a portable phone; another one has a video camera (and we cut to the black-and-white video of that Santa throughout the scene); another sings a grotesque, mocking version of "God Rest Ye Merry, Gentlemen."

The Santa Clauses, no doubt, betray the Christmas spirit, so that this mockery is in line with the earlier sequences of sparkling neon lights, which there only signify the desire to shop. Again the camera not only intrudes, as it does everywhere else, but also represents a Christmas toy, an object of high-tech consumerism just like the telephone. The Santa Clauses do not seem to be mocking the men because they are in bed together; they seem only to be mocking the season. The scene is a kind of surrealistic juxtaposition of private and public (once again the background is a noticeably artificial back projection) where the two realms do not interact in any obvious way. No one is being oppressed here; rather there is a more generic sense of a society out of kilter, where public and private are out of alignment. The two men sleep through most of it, though at the end they awake, with looks that convey something more like quiet surprise than startled offense.

Persecution scenes continue, then, but still ambivalently. The laughter of the mocking Santa Clauses now becomes the laughter of men in a bathhouse. What sort of persecution is this? The protagonist couple now stands forehead to forehead, wearing suits and emphasizing their mirrored images once and for all. The baths are baths inhabited by men, some wearing crowns, which suggests that they must be Romans. The couple is out of place, the center of attention and the object of the mocking laughter, but not obviously uncomfortable. Although we can understand that this is a transposed version of Christ being persecuted by the Romans, the scene itself consists of men in a bathhouse who mock the gay couple, which once again are not circumstances easy to evaluate. The undressed mock the dressed; the promiscuous mock the monogamous; the old mock the young: any of these descriptions apply to this scene, but none allows us to freeze an image of what a victim or what an oppressor is.

After a montage of images—including the king with the feather and the pillow-fight scene with which this book began—we come to the tar-and-feathering scene in a restaurant. This is the most realistically filmed scene in *The Garden*. The handheld camera gives the documentary impression of cinema verité, and the set is an identifiable part of the real world. There is no nondiegetic sound; the sound track rounds these figures into actuality. And the pretty boys are not pretty here, since they are both trussed and gagged from the beginning of the scene. Even before the tarring begins, there are stains on their faces and clothes, as if they have been beaten. The realistic manner of photography suggests that "this could happen," that "this is actuality," but even here, as the scene progresses, it becomes more obviously stylized, more clearly a performance piece.

Why is this frightening scene set in a restaurant? The restaurant table associates this place with the long table of the Last Supper; earlier, the men were welcomed and honored as part of a community. But now the photography suggests that this is the real world; perhaps that other place was a dream or a fantasy. The setting tells us, furthermore, that this is a public humiliation, one not hidden away or closeted. Once again, as with the dons around the table and as in the bathhouse scene, only men take part in this humiliation, although a woman looks on here, as a man looked on when the women attacked the transvestite. Hence there is an anthropological division of the sexes in all of these sequences; men and women never conspire together as couples, which is what we might expect if they were to embody heterosexual oppression at its most transparent.

What the nature of the assault is cannot be exactly determined. We hear only laughter, but no slurs, epithets, or parodies. The leader of the assault has long hair (in contrast to the couple's short hair), and first puts the tar (or some other black substance) around both of their heads. He reaches into his own coat for feathers. This is where the performance aspect begins to become more noticeable. The self-lacerating nature of the assault is implied; the attacker has to disfigure himself. Clothing is also an important motif running throughout the film, and the couple here notably lacks their signature suits. The lead bully rips his coat apart and sticks the flying feathers on both heads, one after the other. His buddies laugh and begin to help. Feathers fly everywhere, and the couple vanishes beneath a layer of feathers. The nonverbal nature of the attack is striking, and may suggest that images and actions speak more powerfully than words. Or in any case, that Jarman has presented this scene in a nondiscursive manner as a means of getting to a deeper sense of what persecution entails.

Just as we realize that there is no language, only laughs, claps, and noises, the men organize themselves into a kind of musical number. They escalate through singing laughter, one by one, until all of the men are whistling a happy song. There is a big finish, the bullies with their arms thrown wide, as if for an audience's approval. The psychology of the scene suggests the way that social bonds are formed at the expense of others; one man's art (song) is created when it turns others into objects (feathery, silent statues). By looking at this scene in such detail, we can see that this is at once a frightening, realistic scene of public humiliation, but also a theatricalized performance that may be construed as a commentary on art. Look at what I am doing! says the bully. This scene again does more than freeze the couple as victims (although this scene and the next come closest to doing that) because Jarman's own art depends on the objectification of this couple. Or, another way of putting it: if Bersani and Dutoit are correct in their assessment of Jarman, then Jarman is already aware of their critique and implicates himself in it. This is why, as we have seen, Jarman himself appears as one of the paparazzi-terrorists.

The monumentalization of the gay couple as archetypal victims occurs when the couple is flogged, beaten, and then tied to crosses. They are frozen, no doubt, but frozen into a borrowed narrative, arguably subverting traditional iconography and associations even as they are brutally beaten. As in *War Requiem*, Jarman intends to create a hallowed space for the dying, a garden of memory and meditation. He borrows from and attacks Christianity at the same time, borrowing its prestige (religious music lends later parts of the film a conventional dignity) and attacking its intolerance. In comparison with the other scenes of persecution we have discussed, the parodic substitution of the couple for Christ is blunt and overt, and one might object to it even on that level. But notice that after these two set pieces, which are the main target of Bersani and Dutoit's objections, the couple reappears, no longer in this transparent relationship to a Christ figure.

198 They now bring a large vessel with a candle in it to the omnipresent table, around which sit men whom we have not met before. A poem emerges over these men, the candle burning before them:

> I walk in this garden
> Holding the hands of dead friends
> Old age came quickly for my frosted generation
> Cold, cold, cold they died so silently
> Did the forgotten generations scream?
> Or go full of resignation

Quietly protesting innocence
Cold, cold, cold they died so silently

Linked hands at four AM
Deep under the city you slept on
Never heard the sweet flesh song
Cold, cold, cold they died so silently
I have no words
My shaking hand
Cannot express my fury
Sadness is all I have,
Cold, cold, cold they died so silently

Matthew fucked Mark fucked Luke fucked John
Who lay in the bed that I lie on
Touch fingers again as you sing this song
Cold, cold, cold they died so silently

My gilly flowers, roses, violets, blue
Sweet garden of vanished pleasures
Please come back next year
Cold, cold, cold I die so silently

Goodnight boys,
Goodnight Johnny,
Goodnight,
Goodnight.[31]

Even as the traditional Christ is nowhere to be seen, the couple returns from the dead, in their own quiet version of Easter. In the Bible, Christ returned from the dead in order to confirm his divine nature and to inspire his disciples to become missionaries of his word ("Go ye into all the world, and preach the gospel to every creature" [Mark 16:15]). The couple in *The Garden* returns from the dead, too, but now as human figures of memory, of angry elegy, of requiem.

Whereas *The Last of England* collaged its apocalyptic pictures into a severe and relentless rhythm that insisted on time, *The Garden* takes us into a place that is less pressured by time, a place of contemplation and memory. In "Gardening, History, and the Escape from Time: Derek Jarman's *Modern Nature*," Daniel O'Quinn shows how Jarman in *Modern Nature* "equates history that is possessed by time with certain kinds of nationalist monumentality."[32] With reference to Jarman's actual garden, O'Quinn writes,

"The sculptured elements of the garden at Dungeness consist entirely of found metal objects and driftwood, which testify to processes of decay."[33] This dialogue with the monumental, which we have discussed at length with respect to *The Last of England* and *War Requiem*, is equally pertinent here.

The Garden, like Jarman's own garden as described by O'Quinn, escapes from time, but without monumentalizing time. It inspires memory and reflection, but without traditional monuments and memorials. The couple's trajectory aims their private affections into situations of public scrutiny, public visibility, and public disaster, into such depths of public discourse that only the most archetypal and monumental narrative of all can comprehend their suffering. But *The Garden* also does everything it can to render such sculptures ethereal and unstable by setting plot adrift. The nighttime conclusion of *The Last of England* is our darkness, our catastrophe, our society in flames; now what are we going to do about it? By contrast, the nighttime conclusion of *The Garden* lets us breathe, and grieve more, and gives us the time to think and mourn and hurt. The same poet, and the same poet's worries, one might say, but walking along different paths.

The final gathering of figures—an old man, the couple, the boy, a woman—stands in contrast, no doubt, to a traditional family. They light papers, as if in remembrance, and there are smiles as the ashes drift into the air. There is only one woman in this last scene, but she organizes the gathering, passes out the food from her basket, and stands above the others. We have seen Swinton gathering things in her basket earlier—mushrooms, rocks—and now, at the end, her basket's things seem magical. We have also seen her pluck chicken feathers into the air, and scream out over a lonely candle. We have seen her sitting in the fields in exactly the pictures that were, in *The Last of England*, taken for the memories of Spencer Leigh. Once gain, when elegy and memory surround Jarman's cinematic expression, he turns archetypally to female figures. The men die in war; the women collect and re-collect. In addition to Swinton, other important female figures in *The Garden* include the flamenco singer, a black-haired young woman who attends her, and a kind of nature spirit dressed in yellow.

The importance of the female figures in *The Garden* is emphasized by a little poem in the middle of the film, read by a female voice:

This is a poppy
A flower of cornfield and wasteland
Bloody red

Sepals two
Soon falling
Petals four
Stamens many
Stigma rayed
Many seeded
For sprinkling on bread
The staff of life
Woven in wreaths
In memory of the dead
Bringer of dreams
And sweet forgetfulness[34]

The dialectic of monumentality and antimonumentality, memory and forgetfulness, is performed here again in this quiet, beautiful poem. At the end of the poem, we see Swinton seem to mouth the words, but her lips are completely out of sync with the sound track; the dream goes on without her. She wears a crown and lies on the ground, a tranquil queen. This is not maternal garb, but she speaks calmly of bread, memory, and color. Once again Tilda Swinton is at the steps, archetypal in her female embodiment of feeling, and performing memory and forgetfulness at once, whether lying on the ground or whirling beneath the bloodred sunset in her shredded wedding dress.

Into the Last, Narrow Rooms:

EDWARD II, WITTGENSTEIN, *and* BLUE

I. MIRRORING POOL AND IRON WALL IN *Edward II*

Never go to the cinema unless it is Dreyer's *The Passion of Joan of Arc*.

JARMAN, PREFACE TO *Wittgenstein*

Whereas *The Last of England, War Requiem,* and *The Garden* seem to group themselves with relative clarity around ideas of anger and elegy, monument and performance, the last three films appear to be much less continuous with one another and also to be less clearly linked to Jarman's previous works. *Edward II* culminates an interest in getting Renaissance poetry up on the screen (as in *The Tempest* and *The Angelic Conversation*), but now the production seems to be all about anger and all too well organized, giving little time to think and lacking our accustomed paths to choose from. *Wittgenstein* seems to drop in out of nowhere, an accidental solicitation. What does this cinematic biography have to do with Jarman's expected set of concerns and ideas, especially coming just after the scorching unforgivingness of *Edward II*? And then the brilliant blue radio program that is *Blue*, a tremendously poignant final film, no doubt, and a superb experiment in cinematic expression. But as a film in a career, beyond its authentic personal pathos, how should we draw it on the map?

Yet most of Jarman's earlier films came into being in a relatively accidental manner—when money showed up, when inspiration hit—and most viewers sense a good deal of continuity between these films even so. On the surface, the final three films do seem to be quite a heterogeneous lot, yet all three, as I will continue to argue, are related in significant ways to elements and concerns of lyric film. Poetry is central to *Edward II*, even though Jarman goes out of his way to say that it is not. Wittgenstein is famously the most poetic philosopher as well as the philosophical inspiration for many twentieth-century poets. And *Blue* is a radio anthology made out of poems. Jarman continues, then, to return to poetry and poetic film, and he returns also to his favorite cinematic images. With some precision, for instance, we may say that the screen of *Blue* is nothing other than a final ocean mirror.

As noted in the earlier discussion of *War Requiem*, Jarman situates *Edward II* in just the way that Owen situated his war poems: by saying, this is not about the poetry. For both artists, their subject matter is too serious for mere poetry: the persecution and sufferings of homosexuals, on the one hand; the horrors of war, on the other. Both artists give us art, rather than documentary, yet they preface their works with gestures that emphasize the content rather than the aesthetic. Jarman's preface to his book *Queer Edward II* reads in part:

> It is difficult enough to be queer, but to be queer in the cinema is almost impossible. Heterosexuals have fucked up the screen so completely that there's hardly room for us to kiss there. Marlowe outs the past—why don't we out the present? That's really the only message this play has. Fuck poetry. The best lines in Marlowe sound like pop songs and the worst, well, we've tried to spare you them . . . [ellipses his].[1]

In a moment of Wildean blasphemy and reversal, Jarman compliments Christopher Marlowe for his "pop songs" and proceeds to erase everything else. Poetry here is not only an inadequate lie but also the elitist, hierarchical opposite of pop. All of Jarman's films have already, to some extent, said "Fuck poetry," in that they invoke poetry as an alternative manner of proceeding, but then refuse to idealize that alternative. When Jarman now says "Fuck poetry," he means once again to deconstruct and deidealize poetry, but he also means to remind us that there is a war on. As uncompromisingly and relentlessly as *The Last of England* brings us that war, it still does so through symbolic images and through extended and oblique performances. *Edward II* is far more specific and assaultive in its broadcast of the war, not because it is much more contemporary or analytical, but because, like a painting by Francis Bacon, it cuts closer to the bone.

As Jarman makes clear in his accompanying text and as later critics have underscored, Jarman severely reduces Marlowe's play to its queer elements. "I chose this play solely for its subject," writes Jarman; "The poetry, like my production values, is of secondary importance" (*Q*, p. 26). The film will conclude by panning across members of OutRage, a final, clear, and contemporary image. Jarman's avowed intent is to appropriate Marlowe's play for the purposes of the tumultuous present: "In our film all the OutRage boys and girls are inheritors of Edward's story" (*Q*, p. 146). Most commentators, for good reason, have followed Jarman's line here by focusing on the sexual content of the film and by giving somewhat less emphasis, therefore, to the film's style and form.[2]

Even as Bersani and Dutoit characterize Jarman's text *Queer Edward II* as essentially Manichean in its representation of power ("*Queer Edward II* is a gay and lesbian rally"),[3] they also lead us toward the idea that Jarman's film is, as usual, more complicated than his accompanying prose might suggest. *Queer Edward II* is dominated visually by slogans on every other page that cry out more loudly than the lines of script. The slogans shout down the poetry, are happily reductive, and support the idea that all is content. But why choose Marlowe at all if one is just going to run down the past ("I have a deep hatred of the Elizabethan past used to castrate our vibrant present," *Q*, p. 112)? Why stage *Edward II* only to disown the poetry? Why not just stage the rally itself?

Marlowe's plot is reduced and reimagined to suit contemporary concerns, but every line, nonetheless, is still poetry. For all the postmodern improvisation with anachronistic costumes and props, no word is spoken that is not Marlowe or Marlovian. The claim that poetry is secondary or only to be "fucked" rings odd and unconvincingly around this exceedingly well-performed and well-articulated film. If the poetry were truly to be sabotaged, one could do more than reduce the lengths of speeches, which occurs throughout; one could also interrupt and wreck the poetry through performance. But this does not happen. The preface sloganizes—"fuck poetry"—but the poetry in the film is performed skillfully and compellingly. The performances, costumes, and settings all belie, in fact, the idea that content is king, since Jarman's *mise-en-scène* throughout recalls the poetic performances and structures that characterize the films from the beginning to the end of his career.

Edward II is reduced through adaptation in order to converse more deliberately with contemporary concerns, but it also unfolds visually and syntactically with poetic openness rather than vis-à-vis linear causality. Even as Jarman adapts Marlowe's play to focus relentlessly on the homoerotic relationship between King Edward and Gaveston, therefore, he situates that relationship by using a visual trope found in earlier films: the doubling pool. Whereas *War Requiem* continually returned to the abstractly located stage of those monumental steps, *Edward II* continually returns to a pool in the depths of Edward's equally abstract and featureless castle. The shimmering, reflecting pool is associated with homoerotic and homosocial relationships in *Sebastiane* and at the end of *War Requiem*. How does it function here?

The minimal sets in all of Jarman's films derive from his limited budgets, to be sure, but they also support an archetypal economy of signification. As in Antonioni, everything counts ("symbolic dust on the desk," *Q*, p. 140), if ambiguously. The film focuses on the queer relationship of Edward and Gaveston, but it does not do so in midair, but amidst visual and verbal metaphors and figures. Jarman's angry subject is evoked necessarily through editing, generic manipulation, set design, and stagings that are not adequately characterized by slogans.

When the film opens we see Edward asleep, and approached by Lightborn with a lantern. Reflections of light play over the room and Edward. We do not see the pool, but the reflections are obviously watery, and quiet sounds of water are heard on the sound track. The script describes the set in this way: "the dungeon is set deep in the earth; a sombre coal cellar. A stagnant pool, the surface of which gleams like beaten lead. Near the edge of the pool, set in the rock, fire issues from the furnace doors" (*Q*, p. 4). The film does not match this description exactly (we never see the gleaming pool in this scene), but what we see in the gloomy darkness does emphasize, just as clearly, elemental fire and water. Lightborn will turn out to be the salvation of Edward, a tender and loving figure who will take the place of Gaveston in Jarman's "happy ending." Visually, the "red hot poker" by which Edward dies in Marlowe's play is transformed into the reflecting pool of homoerotic desire in Jarman's film. In its watery imagery, the opening scene may be said, therefore, both to signal the homoerotic

205

desire around which the narrative revolves and also to look forward to the resolved conclusion.

Lightborn removes a postcard from the sleeping Edward and reads aloud in voice-over, "My father is deceased; come Gaveston." Now Edward awakens and reads it himself (from "memory" as the script has it):

My father is deceased, come Gaveston;
And share the kingdom with thy dearest friend.

(Q, P. 9)

Through the watery reflections, the film thus begins with an echo, an echoing repetition of lines. We hear the doubling. The doubling is finally confirmed and clinched when the scene shifts to two nearly identical sailors in bed. Gaveston enters, carrying two coffee mugs in one hand, and reads the

206

FIGURE 7.1
Momentary doubles
in EDWARD II

two lines once again. The echoing lines and the literal images of erotic doubling are figured once again through the shimmering pool with which we began.

As we will see later in *Wittgenstein*, Jarman loads his spare interiors with readable details. *Wittgenstein*'s rooms are somehow interiors without walls, whereas *Edward II*'s interiors all seem to be rooms in a prison. An archetypal visual opposition runs through *Edward II*, then, which contrasts the soft, cleansing pool to the hard world and walls all around. In a crucial early scene, for example, Edward rejects Isabella's advances in bed. Even here there is, strikingly, a potential doubling between Swinton's Isabella and Edward that is underscored visually by their long red hair.

But the doubling in this instance is violently rent; Edward blocks her advances with an arm and turns his head away, disgusted. Edward proceeds to pound his head against the hard wall, drawing blood. The wedding chamber is thus revealed to be a prison, too, and the sequence suddenly confirms this metaphor by cutting to the dungeon. Here we see a man washing his face in the pool, which is not so much a "stagnant pool" as a clearly formed rectangle of water. The cut causes us logically to assume that this man must be Edward cleaning the blood from his head, but it turns out to be Lightborn. Edward is then revealed to be watching Lightborn from beneath heavy cloaks. In this way, the editing doubles Lightborn and Edward, causing them to switch places for a moment.

The motif of the reflecting pool rises to the level of classical allusion in sequence 18, where the myth of Narcissus is referred to most directly. Here Edward delivers a monologue to his reflection in the dungeon's pool. Even though we are early in the film, Jarman removes a speech from act 5 in Marlowe's play that further embodies the visual theme of doubling and desire:

Two Kings in England cannot reign at once.
But stay awhile, let me be King till night,
That I may gaze upon this glittering crown,
So shall my eyes receive their last content.
My head the latest honour due to it,
And jointly both yield up their wished right.

(*Q*, P. 36)

The speech is illustrated perfectly by the Narcissus motif before us, and we are asked implicitly to connect the relationships of power ("Two Kings") with the relationships of love and sexuality (Edward and Gaveston) that emanate from this glittering pool. The whole play, in Jarman's treatment, hinges on this doubling image. Edward and Gaveston deconstruct and decenter the throne by playing around it, kissing within it, and doubling a kingship which should be inhabited by a single king. Literally, the two kings in this speech are Edward II and Mortimer, as the region breaks apart between them. The mirroring desire of the pool (Edward-Gaveston, Edward-Lightborn) is always set into the context of those stony walls and against the harsh monumentality of Mortimer and his murderous law.

EDWARD II, WITTGENSTEIN, *and* BLUE

Mortimer, indeed, is associated clearly with deadly and fascistic monumentality. When we first see Mortimer, he stands watch with four soldiers over the king's body. The body behind him rests on an enormous rectangular block—sheer regal mass. Dressed like an SS officer, Mortimer is thus linked immediately to the kind of fascist monumentality that nearly brought monumental sculpture to an end in the first part of the twentieth century. Whereas *War Requiem* presents an authentic dialogue between monumentality and performance, *Edward II* sets monument at war with performance. When Bersani and Dutoit speak of the film's Manichean divisions, they have in mind, among other things, the way *Edward II* contrasts a heavy, imprisoning heterosexual tyranny with playful and sparkling homosexual desires.

Later, two consecutive scenes (sequences 33 and 34, reversed in the

FIGURE 7.2
*Monumentality
and oppression*

script relative to the film) once more depend on the deep, archetypal truth of water. Here we see Edward by the pool, surrounded by the iron walls of the dungeon, lamenting the enforced exile of Gaveston:

He's gone, and for his absence this I mourn,
Did never sorrow go so near my heart.

(Q, P. 70)

Derek Jarman and Lyric Film

Edward lies down by the pool, and is again mirrored by his reflection in the water. Then an immediate cut to Gaveston on rocks "by the edge of the sea" (Q, p. 68). Gaveston screams and screams on the rocks, still weirdly dressed in his perfect white dress shirt, just like Edward in the previous scene. We have suddenly moved from dungeon pool to storm-drenched rock. The mirrored pool has broken, and the nightmare of the tempest opens up to fill the breach.

The continuity between Edward's pool and Gaveston's ocean is further elaborated in sequence 42. Now Edward stands in the pool, surely not a straightforward bit of staging but one that reflects Gaveston's oceanic exile through a poignant literalism and identification:

> The wind is good, I wonder why he stays;
> I fear me he is wracked upon the sea.
>
> (Q, P. 86)

After Gaveston is stabbed by Mortimer, Edward delivers an angry monologue, once again hip-deep in the pool. A giant shadow of a welding Lightborn is thrown upon the wall behind him. Now the pool's water suddenly betokens neither a calm oasis of meditation nor even a storm of identification, but becomes rather a pool of angry blood, more like fire than water:

> Edward, unfold your paws
> And let their lives blood slake The Furies' hunger.
>
> (Q, P. 96)

As the blood of war takes precedence, the dungeon becomes associated not with the reflecting pool, but more and more with the fiery oven.

As Jarman's surprise ending works its magic, the pool makes its last appearance. Edward waits for a horrible death (by red-hot poker), which he has apparently just imagined. Edward speaks thus to Lightborn:

209

> These looks of thine can harbour nought but death,
> I see my tragedy written on thy brows.
> Yet stay a while; forbear thy blood hand.
> And let me see the stroke before it comes.
> [And the script adds] Suddenly and unexpectedly Lightborn takes the poker and throws it into the water. He comes over to Edward and kneels and kisses him.
>
> (Q, P. 162)

When the poker is thrown into the water, we hear hisses and weird moans, as if a power is given over. The pool becomes a magic pool and ushers in the dreamlike sequence that concludes the film. That Lightborn would step in for Gaveston as a double for the King's desire has been held in potentiality throughout. Lightborn is the welder who works around the pool, who has power over those visible rivets in the walls. When Edward speaks to his reflection in the pool, he also speaks to Lightborn, who is usually hovering about. Gaveston, Edward, and Lightborn are all joined through the doubling pool and through their relationship to the iron walls around them. Through the simple but powerful images of the set design—reflecting pool and iron wall—the substitution of Lightborn for Gaveston has been prepared.

Although Jarman's preface sets itself angrily against poetry, Gaveston himself is adamantly for poetry, and so, in the end, is the film. The first time we see Gaveston, he waves away the two hustlers making out in bed, claiming a preference for "wanton poets" over soldiers. For Gaveston, it seems, sexuality and desire are worth nothing without culture and art:

> There are hospitals for men like you.
> I have no war, and therefore sir, begon [sic].
> (Gaveston takes a wad of money a passes it to the boys).
> These are not men for me;
> I must have wanton poets, pleasant wits,
> Musicians that with touching of a string
> May draw the pliant King which way I please.
>
> (Q, p. 10)

When Gaveston sends away the two naked men, the contemporary resonance of "hospitals" is strongly felt. In contrast to the generic "soft porn" sexuality of the two hustlers in bed, Gaveston chooses a more cultured, campier homoeroticism. His speech continues:

210

> Music and poetry is his [Edward's] delight,
> Therefore I'll have Italian masques by night
> Sweet speeches, comedies and pleasing shows.
>
> (Q, p. 10)

And over these lines we see a bodybuilder with a giant snake. This entertainment, which is fantastic, elliptical, and fun, illustrates the poetry that Gaveston loves and is crucial to the sensibility of the film—in no way secondary to the subject at hand. There is no homoerotic romance without poetry, and Jarman develops this romance, and their fun, at every turn.

The love of Gaveston and Edward is repeatedly mediated through these entertainments. Watching dance and spectacle clearly inspires their own affections. From a rather realistic and critical standpoint, these scenes may suggest that Gaveston and Edward have nothing better to do than to lounge about conjuring up eye candy at a problematic distance from the actualities of labor and the working class. But read more generously, the scenes show the significant interrelatedness between homoerotic romance and a sustaining context of art and culture.

In their scenes of spectatorship, Edward and Gaveston become an audience like ourselves, and the spectacles become films like *Edward II*. Gaveston and Edward enjoy watching scenes that are more complicated than a naked man or men kissing, although Jarman himself attaches great significance to such simple gestures, since they remain almost absent from the contemporary screen. The happiness of Gaveston and Edward is elaborated through these spectacles and performances; they are so inspired by these moments of expressiveness and creativity that they often participate in the scenes themselves. In an idealistic and romantic reading of these scenes, we might say that the men are transported out of themselves and into their truest selves when art performs its traditional task of transfiguration and ennoblement. Gaveston calls these scenes poetry, the word that Jarman refuses, but Jarman is trying, in the preface, to subvert the academic and the contented at all costs.

The image of the bodybuilder appears in a brief insert of memory or fantasy, a picture superimposed over Gaveston's lines, and the spectacles of poetry have this dreamlike quality throughout. In another scene, Edward and Gaveston watch a pair of men dance on the wide dusty floor before them (sequence 6). These men are dressed identically in black, Gaveston and Edward in white. The dance concludes with a kiss, and when we look back at Gaveston and Edward, they are kissing as well. The throne thus becomes a theater box and also a bed. The dancers are obviously talented and proficient—the scene is meant to convey dancing as an art—and Edward and Gaveston respond with laughter. As Jarman always insisted when making his art films, "we are having a good time here" (*Q*, p. 162). Later, "A poet reads the opening passages of Dante's 'Divine Comedy'" (*Q*, p. 58).

The most remarkable and generically disruptive entertainment or poem is the Cole Porter song sung by Annie Lennox. "Whatever is she doing here?" asks Jarman in his script notes, recognizing that this is, even among heterogeneous artifacts and moods, a strange moment. "Well," Jarman responds, "if you were King for a day who would you have to sing for you" (*Q*, p. 62). Lennox was known for some gender bending in the mid-1980s

(the video for the Eurythmics' "Who's That Girl?" finds her in male costumes), but in *Edward II* she appears not as a diva (the title of her first solo
album, in 1992) but as a tranquil troubadour. She sings "Ev'ry Time We Say
Goodbye" for Gaveston and Edward, which she had already recorded for
Leigh Blake's Cole Porter tribute, *Red Hot + Blue*, and for which Jarman
had already shot a video.

This sequence, in fact, has the feeling of a music video in which Edward
and Gaveston take part for a time, but they are also noticeably absent for
stretches, watching like ourselves. When in the prefatory note Jarman
writes, "The best lines in Marlowe sound like pop songs[,]" this song by
Lennox is surely just what he has in mind. Poetry is again taken out of the
archives and away from the academics; it is asked to matter. This is, therefore, another poem, which Lennox sings for Edward and Gaveston, who
once again enjoy themselves tremendously, dancing and kissing in their
pajamas. Although there may be a feeling that this sequence cooperates
too willingly with music-video glamour, it seems clear that Lennox makes
an affectionate rather than cynical appearance. She sings to the two men
not to increase their box office, but to increase their joy, which ought to be
ordinary and everyday, but for the blindness and violence of the world.

The descent of Annie Lennox into the confines of Marlowe appears
potentially as a liberating anachronism, and Jarman's postmodernist use
of anachronism in *Edward II* has been widely noted. But this breaking
down of linear time is seriously compromised in the film by the restrictions
of space. In what sense is Marlowe outed when there is no "out"? As the
script tells us, every single scene in the film is an "interior." Certainly the
limited budget—although the largest of Jarman's career—accounts for the
limited sets, but the look of *Edward II* has been very deliberately cultivated.
Offsetting the wild and possibly indecorous editing of Marlowe's text, as
well as the ostentatious use of anachronism, therefore, are the repeatedly
prisonlike interiors. Only the merest suggestion of outside light ever man-
ages to stream through the ill-defined windows. In a trashing of *Edward II*
in the gay journal *Christopher Street*, Bob Satuloff calls the film "stultifying, claustrophobic, and mean-spirited."[4] Jarman might accept "mean" if
not "mean-spirited," but the film is clearly designed to be claustrophobic,
and even stultifying in its set design.

One way to read the interiors would be to substantiate the Foucauldian
reading of *Edward II* by Colin MacCabe. "At its heart," writes MacCabe,
"is the constitutive relation which founds the modern English state on a
repressive security apparatus and a repressed homosexuality."[5] Expanding
on this reading would emphasize the degree to which every set, not just

the dungeon scenes, connotes a prison. The film *is* claustrophobic; we're continually trapped in caves. Anachronistically and magically, anything can show up in a cave: conference tables, brass beds, office desks, lecture podiums, even hunting dogs, but the perpetual walls threatens to dampen the magic. A Christmas tree appears, with all the trimmings, but in the next scene the tree is gone; only the walls remain. A Foucauldian reading of the film would emphasize the sense of panopticon or surveillance over all aspects of the interior, interior spaces that are equally subject to power's gaze: prison cell, hospital room, office space, schoolroom, bedroom.

I would read these claustrophobic interiors slightly differently, however, by seeing them as not just cavernous, but literal caves. The walls look like they are cut out of a mountain; the floors are dirt. The effect is somewhat similar to one in Nicholas Ray's *Johnny Guitar*, where Vienna's saloon is set directly into the side of a mountain (we find out later that there is a mine shaft running underneath). When a posse comes to the saloon, we see Vienna (Joan Crawford) playing an immense piano against the backdrop of a rocky wall. This bizarre juxtaposition of cultural artifact and geological backdrop occurs throughout *Edward II*.

And we can read these walls with even further metaphorical specificity. That is, the whole film is buried in a grave. *Edward II* takes place in a crypt. "This ground which is corrupted with their steps," says Mortimer, as he stands before the coffin of the dead king, "shall be their timeless sepulchre, or mine" (Q, p. 48). The whole film takes place indeed, in this timeless sepulchre:

> Edward stands alone at the top of the stone ramp.
> Edward: But what are Kings, when regiment is gone,
> But perfect shadows in a sunshine day?
> I know not, but of this I am assured,
> That death ends all, and I can die but once.
> Come death, and with thy fingers close my eyes,
> Or if I live let me forget myself.
>
> (Q, P. 168)

It critiques the monumental fascism of Mortimer, stages performances of anachronism and fury, but is buried in a vault nonetheless. The ramps up and down in the sets make it look like these people are living in an Egyptian pyramid. When we pan over the OutRage activists at the end, they stand perfectly still, then fade away. They protested and yelled, but now they are ghosts.

Edward II takes place in what Deleuze would call "any space what-

213

soever" ("*espace quelconque*").⁶ Deleuze reads the dislocation of space in Dreyer's *The Passion of Joan of Arc* as implying a fifth dimension, a spiritual realm. *Edward II* also takes place in a strangely archetypal otherworld, in a prison that follows on Genet's *Un Chant d'amour*, in a tomb that descends from the underworld in Cocteau's *Orpheus*. Although at one point Mortimer can hear, as if in the next room, Gaveston bouncing up and down on the throne, there is no way to map out the relationship of any room to any other room. Yet the spatial perspective of any space in particular is perfectly clear and visible. There is no distortion in presentation or framing, as there always is in Dreyer's *Joan*. *Edward II* presents us with a clear, undistorted series of tomblike interiors as it meditates on politics from an abstract perspective that might formerly have been occupied by religion. It is not too much to say that politics is religion for Jarman at this point, an idea only reconfirmed when we remember that *Edward II* follows directly upon *The Garden*.

Francis Bacon, one of the most important figures in twentieth-century painting, is necessarily in the background of Jarman's visual imagination throughout his career. A fellow Londoner ("I really feel for Francis Bacon when I pass him in Compton Street. I hope I'm wearing a leather jacket in my 70s"),⁷ bohemian, and homosexual, Bacon painted images from which Jarman's cinematic compositions sometimes derive. And like Jarman, Bacon, who was dissatisfied with the "decorations" of abstract modernism, aimed for a visceral, emotional response in his viewers. Clearly the staging of the pope's audience in *Caravaggio*—white light surrounding the pope like the "space-time" cubes in Bacon's series of screaming popes—is modeled on the work of the British painter. The golden thrones that stand amidst a world of suffering are also part of the reservoir of images that course through *Edward II*.

The most Baconian image is found in sequence 62. The script reads, "Edward stands victorious over his naked captive—crucified on sides of beef" (*Q*, p. 128). The dangling beef had been discovered earlier by little Prince Edward, and such an image is not unknown in film—viewers will remember slabs of beef in the meat lockers of film noir or in recent police thrillers. Yet hanging there in the middle of an undefined, abstract room, this is clearly Bacon meat.⁸ *Painting, 1946* is only one of several key Bacon paintings that juxtapose a butchered carcass with images of crucifixion. In Bacon, we seem to have at least a basic sense of these carcasses. For example, he himself said:

> Well, of course, we are meat, we are potential carcasses. If I go into a butcher's shop I always think it's surprising that I wasn't there instead

214

of the animal. . . . we give this purposeless existence a meaning by our drives.[9]

Bacon's crucified carcasses and screaming popes embody nightmarish suffering and abysmal terror. But how does Jarman, clearly working through Bacon's visual territory, deploy the golden thrones and sides of beef? How does Jarman reconfigure the Baconian interior?

Jarman's notes in the script suggest that the church is to blame for this particular side-of-beef crucifixion: "'Peace-loving' Archbishop Carey had SAS marksman all over Canterbury Cathedral for his enthronement" (Q, p. 178). This is self-righteous violence, then, on the part of Edward, the violence of revenge, the violent reply to violence that Bersani and Dutoit point to as a critical flaw in Jarman's films. But Jarman cannot, in this film, be asking us to sympathize with the character of Edward here; he goes so far as to dress Spencer and Edward in butcher's aprons.

The persecution of Edward and Gaveston drives Edward into unrecognizable forms of "creativity" and self-representation. Edward slowly combs the hair of the policeman strung up on the beef, the culminating mockery in a scene that represents Edward as outside the human—never mind the humane—driven beyond any conceivable identification or sympathy. In the next scene, Spencer and Edward, "drenched in blood, undress, [and] wash with water from a bucket" (Q, p. 130). They laugh insanely to themselves as Kent confirms their butchery:

A brother? No a butcher of my friends!
Proud Edward, dost thou banish me thy presence?

(Q, P. 130)

Jarman's staging (Edward in a butcher's apron) literally takes the side of Kent, and Edward himself is here bloody, savage, wordless; he only spits at Kent. Edward in this guise is not a revenge hero who is compelling or dignified in any least respect.   215

The heterosexist gang of Isabella and Mortimer is attended by its own violences, and the mean-spiritedness of Edward is no doubt intended to be justified by the horrific actions of his enemies. Notably, Jarman depicts Mortimer in bed with "3 wild girls"; they grind into his back with their leather stiletto heels. Perhaps we are supposed to see that Edward's bloodthirsty violence is sparked by a lover's rage, whereas Mortimer's just lusts for power (and sadomasochistic sex). In a western, Mortimer would be gun-crazy, and he responds to Gaveston's aggressive verbal defenses ("Base leaded Earls that glory in your birth, / Go sit at home and eat your tenant's beef" [Q, p. 92]) by stabbing him. Isabella is later shown taking target practice at a hanging deer carcass, and both Mortimer and Isabella are depicted as absolutely vicious in their homicidal wrath, Isabella going so far as to bite into Kent's neck like a vampire.

Although Jarman's camera does not distort bodies and space the way a painting by Bacon does, the macabre violence at the center of Bacon, substantiated by images of crosses and carcasses, crosses paths with the vengeful anger in Jarman's *Edward II*. Although there is more political narrative in Jarman than there is in the existential horror of Bacon, Jarman still makes Edward and Gaveston much less sympathetic than he might, making an act of violence seem neither justifiable nor unjustifiable, but rather more like one more act of brutality in a bloody, death-swamped world.

Violence finally comes to a magical resolution when Isabella and Mortimer are covered in flour and set in a cage. Some of Bacon's screaming popes scream from inside cubes or cages, and this final toylike cage literalizes all the prisons and claustrophobic caverns in the film. Little Prince Edward, wearing earrings, dances on the cage and listens to the "Dance of the Sugar Plum Fairy." King Edward awoke from his nightmare, moments earlier, to watch Lightborn throw down his red-hot poker into the reflecting pool. Mortimer will be executed in the Tower, but for now he sits like a pale, powdery ghost in his emblematic cage. *Edward II* is full of anger, outraged, but the difference between desire's anger and power's anger is not always clear. So the film stabs and howls into space and then buries itself beneath a mile of thick earth. The ghosts at the end of *Edward II* are surely related to the ghosts in *War Requiem*. Yet whereas *War Requiem* focused mostly, and most successfully, on the requiem, *Edward II* gives us, most poetically, the war.

II. *Wittgenstein* AND TRANSPARENCY

What it is that is deep about magic would be kept.

WITTGENSTEIN, *Remarks on Frazer's* GOLDEN BOUGH[10]

There is only one poem in *Wittgenstein*, a satirical poem about Ludwig:

For he talks nonsense, numerous statements makes,
Forever his own vow of silence breaks:
Ethics, aesthetics, talks of day and night,
And calls things good or bad, and wrong or right.
Who, on any issue ever saw

Ludwig refrain from laying down the law?
In every company he shouts us down,
And stops our sentence stuttering his own;
Unceasing argues, harsh, irate and loud,
Sure that he's right, and of his rightness proud,
Such faults are common, shared by all in part,
But Wittgenstein pontificates on Art.

(W, PP. 110–112)

A clumsy descendant of Alexander Pope's heroic couplets, it is a horrible poem by any standards, read by the not obviously literary Lady Ottoline Morrell (Tilda Swinton). This unique and hideous poem reminds us that the subject matter of *Wittgenstein* may not so readily translate to a species of lyric film. Wittgenstein is not only a terrifically abstruse philosopher (rather than a poet), but he is also seen here as an arguer, a proud pontificator who lays down the law. Such a figure seems bent on the monumental rather than the performative. And such a heroic figure, splendid in his isolated genius, seems out of place or unidiomatic in Jarman's cinema. For having seen what we have seen thus far, we can only ask, where is the mirror?

Many of Jarman's films do not focus on a single heroic personage (*The Last of England, War Requiem, The Garden*); on the contrary, they divide our attention between numerous figures, with the effect of emphasizing heterogeneous textures and focal points rather than clear structures with centers. Even prominent title characters, such as Caravaggio or Edward, are mirrored and replicated by other characters. Caravaggio and Edward powerfully control the perspective and shape of their narratives, but they still find themselves in much closer relation to the world and the people in that world than Wittgenstein. Wittgenstein, it is true, is another important figure in Jarman's homosexual pantheon, to be added now to Wilfred Owen, Benjamin Britten, and Christopher Marlowe, but this homosexual desire is not presented through mirroring. And *Wittgenstein* is one of the few Jarman films without a serious poem in it.

But of course all of the issues that poetry raises—the formation of public and private languages, the possibilities of communication, the necessity of interpretation, the trajectory of logic—are all issues central to Wittgenstein's projects, and so are brought onto the screen in this film. Wittgenstein is, in his own aphoristic and fragmented way, a poetic philosopher, indeed, and a tremendously important influence on poets, novelists, artists, and composers in the twentieth century. In *Wittgenstein's Ladder: Poetic Language and the Strangeness of the Ordinary* (1996), Marjorie Perloff enumerates how astonishingly often twentieth-century poets and artists either turn directly to Wittgenstein—to fictionalize his life or quote from the *Tractatus*—or else create Wittgenstein-like texts by working through issues of language and society in a manner akin to his own.[11] "Philosophy ought really to be written only as a form of poetry," writes Wittgenstein in *Culture and Value*, and Perloff's writers, from Gertrude Stein to Robert Creeley and Charles Bernstein, may be seen as working with such an idea in mind. If we recall how often Wittgenstein went about deidealizing philosophy, we can more readily turn his epigrams toward Jarman: "Cinema ought really to be made only as a form of poetry."

At the end of his career, at the end of his life, Jarman's poetic interest in mirroring takes a turn. In *Wittgenstein*, Wittgenstein is obviously not the mirror of anyone else. Bertrand Russell and John Maynard Keynes are of his age, but not in his league and visually quite out of his spectrum. These characters are played with dignity by men in such bright colors that they clearly are out of Wittgenstein's field of contact. Johnny (Kevin Collins), a fictive amalgamation of Cambridge philosophy graduate students, goes to movies with Wittgenstein, is Wittgenstein's desire, but, in contrast to nearly everything we have seen in Jarman so far, shares absolutely nothing in common with Wittgenstein visually. No figure in the film mirrors Wittgenstein. Instead, the key to understanding *Wittgenstein* both visually and figuratively is now transparency. Jarman is quite clear about this in his preface to the script:

> I explore Wittgenstein through Newton's prism: his "glasse works." It is through transparency that the world is discovered. The camera lens.
>
> (W, p. 64)

The look of the entire film is an exact retort to the sets in *Edward II*. If Jarman's adaptation of Marlowe is buried in a timeless sepulchre, under pyramids of suffering and oppression, *Wittgenstein* takes place in a set of timeless interiors absolutely without walls. *Edward II* is staged beneath a mountain of power and hatred; *Wittgenstein* takes place in a world of thought, in a series of open interiors without horizons. Jarman writes, "The floors and walls of the small studio draped like a funeral. A black infinity" (W, p. 68). *Edward II*, in its bouts of horrific violence or in Mortimer's standing in front of the king's raised coffin, may easily strike a viewer as funereal or as draped with death's hangings. But *Wittgenstein*'s drapes seem to create, instead, a night of possibility or infinity rather than death: "My film does not portray or betray Ludwig. It is there to open up" (W, p. 67).

The walls all come down, transparently, in absolute contrast to *Edward II*, so that the scenes take place not underground, but rather in outer space:

> And the black? The black annihilates the decorative and concentrates so my characters shine in it like red dwarfs—and green giants. Yellow lines and blue stars.

(W, P. 67)

Some reviewers took Jarman's incorporation of a green Martian for campy excess or excrescence, but seen in this cosmic light, the Martian's appearance is far from whimsical. He's there to tell us exactly where *Wittgenstein* is coming from. Terry Eagleton's original script for *Wittgenstein* sports, of course, no Martians, but Eagleton's world is three-dimensional, realistic, and full of psychological explanations. Jarman's Martian not only provides Wittgenstein with an internal interlocutor (and another self who is, once again, strikingly not a mirrored self), but also serves to insist, in effect, that this darkness all around is not just the night, but, indeed, outer space. The Martian's character is comical and random, but figuratively of utmost importance, and he even speaks the last lines. Although the film takes us to particular, named places in Wittgenstein's life (Norway, Cambridge, Moscow University, Ireland), the presence of the Martian opens up these geographical coordinates and asks us implicitly to see the floating interiors as larger dimensions, dimensions even beyond our world.

Wittgenstein not only reorients space, then, taking place in any outer space whatsoever, but it also reorients time. If the green Martian is the clearest indicator that cinematic space is open, fluid, then the appearance of the young Wittgenstein indicates that time is equally open to redirection and reorientation. Whereas Wittgenstein has any number of conversations with the Martian—indeed, the Martian always appears with Wittgenstein, never by himself—young Wittgenstein nearly always appears by himself and never talks to his older self. Time is not linear, but it is still partitioned.

Young and older Wittgenstein share the screen only rarely. When Russell and Wittgenstein leave the room after talking about an imaginary rhino beneath the table, young Wittgenstein "crawls out from beneath the table wearing a yellow rhinoceros horn" (W, p. 78). Or Wittgenstein may do a voice-over while young Wittgenstein "licks a blue ice lolly in the cinema" (W, p. 106). In an early scene young Wittgenstein marches through a World War I scene carrying a banner that reads "The World is Everything That is the Case" (W, p. 86) and walks right by the adult Wittgenstein, who is firing his machine gun in the trenches. But this is as close as they ever come, and even then we realize that they clearly inhabit separate worlds. They never talk to each other; Wittgenstein never directly consults his childhood. Amidst much chronological and spatial wildness, then, amidst moments of temporal and spatial blending and overlap, we always have a sense that there are boundaries, that each self is, to some degree, a coherent solidity unto itself.

Time is significantly loosened and uncoiled, subjected to a magical vision not unlike that found in Paradjanov's *The Color of Pomegranates*. In Paradjanov the simultaneous present of the young poet and older poet was an emblem in itself of the prophetic and time-transcending powers of both poet and filmmaker. The use of the young and the old Wittgenstein powerfully recalls these figurative gestures from Paradjanov, which we earlier remembered also with respect to the end of *Caravaggio* when the young painter seems to look onto his older self. But despite the reorientation of linear chronology and the substitution of the emblematic gesture for psychological or historical explanation, there is a fatalism in both Jarman and Paradjanov.

Lyric film may disrupt time, but *The Color of Pomegranates*, *Caravaggio*, and *Wittgenstein* all end up at a deathbed, at the finality of death. Thus for all the open and poetic treatment of time and space in *Wittgenstein*, the film still begins with a birth ("Hello. My name is Ludwig Wittgenstein. I'm a prodigy. I'm going to tell you my story. I was born in 1889 to a filthy rich family in Vienna" [*W*, p. 70]) and ends with a death. It is a brilliant impossibility to have young Wittgenstein narrate—posthumously—his biography. But the poetic freedom of such a representation will never save the older Wittgenstein from having to die all over again. Time and space are therefore open, in many respects, but at the same time, lives and selves still are seen to possess boundaries and to move within certain limitations.

These boundaries and limitations are precisely what is at stake in *Wittgenstein*, but they are now set in a black world of transparency, in contrast to the mountainous prisons of *Edward II*. Wittgenstein's philosophy of language, as the film represents it, is one that constantly explores its own limitations:

> Wittgenstein: I used to believe that language gave us a picture of the world. But it can't give us a picture of how it does that. That would be like trying to see yourself seeing something. How language does that is beyond expression. That is the mystery. That was all wrong. Language isn't a picture at all.
> Russell: What is it then?

Wittgenstein: It's a tool; an instrument. There isn't just one picture of the world, there are lots of different language games. Different forms of life, different ways of doing things with words—they don't all hang together.

Russell: What do you mean?

Wittgenstein: All I mean is 'The limits of my language are the limits of my world.' We keep running up against the walls of our cage. I'm terribly sorry—you have a worthless teacher today. I'm all cleaned out. Please forgive me.

(W, P. 118)

Most of this exchange is drawn from several passages in Eagleton's original script, but Jarman has added the first two sentences in Wittgenstein's third speech. These two lines are directly quoted from Wittgenstein and provide a visual grounding for the abstract idea elsewhere. Jarman set Mortimer and Isabella in an emblematic cage at the end of *Edward II*, and he now puts Wittgenstein in a cage toward the end of this later film. Are there walls or not? And if there are walls, what are they? In *Edward II* surely the walls are walls of power, of repression. The walls of the cage in *Wittgenstein*, however, must be something more like the walls of our thought. But Jarman interestingly grounds Wittgenstein's thought-world and his thought-walls with social specificity.

We might expect that Wittgenstein in his cage would speak a monologue about public and private language, but instead he gives the film's most extended meditation on his homosexuality:

Wittgenstein: Philosophy is a sickness of the mind. I mustn't infect too many young men. How unique and irreplaceable Johnny is. And yet how little I realise this when I am with him. That's always been a problem. But living in a world where such a love is illegal and trying to live openly and honestly is a complete contradiction. I have known Johnny three times. And each time I began with a feeling that there was nothing wrong. But after, I felt shame.

(W, PP. 130–32)

As Wittgenstein broods over his sexuality, the scene shows us a kind of parodic doubling, as Wittgenstein sits in a cage along with a parrot, who is in a smaller cage. Jarman here reads "the walls of our cage" as indeed the walls of power and intolerance, "a world where such a love is illegal." In this sequence Jarman suggests that Wittgenstein's desire to think in a "com-

221

mon language," and not with reference to "private meaning," originates in his homosexuality.

He furthers this suggestion by showing Wittgenstein in the very next scene philosophizing to Johnny in their bed:

> Wittgenstein: Well, for many years at the centre of philosophy was a picture of the lonely human soul, brooding over its private experiences.
> Johnny: Yeah, everyone knows that.
> Wittgenstein: This soul is a prisoner of his own body, and he is locked out from contact with others by the walls of their bodies. I wanted to get rid of this picture. There is no private meaning. We are what we are only because we share a common language and common forms of life. Do you understand what I'm saying? Do you understand what I'm saying?
>
> (W, P. 132)

In Eagleton's script, Wittgenstein gives a similar lecture to a mechanic, who has absolutely no idea what the great philosopher is talking about. By contrast, in Jarman's version, even though Johnny is speechless at the end, there is at least the possibility that the philosophy student can follow what Wittgenstein is saying. This is not a philosophy of the bedroom, as in Sade, but it is a philosophy that at least in part originates in the bedroom, in the ways that sexual identities have to do with private and public relationships and communication. Jarman does not press these biographical or sexual explanations for the philosophy too much, but he does allow us to see potential connections. He opens up Wittgenstein's thought in these various directions.

Wittgenstein, like so many of Jarman's films, aims toward the mirror and the sea. The last four scenes, in fact, although set amidst black infinity, occupy quite deliberately this idiomatic and now familiar territory. Scene 50, "A Stroll in the Rain," quietly invokes the watery elements: "Wittgenstein and Keynes are walking beneath a large green umbrella" (W, p. 138). An undoubted sense of an ending is felt, and Wittgenstein says, "I'm going to Ireland to live by the sea." In scene 51, "Ireland," "Wittgenstein sits in a green deck chair," (W, p. 138) and we hear the waves of the ocean on the sound track. The very last scenes in Eagleton's script are set by the sea as well, but there the effect seems Tennysonian, melancholy, merely scenic. "I'll just go and say goodbye to the sea," says Wittgenstein in Eagleton's version (W, p. 61). Or, in Eagleton's next sequence, "Wittgenstein comes through the door of the cottage, and stares at the sea" (W, p. 61). Jarman's watery

222

elements, by contrast, accumulate to something more than naturalism or oceanic elegy. Jarman plays on the visual motif like a composer of music so that the tune becomes more than just the tune. As Jarman's Wittgenstein sits in his deck chair, surrounded by darkness and the sounds of the ocean, a student approaches. The student wears a shiny black raincoat. Using the sparest means, Jarman adds one more watery element to the visual mix. The raincoat has nothing to do with oceanic elegy or melancholy; it does not indicate farewell. Instead it appears as a visual rhyme: umbrellas, raincoat, water, sea. All are linked images, overdetermined and improbable in their collective appearance, which, with variable effect, emphasize the aqueous.

The watery images now form almost inevitably into mirrors. In his version of the script, Eagleton writes a beautiful description of Wittgenstein's icy world of thought, which Jarman takes over almost without emendation:

> Let me tell you a little story. There was once a young man who dreamed of reducing the world to pure logic. Because he was a very clever young man, he actually managed to do it. It was beautiful. A world purged of imperfection and indeterminacy. Countless acres of gleaming ice stretching to the horizon. So the clever young man looked around the world he had created, and decided to explore it. He took one step forward and fell flat on his back. You see, he had forgotten about friction. The ice was smooth and level and stainless, but you couldn't walk there. So the clever young man sat down and wept bitter tears. But as he grew into a wise old man, he came to understand that roughness and ambiguity aren't imperfections. They're what make the world turn. He wanted to run and dance. And the words and things scattered upon this ground were all battered and tarnished and ambiguous, and the wise old man saw that that was the way things were. But something in him was still homesick for the ice, where everything was radiant and absolute and relentless. Though he had come to like the idea of the rough ground, he couldn't bring himself to live there. So now he was marooned between earth and ice, at home in neither. And this was the cause of all his grief.

(W, P. 142)

In Eagleton this speech is delivered by Keynes at Cambridge, before Wittgenstein goes to Ireland. There, the story serves as an accusation. It is a figurative explanation of Wittgenstein's restlessness, which Keynes puts more straightforwardly thus: "I think you're suffering from a potentially terminal case of moral integrity. We're all wilting in the glare of your remorseless

223

honesty" (W, p. 54). In Jarman, however, the parable is spoken over the dying Wittgenstein, who is already in Ireland. The story serves as the first coherent narrative interpretation of Wittgenstein's life and thought.

According to this parable, all of Wittgenstein's desire is directed toward the smooth surface of that glass. Keynes understands this glass to be an idealistic mistake, an impractical delusion, but Jarman's images refuse to substantiate Keynes's critique. While the story continues in a voice-over, we see the young Wittgenstein carry one of his philosophical banners past a snowman. The snowman is stodgy and ordinary; it scarcely indicates the gleaming danger of the ice. Although Keynes judges that the philosopher is "marooned between earth and ice," we see the young Wittgenstein, wearing large plastic wings, come floating up on two dozen white balloons. Jarman's images lyrically subvert Keynes's condemnation of the glass, for Jarman knows how many magical properties occur in reflections.

In a way, then, it is "pure logic" when the next sequence shows us the Martian sitting at the foot of Wittgenstein's bed. As the script indicates, "He holds a prism which refracts the light" (W, p. 143). The gleaming ice has become a glass. The Martian sits in for an angel, a messenger who travels between worlds. But he says, "Hail Chromodynamics, Lord of Quantum," rather insanely and yet also perfectly. Hail the God of color, of light, of film. This is the glass that has shown us—randomly? precisely?—*Wittgenstein*'s magnificent world of color. This is glass that Jarman honors for its transparency as opposed to its reflectiveness. Here the prism refracts blindingly, like the mirrors in *The Art of Mirrors*. The Martian teases us by representing both ambiguity and perfect simplicity:

> Concerning the philosopher Ludwig Wittgenstein. Deceased. The solution to the riddle of life in space and time lies outside space and time. But as you know and I know, there are no riddles. If a question can be put at all, it can also be answered.

(W, P. 144)

We cannot come to easy conclusions about Wittgenstein's life and thought; we certainly cannot sum it up in a story. On the other hand, there are answers, transparent answers. The Martian serves to resist closure, to offer an otherworldly alternative to Keynes's pragmatic critique, but we can also see the Martian as lyrically criticizing Wittgenstein (he is an alternative to Keynes, but also a parallel to him) by offering lyrical simplicity for the rigors of Wittgenstein's life.

Although in his preface Jarman announces certain kinds of solidarity with Wittgenstein ("The forward exploration of Colour is Queer"), the film *Wittgenstein* serves as a critique of Wittgenstein as much as a celebration. The way that Jarman situates the comments of both Keynes and the Martian shows that the criticism, or the representations of criticism, will not be too overt or heavy-handed, yet there is a strong sense that Jarman's differences with Wittgenstein do find some expression in these characters. The obsessive rigor of Wittgenstein, although expressed often in enigmatic fragments, seems antithetical to the drift and associative movements in Jarman's cinema. The *Tractatus* fragments are condensed and elliptical, but we would not say that Wittgenstein's entries are linked, one to another, like the elements of a dream. There are moments when Wittgenstein and Jarman may seem to verge toward one another as imaginative thinkers, but in the final account, it seems that surely they swerve away. Hence, perhaps, the title of Jarman's preface: "This is not a Film of Ludwig Wittgenstein."

Jarman may take on the *Wittgenstein* script only to distance himself from his subject, but Wittgenstein also leads to a crisis in Jarman's own aesthetic sensibility. Jarman likes to assemble cinematic elements through half-conscious and seemingly random association. For example, when the narrator tells us of Wittgenstein's going to Manchester University to study aeronautics, the visuals show us: "Older Wittgenstein wearing kite wings picks up two lawn mower sprinklers and holds them out like the propellers of a plane. The light catches the swirling water like a Catherine wheel" (*W*, p. 76).

This is a delightfully weird image, and Jarman's description exactly underlines his interest in light on water. It has not been noticed, however, that this picture has been stolen directly—as a poet steals—from an analogy in Ray Monk's biography of Wittgenstein:

> Though still convinced he had neither talent nor taste for aeronautical engineering, Wittgenstein persevered with his attempts to design and construct an aircraft engine. Plans of his proposed engine survive, and show that his idea was to rotate the propeller by means of high-speed gases rushing from a combustion chamber (rather in the way that the pressure of water from a hose is used to turn a rotating lawn sprinkler).[12]

We are familiar with this kind of associationist logic from any number of Jarman's films, from what we know about how images got onto the screen and how they were edited together.

But Wittgenstein provokes a crisis in Jarman, a crisis around the ideas of depth and surface. Poetic links and associationist logic are mysterious, deep, difficult to trace, only partly legible. The sphinx, the magician, John

Dee's hieroglyphics, Prospero's symbols, even the graffiti in *Jubilee* all point toward a language only partly understood by ordinary means. Even the cover photo for the Eagleton and Jarman scripts, which was widely reproduced, shows us Wittgenstein as a kind of Prospero figure who stands before a blackboard covered with German phrases, marks, and erasures, which must surely imply, altogether, great power of thought.

Yet Wittgenstein's rigor often leads him to question these metaphors of depth, to deconstruct (to use a later vocabulary) the surface-depth distinction. The many discussions of transparency in Wittgenstein's *Remarks on Colour* can only complicate enormously the conventional usages of "surface" and "depth":

> In the cinema we can sometimes see the events in the film as if they lay behind the screen and it were transparent, rather like a pane of glass. The glass would be taking the colour away from things and allowing only white, grey and black to come through. (Here we are not doing physics, we are regarding white and black as colours just like green and red).—We might thus think that we are here imagining a pane of glass that could be called white and transparent. And yet we are not tempted to call it that: so does the analogy with, e.g., a transparent green pane break down somewhere?[13]

Remarks on Colour is built out of these brilliantly difficult paragraphs that stare remorselessly at the ways we talk about color, its properties and elements, its grammar. To a filmmaker utterly absorbed—one might say saturated—in thoughts about color, whose favorite British director is the equally color-obsessed Michael Powell, these unfoldings and dissections of the language of color can only leave a powerful impression.

In Monk's description, Wittgenstein's objections to metatheories lead to a poetical way of thinking, to a process of thought that is, indeed, associationist at heart:

> After the fog had cleared there could be, for Wittgenstein, no question of meta-theories, of theories of games. There were only games and their players, rules and their applications: "We cannot lay down a rule for the application of another rule." To connect two things we do not always need a third: "Things must connect directly, without a rope, i.e., they must already stand in a connection with one another like the links of a chain." The connection between a word and its meaning is to be found, not in a theory, but in a practice, in the use of the word. And the direct connection between a rule and its application, between

the word and the deed, cannot be elucidated with another rule; it must be *seen*: "Here *seeing* matters essentially: as long as you do not see the new system, you have not got it." Wittgenstein's abandonment of theory was not, as Russell thought, a rejection of serious thinking, of the attempt to understand, but the adoption of a different notion of what it is to understand—a notion that, like that of Spengler and Goethe before him, stresses the importance and the necessity of "the understanding that consists in seeing connections."[14]

In addition to descriptions like this, Jarman would have read in Monk's biography Wittgenstein's comments on deep magic, and of his impatience with Frazer's *The Golden Bough* for trying to explain everything: "The wealth of facts which Frazer had collected about these rituals would, Wittgenstein thought, be more instructive if they were presented without any kind of theoretical gloss and arranged in such a way that their relationships with each other—and with our own rituals—could be *shown*."[15] Jarman's immersion in Wittgenstein may have been intuitive, selective, critical, and self-seeking, but it leads to a substantial change in his own aesthetics. In *Wittgenstein* and *Blue* Jarman seems to learn another name for poetry. Jarman learns that an associationist manner of proceeding is not necessarily to be imaged as a sphinx, aligned with mystery and all things strange. Instead, poetry might be aligned with transparency. Coming to Wittgenstein causes Jarman to refigure, rename, and resee what poetry is, and *Wittgenstein*, *Chroma*, and *Blue* all reflect this knowledge.

III. *Blue*: A PARABLE OF THE BLIND POET

If the doors of Perception were cleansed then everything would be seen as it is.

BLAKE (AS QUOTED IN *B*, P. 12)

Derek Jarman's final film, *Blue* (1993), poignantly records Jarman's meditations on losing his sight and his life to AIDS. Testing the boundaries of what cinema dares to do, Jarman shows the audience only a wavering screen of blue for the entirety of the 76-minute film. As a movie that is all sound track, *Blue* might be thought of as a species of radio, where we would read the film into a tradition of radio plays by Samuel Beckett or Harold Pinter.[16] Following this book's focus on poetry, however, I will read the film as a poetry video.

Since the lyrical films by Deren and Brakhage that Sitney writes about so definitively in *Visionary Film*, there have been ongoing attempts to integrate or analyze the poetic by means of video or film. With the rise of music television in the 1980s, there have emerged any number of straightforwardly parallel poetry videos with, instead of three minutes of rapidly edited music, a condensed plot and visual annotation, the visuals cut according to a poem. The most noteworthy of these enterprises may be the television series called *The United States of Poetry* (1996), produced by Bob Holman, a coorganizer also of slam poetry contests and the Nuyorican poetry café in New York city. The intention in these videos, as in slam poetry (which has inspired movies such as *Slam* [1998]), is to popularize poetry beyond the narrow corners of academia through music, pictures, and, overall, a spontaneous good time.[17] Poetry has also been incorporated and meditated on by any number of recent artists in video, in either experimental films or gallery installations. Artists such as Bill Viola, Mary Lucier, and Woody and Steina Vasulka all self-consciously explore the lyrical in their work.[18] Bill Viola's writings and videos such as *The Reflecting Pool* (1977) and *Ancient of Days* (1979) are particularly interesting in regard to their exploration of time, memory, and mystical consciousness.[19]

According to Tony Peake, *Blue* evolved from a kind of performance piece called "Symphonic Monotone," in which Jarman and Tilda Swinton, dressed in blue, sat at a table and recited poetry and monologues. A movie screen "was suffused in IKB, the Yves Klein blue, on which, at intervals, was projected a series of slides: images from Jarman's super-8s and of passages from an essay on blue."[20] And Jody Graber, "the young prince in *Edward II*, handed pebbles painted blue and gold to various audience members."[21] *Blue*, the film, emerges as a kind of happening, and would not seem out of place in a gallery installation in any major city in the world. But *Blue* is a feature-length experiment—no mere happening or installation—and it makes its most testing claims by juxtaposition with other feature-length films. *Blue* is a feature-length poetry video that continues to work through Jarman's ideas about poetry and art.

The script of *Blue* is embedded in Jarman's book *Chroma: A Book of Color* (1994), so let us characterize that text first, before turning to the film itself. In form and content, *Chroma* is related to Jarman's earlier journals, such as *Dancing Ledge, Kicking the Pricks*, and *At Your Own Risk*, in that it is built out of nonnarrative blocks and contains numerous autobiographical sections that, once again, include meditations on childhood, art, and gay identity. However, compared to the earlier texts, *Chroma* is organized more obviously as a book about something; it is more than chronological journal entries. *Chroma* uses colors and ideas about colors to frame entries that are sometimes straightforwardly autobiographical, but that also consist of quotations (from Aristotle, Pliny, Van Gogh, or Wittgenstein, for example), snatches of art criticism or opinion, historical reflections on color and light, and a variety of other forms of commentary and speculation.

Chroma is a species of "cut-up"—the word Jarman uses to describe his work with Britten's *War Requiem*—and, more specifically, a kind of critical collage that is more familiar from American experimental writing. Jarman's early poems showed his rough-and-ready familiarity with the American Beats, and William Burroughs stands as an origin for cut-up writing. Closely related to *Chroma* are works like Charles Olson's *Call Me Ishmael*, Susan Howe's *My Emily Dickinson*, and Louis Zukofsky's *Bottom: On Shakespeare*, which use collages of different kinds of quotations and commentaries to create a text which is about Melville, Dickinson, or Shakespeare, but in a different manner than usual academic criticism. Zukofsky's *Bottom* contains dozens of passages from Wittgenstein, and may be said to embody the visual sense of arrangement and association that Wittgenstein would have preferred to see in Frazer. Jarman's *Chroma* is more autobiographical than these texts and also less forced and ingenious. It shares their common impulse to talk about art critically, intellectually, but without the academic requirements of objectivity or argument. All of these works are wide-ranging commentaries without theses.

The meditations on color in *Chroma* range through regions that we would ordinarily associate with the aesthetic and the political. The whole treatise is, on the one hand, a meditation on abstract color by a painter and filmmaker; yet it is, at the same time, a set of powerfully activist statements by a gay man dying of complications from AIDS. The meditations on color evoke quotations and commentary by artists and art historians such as Alberti, Leonardo, Malevich, and Kandinsky. Yet the colors also start to take on contemporary political dimensions.

For instance, the section called "Alchemical Colour" begins: "consider the world's diversity and worship it" (*CH*, p. 75). The spectrum of colors at one point signifies a politics of multiculturalism—a "rainbow coalition." The collection of thoughts on white is titled "White Lies," and the spectre of white power haunts the whole section ("White has great covering power. The white washed family does not question the bride's blushes beneath the veil," *CH*, p. 12). In Jarman's shaping, white is close to the beginning, and black is close to the end. "White Lies" is the first section after the introduction, and "Black Arts: O Mia Anima Nera" is the fourth section from the end. For black is the eternity into which Jarman travels. "Black is beautiful" (*CH*, p. 140); "Burning the white brings us black" (*CH*, p. 141). The collage of quotations and opinions in this book gives an impression that abstract color resonates subjectively with each viewer, yet with a subjectivity more broadly social and historical than any particular, individual self. Thus even though *Chroma* contains the poignant testimony of a dying individual, the autobiographical collage becomes yet another of Jarman's re-formations or re-presentations of that subjectivity, a re-formation that complicates the subject through multiple voicings, quotations, and juxtapositions.

As usual, hand in hand with this complex presentation of self—neither autobiographical nor anonymous, neither entirely singular nor collective—is an emphasis on poetry. *Chroma* begins with a Jarman poem for an epigraph, and it concludes with a long poem, which we will examine momentarily. As in the earlier journals, *Chroma* includes entire poems by Jarman and excerpts from poems by others (the introduction concludes, for instance, by quoting Christina Rossetti's "What Is Pink?"). Once again, the emphasis on poetry is aligned with the nonnarrative continuity of the text. As in the films, the incorporation of poems in *Chroma* indicates the way that the text represents and evaluates its own coherence. Poems also indicate to us how we need to read and understand the text. Poetry best expresses sentiments that do not cohere according to linear argument and that do not inhabit a region of statement or univocality. We may also note that "Into the Blue," the section that contains the reading script for the film *Blue*, is even more noticeably filled with poems than the rest of the book.

"Alchemical Colour" is located halfway through, and "The Romance of the Rose" and "The Sleep of Colour" are placed before that. Jarman has certainly not given up on his alchemical and Jungian mysteries, but the sections seem to develop away from layers and shadows ("Shadow is the Queen of Colour" is the third section) toward shining light and transparency. "Black Art," the fourth section from the end, begins with Ad Reinhardt's *The Quintessential Mystery of Black* in order to revise our sense of black magic and alchemical quintessence. "Silver and Gold," three sections from the end, again works with alchemical elements (gold is the goal of alchemical transmutation), but ends up on "silver" ("silver lining lurks," *CH*, p. 144). As in *Caravaggio*, "gold" can only be celebrated halfway: it glitters spectacularly, but it is too much money ("Yves Klein throwing gold into the Seine," *CH*, p. 143). "Iridescence," the penultimate section, aims toward translucence, "shimmering bubbles" and "mother of pearl" (*CH*, p. 146).

The final section of *Chroma* is titled "Translucence." After the spectrum of colors has been ranged through, a colorlessness, a species of transparency, is attained. This reflects the new consciousness that we found present in *Wittgenstein*. The mirror-and-ocean imagery that we have seen throughout Jarman's works is once again close at hand, but transformed. The first quotation in *Chroma*, in fact, is from Milton's *Comus*, the invocation to Sabrina: "under the glassy, cool, translucent wave . . . Listen and appear to us / In name of great Oceanus, / By the earth-shaking Neptune's mace" (*CH*, p. 147). Translucence has now become more about glass than mirror, more about transparency than reflection. The emphasis is on our seeing beyond ourselves rather than seeing ourselves over again. In what is essentially a quote from his preface to *Wittgenstein*, Jarman writes, "Glass is the key to the exploration of our world" (*CH*, p. 147). Yet glass may be a tool not only for discovery (microscope, telescope), but also for obliteration. "Where did glass appear in my films?" asks Jarman (*CH*, p. 148). And he recalls "the prisms in the centre of the *Shadow of the Sun* and *The Art of Mirrors*. In Wittgenstein, Mr. Green, the Quark of Charm and Strangeness, flashes a halo of light back into the camera. Light obliterates the image" (*CH*, p. 149). Translucence therefore is double-edged as well, lying on the surface, pure as Sabrina, yet as deep as the ocean. It lies beyond color, as one transcends light, yet leaves us, perhaps, in darkness. "Glass is the salt of the intellect—a seeing through, its transparency pushes into dark corners" (*CH*, p. 148).

To conclude the section called "Translucence," and *Chroma* as well, Jarman recalls having had tea with architect Philip Johnson—not the most revolutionary figure one can imagine—and then provides an extended poem, a poem without a title but presumably about translucence. The idea of transparency, the absence of weighted color, allows the poem to narrate, among other things, a sex change; gender becomes fluid, adrift. A kind of dream vision ("translucent in my ghostly eye") emerges in childlike language ("The stars shine through him / Bright as a child's sparkler").

> Mr Seethrough is transparent
> Pellucid as a shrimp
> Lustrous glass aorta
> Opening and closing
> Diaphanous Medusa
> Umbrella of the deep.
>
> (CH, P. 149)

The language is that of a children's story ("Mr Seethrough"), but surely this is an adult myth or allegory. Mr. Seethrough himself is an oceanic spectacle, and we are told that he does not hide, but instead enjoys playing in the light, "Even on sunny days / Dancing in the ripples" (*CH*, p. 149).

His oceanic fluidity allows him to change his sex and so to change the children's story into something more:

> He waits for the sun to set
> Then walks the corridor again
> Today he's changed his sex
> She wears a dress of silk gossamer
> So fine that any bride
> Could pull it through a wedding ring
> A dragon fly
> With ultraviolet wings
> Her dress rustling
> As she vanishes behind
> The diamond window pane
> In the mirrors on the wall
> She is not seen at all.
>
> Will she be my Mr Seethrough?
>
> (CH, P. 150)

As the lines aim toward that mirror into which everything vanishes, nature ("a dragon fly") and culture ("a dress of silk gossamer") are drawn on to provide images of authentic beauty; these images do not seem restless or ironic. Genders and relationships thus turn together and oscillate in a pleasant sort of oblivion. From the ripples of the ocean to the "flaring glassy chandeliers," the poem drifts and sparkles its way toward a celebration of absent form:

> As she disappears
> I toast my ghost
> In acqua [sic] vite
> Luminous presence
> Here and gone.
>
> (CH, P. 151)

These bright waters of life indicate both absence and presence, self and oblivion, and with that, both poem and book conclude.

There are still six more sections ("Isaac Newton," "Purple Passage," "Black Arts," "Silver and Gold," "Iridescence," "Translucence") in *Chroma* after "Into the Blue," yet the film *Blue* evokes the same feelings of finality and transcendence as "Translucence." Filled with some of Jarman's last public thoughts, this unique, imageless film is manifestly a farewell to film as well as a farewell to life. The blue screen signifies Jarman's blindness, but that it is blue (not black or white or gray) also seems to look beyond blindness and even beyond life. The blue screen is itself not only an alternative form of film, but an alternative visual world—the logical end to the hypothetical inventions and envisionings of lyric film. Jarman's relentlessly blue screen thus joins those other alternative visions: Cocteau's ruined underworld, Pasolini's deserts.

Jarman expressly intends *Blue* as an homage to Yves Klein. We can easily see how Jarman would have been drawn to Klein's speculative musings, which always rely on something very like the language of alchemy for their ambitious and cosmic generalizations. In 1957 Klein began painting with IKB (International Klein Blue)—more or less the same shade as Jarman's *Blue*—as a means of working out his ideas about color and the void. The monochrome panels he created allow the viewer to conjure various emotions and ideas, but responses associated with sky and sea are never too far away. Klein conceived the color as conveying a transcendental aspect of life, but he also employed metaphors of water and ocean when speaking of his blue. "I believe that one can speak here of an alchemy of painting, born from the tension between each passing instant and the material [the pictorial material]. The suggestion of a bath in a space vaster than infinity. The blue is the invisible made visible."[22] The oceanic qualities of this blue come through in many descriptions by critics ("Saturated in blue, the panels give one the impression of being immersed deep down in the ocean, or else that one is gazing up at a constellation of stars in an electric blue sky"),[23] and Klein would create a blue *La Vague* (*The Wave*, 1957), as a model for the walls of the Musiktheater Gelsenkirchen. In his own cosmic humor, he once sent out a letter which suggested that one of the world's seas be colored blue and renamed the Blue Sea.[24] That Klein's blue is both naturalistic like an ocean and yet absolutely artificial looks ahead toward the always-constructed nature in Jarman. Perhaps the best word to describe Klein's blue captures both this oceanic quality as well as the artifice: ultramarine.

Jarman's film *Blue* is a collection of poems (printed as lineated poems in *Chroma* and also in the text for *Blue*), journal entries, aphorisms, and miniature narratives, which are mostly read by Nigel Terry, the voice of poetry in *Caravaggio* and *The Last of England*.[25] The blue screen carries Jarman's interrogation of cinematic imagery to its logical extreme, and the continuity of the voice track is episodic, a collage. The film is autobiographical, no doubt, but once again the projected subjectivity tends to divide rather than unify. The film rounds Jarman's floating, oceanic career to a close by concluding with ocean sounds and the sea drift of elegy.

As is usual in Jarman's works, *Blue* plays with form self-consciously, working through a literary tradition and making allusive references, but also laying claim to open form and heterogeneous material. Thus the film begins with what is identifiably an invocation:

> You say to the boy open your eyes
> When he opens his eyes and sees the light
> You make him cry out. Saying
> O Blue come forth
> O Blue arise
> O Blue ascend
> O Blue come in
>
> (*B*, P. 3)

This apostrophe to blue begins the film like a classical ode or classical epic. It also has the immediate effect of disorienting the subject of the film, which we might have thought was Jarman. Who is "you"? Jarman seems at once to be the "you" and "the boy," and even, potentially, "blue," for that matter. Blue becomes a beautiful distraction from the tragedy before us, a "dallying," like the flowers in Jarman's garden. And indeed, just as the film begins with the traditional apostrophe of poetic invocation, it concludes with a readily identifiable elegy. The last line, "I place a delphinium, Blue, upon your grave" (*B*, p. 30), would not be found out of place in Shelley's "Adonais" or Swinburne's "Ave Atque Vale." The poet begins by invoking another, who is himself, and ends by mourning for another, who is also himself. Blue connotes the blue sky and the blue ocean that allow a journey away from the self and then back.

Although surprisingly traditional poetic elements frame the film, then, there are also numerous self-conscious appeals to open form and the absence of closure, gestures we recall also from the poem that begins *The Garden*. A series of aphorisms, for instance, are brought forward that equate the flowing sensibility of Blue with boundlessness and freedom:

> The image is a prison of the soul, your heredity, your education, your vices and aspirations, your qualities, your psychological world.
> I have walked behind the sky.
> For what are you seeking?
> The fathomless blue of Bliss.

234

To be an astronaut of the void, leave the comfortable house that
imprisons you with reassurance, Remember,
To be going and to have are not eternal—fight the fear that engenders
the beginning,
the middle and the end.

For Blue there are no boundaries or solutions.

(*B*, PP. 15–16)

The blue on the screen thus becomes, in the voice-over's reading,
an emblem of freedom obtained from the confines of form, as well as a
description of the fluid continuity of the film. Yet the dogmatic extremes
of antiform announced here are not, in fact, entirely followed by the film.
Although different episodes are unclearly related and chronology is definitely broken apart, there is still not a complete absence of form, as the traditional gestures at the beginning and end make clear. There are also local
rhythms and larger effects that contribute to some measure of coherence
in the film, even if they are not easily pinned down to a plot. The recurrent voice of Nigel Terry, the playing with ideas about blue, and the illness
of Derek Jarman at the heart of the film all provide a strong framework
around which episodes and scenes may revolve.

As the career continues, Jarman's sound tracks are more and more
complexly and interestingly related to the visual images on the screen. In
Blue there is a three-way relationship between the blue screen, the voice-
overs, and the other sounds on the sound track. After the credits, a ringing
bell coincides with the appearance of the blue screen, and we hear a series
of discordant chimes at varying intervals. The tolling of the bell in *War
Requiem* and the ticking of the clock in *The Angelic Conversation* are at the
edge of sonic reference here. We are called to attention, as if by a Buddhist
chime or by an alarm clock, but the sounds accumulate to minor chords
and a very restless first impression. When Nigel Terry reads the film's
invocation, an oboe attends with an ascending sound-painting, annotating
the voice-over in a conventional, supportive manner. Ambient sound then
provides a documentary effect in the next sequence ("I am sitting with some
friends in this café drinking coffee," *B*, p. 3), as we can hear clinking cups
and glasses.

But we also realize that the sound-space is entirely imaginary, when the
sound of bombs accompanies the daily news report ("the war wages across
the newspapers and through the ruined streets of Sarajevo"). The sound
splices that occur occasionally in *Caravaggio* (when a crowd roars upon the

235

mention of the Colosseum) are now the rule in *Blue*. Once again sound does not support a three-dimensional world, but rather appears as supporting or contrasting annotation, and so allows fluid and instantaneous movement between radically disconnected points. The insistence on an abstract world of the mind rather than a mappable space of three dimensions is clinched in the next two fragments (I have added sound descriptions to the script below):

> I step off the kerb and a cyclist nearly knocks me down. [ring of bicycle bell, angry voice: "Look where the fuck you're going"]. Flying in from the dark he nearly parted my hair.
>
> I step into a blue funk.
> [crashing of metal doors, as if of a prison]
>
> (*B*, p. 3)

The movement between real and abstract worlds could not be enacted more clearly or deliberately.

Blue moves back and forth between documentary and imaginative sound-spaces, between journal entries and poems. Medical entries such as

> the doctor in St. Bartholomew's Hospital thought he could detect lesions in my retina—the pupils dilated with belladonna—the torch shone into them with a terrible blinding light
>
> (*B*, p. 4)

alternate with heartfelt, sentimental poems:

> I'm walking along the beach in a howling gale—
> Another year is passing
> In the roaring water
> I hear the voices of dead friends
> Love is life that lasts forever.
> My heart's memory turns to you
> David. Howard. Graham. Terry. Paul. . . .
>
> (*B*, p. 5)

But despite the fact that the film is grounded in the merciless fact of a dying man, the film transcends one individual's suffering or even his story. The *Blue* screen that stares relentlessly upon us refuses the real and demands to be read as a metaphor. "Blue transcends the solemn geography of human limits" (*B*, p. 7). The film offers various readings of blue, which has the overall effect of assuring us that there can be no one way of reading:

Derek Jarman and Lyric Film

The blood of sensibility is blue
I consecrate myself
To find its most perfect expression

(*B*, P. 8)

Blue is transcendence. Blue is blood. Unchanging blue is a kind of blindness.
Blue is a visual absence, a nothingness before the abyss of death. Blue is the
infinite sea around Jarman's hospital room.

I fill this room with the echo of many voices
Who passed time here
Voices unlocked from the blue of the long dried paint
The sun comes and floods this empty room
I call it my room
My room has welcomed many summers
Embraced laughter and tears
Can it fill itself with your laughter
Each word a sunbeam
Glancing in the light
This is the song of My Room

(*B*, P. 10)

As the film drifts toward the conclusion, Jarman provides an extended narrative of a trip to St. Mary's Hospital. In the waiting room—"Hell on earth
is a waiting room" (*B*, p. 11)—is a little man who resembles Jean Cocteau.
"He looks like Jean Cocteau without the poet's refined arrogance" (*B*, p.
27). "Jean Cocteau takes off his glasses." The sequence concludes: "As I
left St. Mary's I smiled at Jean Cocteau. He gave me a sweet smile back"
(*B*, p. 28).

It is not an accident that Cocteau looms up at the end of *Blue*, for Cocteau is the poet of the mirror and the sea. *Blue* may be painted over with
Kleinian blue, but it is born, like all of Jarman's work, from the cinematic
poetry of Jean Cocteau. *Blue* reflects on the mirrors and the seas of Cocteau, the mirror that turns to ocean: "I smiled at Jean Cocteau. He gave a
sweet smile back."

And so *Blue* ends all in ocean, in the drift of blue reverie, otherworldly
dream, the drowning deep following upon the tempest:

Pearl fishers
In azure seas
Deep waters

Washing the isle of the dead
In coral harbours
Amphora
      Spill
    Gold
Across the still seabed
We lie there
Fanned by the billowing
Sails of forgotten ships
Tossed by the mournful winds
Of the deep

(B, PP. 28–29)

Blue is now oceanic dissolution, the drift of death, but also the dissolution of individual into community, as "I" becomes "our":

Our name will be forgotten
In time
No one will remember our work
Our life will pass like the traces of a cloud
And be scattered like
Mist that is chased by the
Rays of the sun
For our time is the passing of a shadow
And our lives will run like
Sparks through the stubble

This last poem is extraordinarily beautiful and poignant, accompanied by a quiet guitar and the sounds of ocean. The oboe that arose at the beginning ("O Blue come forth") joins briefly, as does a cello, to make a classical-sounding quartet (Satie provides the background for the St. Mary's sequence with Jean Cocteau).

An entirely blue screen with classical music. A radical and traditional cinema. A beautiful elegy for men dying of AIDS. A revolutionary and simple poem. The cinema of poetry that rearranges life's stories and takes us into ever more challenging other places, now bows out, in the soft sounds of ocean and the return of the gleaming bells.

I place a delphinium, Blue, upon your grave.

238

Derek Jarman and Lyric Film

Notes

CHAPTER ONE

1. Derek Jarman, *Modern Nature* (Woodstock, N.Y.: The Overlook Press, 1991, 1994), p. 170.

2. Jarman, *Modern Nature*, p. 199. Emblemata are emblems, deriving ultimately from emblem books, which originated in 1531 with the publication of *Emblematum Liber* by Andreas Alciatus. Emblem books were used as visual dictionaries by artists, the most famous being *Iconologia* by Cesare Ripa (1593). Jarman's well-known attraction to the Renaissance, then, appears not just in his restaging of Marlowe and Shakespeare, but here as well.

3. Derek Jarman, *War Requiem* (Boston: Faber and Faber, 1989), p. xi.

4. Derek Jarman, *Derek Jarman's* Caravaggio: *The Complete Film Script and Commentaries* (London: Thames and Hudson, 1986), p. 133.

5. On classic narration, see David Bordwell, Janet Staiger, and Kristin Thompson, *The Classical Hollywood Cinema: Film Style and the Mode of Production to 1960* (New York: Columbia Univ. Press, 1985); "causality is the armature of the classical story" (p. 13). Bordwell contrasts "classic narration" with "art-cinema narration" in *Narration in the Fiction Film* (Madison, Wisc.: Univ. of Wisconsin Press, 1985). Art-cinema film, according to Bordwell, loosens causality and exhibits character more subjectively or expressionistically than Hollywood film (p. 207). Thompson argues that the paradigm continues to hold for recent Hollywood films in *Storytelling in the New Hollywood: Understanding Classical Narrative Technique* (Cambridge, Mass.: Harvard Univ. Press, 1999).

6. An excellent preliminary history of avant-garde cinema is A. L. Rees, *A History of Experimental Film and Video* (London: British Film Institute, 1999), which includes a section on "cine-poems and lyric abstraction" (pp. 33–35) and an evaluation of the place of Jarman and Greenaway in avant-garde cinema (pp. 98–103).

7. Quoted by Marjorie Perloff as one of two epigraphs to her book *Wittgenstein's Ladder: Poetic Language and the Strangeness of the Ordinary* (Chicago: Univ. of Chicago Press, 1996).

8. "Poetry and the Film: A Symposium," in *Film Culture Reader*, ed. P. Adams Sitney (New York: Praeger, 1970; rpt., New York: Cooper Square Press, 2000), pp. 171–186 in the reprint edition. The symposium was held October 28, 1953; the Deren quote is taken from page 183.

9. For examples of recent film analyses in Russian formalist mode, see Lawrence Michael O'Toole and Ann Shukman, eds., *Film Theory and General Semiotics*, Russian Poetics in Translation, Volume 8, (Oxford: Russian Poetics in Translation; distributed by Holdan Books), 1981.

10. Tracy Biga, "The Principle of Non-Narration in the Films of Derek Jarman," in *By Angels Driven: The Films of Derek Jarman*, ed. Chris Lippard (Westport, Conn.: Praeger, 1996), pp. 12–30.

11. Derek Jarman, *Kicking the Pricks* (Woodstock, New York: The Overlook Press, 1997; orig. pub. as *The Last of England* [London: Constable Robinson, 1987]), pp. 185–187.

12. Leo Bersani and Ulysse Dutoit, *Caravaggio* (London: British Film Institute, 1999), p. 49.

13. Lawrence Driscoll, "'The Rose Revived': Derek Jarman and the British Tradition," in Lippard, *By Angels Driven*, pp. 65–83.

14. James Agee, *Agee on Film* (Boston: Beacon Press, 1958), p. 314.

15. Tom Gunning, *D. W. Griffith and the Origins of American Narrative Film: The Early Years at Biograph* (Urbana and Chicago: Univ. of Illinois Press, 1991).

16. Gunning, *D. W. Griffith*, p.175.

17. Martin Williams, *Griffith: First Artist of the Movies* (New York: Oxford Univ. Press, 1980), p. 58.

18. For a detailed description of a parallel impulse toward *film d'art*, with a particular emphasis on poetry, see William Uricchio and Roberta E. Pearson, "Literary Qualities: Shakespeare and Dante," in *Reframing Culture: The Case of the Vitagraph Quality Films* (Princeton, N.J.: Princeton Univ. Press, 1993), pp. 65–110.

19. Scott Simmon, *The Films of D. W. Griffith* (New York: Cambridge Univ. Press, 1993), p. 145.

20. For a good reading of the relationship between the epigraph from Dante and the neorealistic film that follows, see Maurizio Viano, *A Certain Realism: Making Use of Pasolini's Film Theory and Practice* (Berkeley, Calif.: Univ. of California Press, 1993), pp. 71–72.

21. "Lindsay elaborates the notion of film as a new American hieroglyphic, paving the way for a democratic culture as envisioned by Whitman," Miriam Hansen, *Babel and Babylon: Spectatorship in American Silent Film* (Cambridge, Mass.: Harvard Univ. Press, 1991), p. 193. In *The Art of the Moving Picture* (1915; revised 1922; reprint, New York: Liveright, 1970), Lindsay himself reads the structure of *Intolerance* as "ungrammatical as Byron, but certainly as magnificent as Byron" (p. 11).

240   22. For a reading of the cradle from the perspectives of gender and structure, see "Riddles of Maternity" in Hansen, *Babel and Babylon*, pp. 199–217.

23. Williams, *Griffith*, p. 110.

24. On the influence of the soft-focus in *Broken Blossoms* (cameras by Billy Bitzer and Henrik Sartov), see Bordwell et al., *Classical Hollywood Cinema*, p. 287.

25. Richard Schickel, *D. W. Griffith: An American Life* (New York: Simon and Schuster, 1983), p. 391.

26. Schickel, *Griffith*, p. 394.

27. Ibid.

28. Thomas Burke, "The Chink and the Child," in *Limehouse Nights* (New York: McBride and Company, 1917). "Cheng was a poet. He did not realise it" (p.16).

29. It might also be worth recalling how drearily conventional poems were at the time, even in well-known and influential journals such as Harriet Monroe's *Poetry*. Taken more or less at random, here is the first stanza from Dorothy Dow's "Handful of Ashes" (*Poetry*, 1921):

Beauty that shakes in lights,
Beauty that gleams in mists,
Loveliness of still night.
Gold of the stars that twists,
Ribbon-like into the sea . . .
Beauty is calling me.

30. Gina Marchetti, *Romance and the "Yellow Peril": Race, Sex, and Discursive Strategies in Hollywood Fiction* (Berkeley, Calif.: Univ. of California, 1993), p. 42.

31. On Pasolini's exoticism, see Chris Bongie, *Exotic Memories: Literature, Colonialism, and the Fin de Siècle* (Stanford, Calif.: Stanford Univ. Press, 1991). On lyricism and exoticism, see also Burlin Barr, "Lyrical Contact Zones: Representation and the Transformation of the Exotic" (Ph.D. diss., Cornell Univ., 1999).

32. With less generosity toward Griffith, Marchetti views the tragic conclusion more through what happens to Cheng, i.e., he is punished by death for desiring the white woman. Again, since Griffith is dealing with such stereotypes, and in view of how similar narratives characteristically work, it is hard to controvert such a reading.

33. Christian Metz, "The Modern Cinema and Narrativity," in *Film Language: A Semiotics of the Cinema*, trans. Michael Taylor (Chicago: Univ. of Chicago Press, 1991), pp. 185–227. Further references to this article will be given in parentheses.

34. Collected in Richard Abel, *French Film Theory and Criticism: A History/ Anthology, 1907–1939*, 2 vols. (Princeton, N.J.: Princeton Univ. Press, 1988).

35. On the role of poetic composition in French impressionism, see scattered remarks in Richard Abel, "The Narrative Avant-Garde," in *French Cinema: The First Wave, 1915–1929* (Princeton, N.J.: Princeton Univ. Press, 1984), pp. 279–526.

36. In the definitive work on German expressionistic film, *The Haunted Screen: Expressionism in the German Cinema and the Influence of Max Reinhardt* (trans. Roger Greaves, [Berkeley, Calif.: Univ. of California Press, 1969]), Lotte Eisner reminds us of how often expressionistic cinema is conceived in terms of "visions" (p. 10); such films may also be thought of as *stimmungbilder*, or "mood pictures" (p. 152). There are a number of actual poets and poems in these films, which include Leni's *Waxworks* (p. 87) and Wegener's *Pied Piper of Hamelin* (p. 47). When Godard calls Murnau a "poet" ("There was theatre [Griffith], poetry [Murnau], painting [Rossellini], dance [Eisenstein], and music [Renoir]"; *Godard on Godard: Critical Writings by Jean-Luc Godard*, eds. Jean Narboni and Tom Milne, trans. Tom Milne [New York: Da Capo, 1986], p. 64), he actually means something rather concrete, considering that Murnau made films like *Faust* (1926), based on Goethe's lyric drama, and *Sunrise: A Song of Two Humans* (1927), whose subtitle signals a lyric genre; he also often deployed poetry-like title cards.

37. See Tom Gunning, *The Films of Fritz Lang: Allegories of Vision and Modernity* (London: British Film Institute, 2000), which begins with a reading of Hölderlin's "The Poet's Vocation," as quoted in Godard's *Contempt*.

38. In *Kino: A History of the Russian and Soviet Film* (3rd ed. [Princeton, N.J.: Princeton Univ. Press, 1983]), the still-standard history of Soviet film, Jay Leyda writes, "Dovzhenko was not the inventor of a new film language of 'illogical' connections, for Kuleshov's 'creative geography' had been used even by Vertov, and Pudovkin's emotional symbols and the 'intellectual' vaults of [Eisenstein's] *October* had all suggested a new form. Dovzhenko was the first to lift all the suggestions to the level of mature poetry." (p. 252). On the poetry and literature contemporary with Dovzhenko's cinematic poetry, see George S. N. Luckyj, *Literary Politics in Soviet Ukraine, 1907–1934,* rev. ed. (Durham, N.C., and London: Duke Univ. Press, 1990). Because of my own linguistic limitations, I refer in this section only to translations of Russian texts and relevant non-Russian criticism.

39. Alexander Dovzhenko, *The Poet as Filmmaker: Selected Writings*, ed. and trans. Marco Carynnyk (Cambridge, Mass.: MIT Press, 1973).

40. "Autobiography," in Dovzhenko, *Poet as Filmmaker*, p. 21.

41. Quoted by Carynnyk in Dovzhenko, *Poet as Filmmaker*, p. xvii.

42. "Classic Plastics (and Total Tectonics)," in Sitney, *Film Culture*, pp. 387–392.

43. Andrey Tarkovsky, *Sculpting in Time: Reflections on the Cinema*, trans. Kitty Hunter-Blair (Austin, Tex.: Univ. of Texas Press, 1989), p. 21.

44. Natan Abramovich Zarkhi, trans., *Mother: A Film by V. I. Pudovkin; Earth: A Film by Alexander Dovzhenko* (New York: Simon and Schuster, 1973), pp. 91–92. Vance Kepley also considers this section of the film "the most lyrical sequence" (*In the Service of the State: The Cinema of Alexander Dovzhenko* [Madison, Wisc.: Univ. of Wisconsin Press, 1986], p. 81).

45. This contrast is noted by Marcel Oms, *Alexandre Dovjenko* (Lyon: Société d'études, recherches et documentation cinématographiques, 1968), p. 34.

46. Zarkhi, *Mother; Earth*, p. 98.

47. Barthélemy Amengual, *Alexandre Dovjenko* (Paris: Editions Seghers, 1970), pp. 62, 64.

48. Almost the only text on Paradjanov is by Patrick Cazals, *Serguei Paradjanov* (Paris: Éditions de l'Étoile (Cahiers du Cinéma), 1993). I rely on this superb critical work for biographical information and, as noted, interpretive suggestions. Page numbers from this text are cited parenthetically.

49. Both Pasolini and Fellini defended asynchronization and post-dubbing at the level of a theory, though they first used the practice as a means of economizing.

50. Angela Dalle Vacche, *Cinema and Painting: How Art Is Used in Film* (Austin, Tex.: Univ. of Texas, 1996).

51. Jarman, *Kicking the Pricks*, p. 81.

52. For a good description, see Vida T. Johnson and Graham Petrie, "Tarkovsky's Aesthetics," *The Films of Andrei Tarkovsky: A Visual Fugue* (Bloomington,

Ind.: Indiana Univ. Press, 1994), pp. 31–40; see also Maya Turovskaya, *Tarkovsky: Cinema as Poetry*, trans. Natasha Ward, ed. Ian Christie (Boston and London: Faber and Faber, 1990).

53. Tarkovsky, *Sculpting in Time*, pp. 19–20.

54. Ibid., p. 21.

55. Mark Le Fanu, *The Cinema of Andrei Tarkovsky* (London: British Film Institute, 1987), p. 84.

56. Tarkovsky, *Sculpting in Time*, p. 101.

57. Ibid., p. 143.

58. In his discussion of the "Newsreel Sequences," Le Fanu emphasizes the "eternity" of the sky over the soldiers' heads and the water having "the placidity of dreams" (p. 77). After the chaotic scenes of the Spanish Civil War, the camera "focuses on a little girl seated on a suitcase, long enough to register the moment when her charming smile changes into a frown of bewilderment" (p. 77); "The whole film, it could be said, 'comes together' at this instant[.]" Here again my emphasis differs: I feel more frown than smile; I recall the atom bomb as much as I recall this child; I think that Le Fanu overidealizes the film's power to "unify."

59. Tarkovsky, *Sculpting in Time*, p. 143.

60. On Tarkovsky and water, see Johnson and Petrie, *Films of Tarkovsky*, pp. 204–209, and Antoine de Baecque (on Tarkovsky's "poésie de l'éau"), *Andrei Tarkovsky* (Paris: Editions de l'Étoile (Cahiers du Cinéma), 1989), pp. 23–32.

61. Johnson and Petrie, *Films of Tarkovsky*, p. 118.

62. Jean Cocteau, *The Art of Cinema*, ed. André Bernard and Claude Gauteur, trans. Robin Buss (New York: Marion Boyars, 1992), p. 51.

63. Cocteau, *Art of Cinema*, pp. 68–69.

64. Geoff Andrew, *The "Three Colours" Trilogy* (London: British Film Institute, 1998), p. 69.

65. Russell Banks, *The Sweet Hereafter* (New York: HarperCollins, 1991), p. 91.

66. In his review of *The Sweet Hereafter*, Tony Rayns refers to Nicole's "rationally inexplicable decision to scuttle the lawsuit" (*Sight and Sound* 7, [Oct. 1997]: p. 61).

67. "The entire sequence imparts a sense of creepy lyricism," writes Egoyan, quite rightly, of the meeting of Nicole and her father in the barn (Atom Egoyan, "Recovery," *Sight and Sound* 7, [Oct. 1997]: p. 21).

68. So argues David Gardner in "Perverse Law: Jarman as Gay Criminal Hero," in Lippard, *By Angels Driven*, pp. 31–64.

69. Le Fanu argues in *Cinema of Tarkovsky* that the key couple is not Orpheus and Eurydice, or even Orpheus and the Princess, but rather Orpheus and Heurtebise (p. 106). For Cocteau's *Orpheus* in a gay context, see also Richard Dyer, *Now You See It: Studies on Lesbian and Gay Film* (New York: Routledge, 1990), pp. 64–74.

70. Jarman, *Kicking the Pricks*, p. 60.

71. P. Adams Sitney, *Visionary Film: The American Avant-Garde, 1943–1978*, 2nd ed. (New York: Oxford Univ. Press, 1979).

72. Sitney, *Visionary Film*, p. 142.

73. See VeVe A. Clark, Millicent Hodson, and Catrina Neiman, *The Legend of Maya Deren: A Documentary Biography and Collected Works*, vol. 1, part 1, *Signatures, 1917–1941* (New York: Anthology Film Archives/Film Culture, 1984).

74. Stan Brakhage, *The Brakhage Lectures: Georges Méliès, David Wark Griffith, Carl Theodore Dreyer, Sergei Eisenstein* (Chicago: The GoodLion, 1972). The material originally appeared in issues 11, 13, 14, and 15/16 of *Caterpillar*, one of the most important purveyors of experimental poetry and prose in the 1970s.

75. Sitney treats the birth films *Window Water Baby Moving* and *Thigh Line Lyre Triangular* in *Visionary Film*, pp. 150–153.

76. Jane Giles, *The Cinema of Jean Genet: Un Chant d'amour* (London: British Film Institute, 1991).

77. Jean Genet, *The Selected Writings of Jean Genet*, ed. Edmund White (Hopewell, N.J.: Ecco Press, 1993), p. viii.

78. Giles, *Cinema of Genet*, pp. 18–24.

CHAPTER TWO

1. Quoted by Charles Simic, *Dime-Store Alchemy: The Art of Joseph Cornell* (Hopewell, N.J.: Ecco Press, 1992), p. 13.

2. Tony Peake, *Derek Jarman: A Biography* (Woodstock, N.Y.: The Overlook Press, 2000), p. 177.

3. This information is taken from online catalogue descriptions from the United States Library of Congress.

4. This photograph is reproduced in Christopher Wood, *Victorian Painting* (Boston and New York: Little, Brown and Co., 1999), p. 200.

5. Blake Morrison and Andrew Motion, eds., *The Penguin Book of Contemporary British Poetry* (New York: Penguin, 1982).

6. On the Beats and the Promised Land, see Peake, *Derek Jarman*, p. 96. The poet Robert Farnsworth hears in Jarman's tired, hypnotic manner the early verse of T. S. Eliot, and, indeed, Eliot's poetry and monotone delivery must be a context for Jarman's poems from *A Finger in the Fishes Mouth* to *The Last of England* (Farnsworth in conversation with the author).

7. Thomas E. Yingling, *Hart Crane and the Homosexual Text: New Thresholds, New Anatomies* (Chicago and London: Univ. of Chicago Press, 1990).

8. Derek Jarman, *Blue: Text of a Film* (Woodstock, N.Y.: The Overlook Press, 1994), p. 30.

9. Mark Doty, *My Alexandria: Poems* (Urbana, Ill.: Univ. of Illinois Press, 1993).

10. Alexander Pope, *The Rape of the Lock*, canto 4, lines 53–54.

11. Peake, *Derek Jarman*, p. 178.

12. For good general history of queer studies (with bibliography), see Annama-

rie Jagose, *Queer Theory: An Introduction* (New York: New York Univ. Press, 1996).

13. Steven Bruhm, *Reflecting Narcissus: A Queer Aesthetic* (Minneapolis: Univ. of Minnesota Press, 2001); Dyer discusses homosexual contexts for Cocteau's mirrors in *Now You See It*, p. 67ff.

14. "Jewly" is a clumsy adverb that contains "jewel," but presumably not "Jew." Not a successful neologism.

15. Earl Jackson, Jr., *Strategies of Deviance: Studies in Gay Male Representation* (Bloomington and Indianapolis: Indiana Univ. Press, 1995).

16. A point made by Robert Stam in *Film Theory: An Introduction* (Malden, Mass.: Blackwell, 2000), p. xx.

17. Luce Irigaray, *Speculum of the Other Woman*, trans. Gillian C. Gill (Ithaca, N.Y.: Cornell Univ. Press, 1985), p. 133.

18. Luce Irigaray, *Marine Lover of Friedrich Nietzsche*, trans. Gillian C. Gill (New York: Columbia Univ. Press, 1991).

19. See Tamsin Lorraine, "Shattering Mirrors," in *Irigaray and Deleuze: Experiments in Visceral Philosophy* (Ithaca, N.Y.: Cornell Univ. Press, 1999), pp. 90–109.

20. See, for instance, Judith Butler, *Gender Trouble: Feminism and the Subversion of Identity* (New York: Routledge, 1990), p. 13.

21. Leo Bersani, *Homos* (Cambridge, Mass.: Harvard Univ. Press, 1995), p. 66.

22. *A Journey to Avebury* (1971), *Garden of Luxor* (1972), and *Art of Mirrors* (1973) are additions to the Kino Video DVD edition of Jarman's *Tempest* (2000).

23. See Janet Bergstrom, ed., *Endless Night: Film and Psychoanalysis, Parallel Histories* (Berkeley, Calif.: Univ. of California Press, 1999). T. Jefferson Kline, in *Bertolucci's Dream Loom: A Psychoanalytic Study of Cinema* (Amherst, Mass.: Univ. of Massachusetts Press, 1987), aligns film and dreaming in all of Bertolucci's works up to the time of the book's publication. See also Robert T. Eberwein, *Film and the Dream Screen: A Sleep and a Forgetting* (Princeton, N.J.: Princeton Univ. Press, 1984).

24. For Munsterberg's works, see *Hugo Munsterberg on Film: The Photoplay: A Psychological Study and Other Writings*, ed. Allan Langdale (New York: Routledge, 2002); Siegfried Kracauer, *From Caligari to Hitler: A Psychological History of the German Film* (Princeton, N.J.: Princeton Univ. Press, 1947).

25. "The 'core texts' of Jungian psychology" are more or less absent from reading lists and curriculum descriptions," writes Andrew Samuels in *The Cambridge Companion to Jung*, ed. Polly Young-Eisendrath and Terence Dawson (Cambridge: Cambridge Univ. Press, 1997), p.1.

26. Jean Mitry, *Semiotics and the Analysis of Film*, trans. Christopher King (Bloomington and Indianapolis: Univ. of Indiana Press, 2000), p. 196. Brian Lewis discusses the important role of poetry in Mitry's work in "In Defense of Symbol: Film Aesthetics and Symbolist Poetics," *Jean Mitry and the Aesthetics of the Cinema* (Ann Arbor, Mich.: UMI Research Press, 1984), pp. 97–116.

27. *Seven Sermons to the Dead* is included in *The Gnostic Jung: Selections from the Writings of C. G. Jung and His Critics*, ed. Robert A Segal (Princeton, N.J.: Princeton Univ. Press, 1992); C. G. Jung, *Alchemical Studies*, ed. Gerhard Adler, trans. R. F. C. Hull, Collected Works of C. G. Jung, vol. 13 (Princeton, N.J.: Princeton Univ. Press, 1968).

28. Peake, *Derek Jarman*, p. 314.

29. On Jarman and alchemy, see Peake, *Derek Jarman*, p. 191.

30. Carolee Schneemann, "Kenneth Anger's 'Scorpio Rising,'" in Sitney, *Film Culture Reader*, p. 277.

31. Kenneth Anger, "Modesty and the Art of Film," *Cahiers du Cinéma* 5, Sept. 1951. This translation is by David Wilson.

32. C. G. Jung, *Memories, Dreams, Reflections*, comp. and ed. Aniela Jaffé, trans. Richard and Clara Winston (New York: Vintage, 1965), p. 151.

33. James Hillman, *Re-Visioning Psychology* (New York: Harper and Row, 1975), p. 93. On Hillman, see Elizabeth M. Baeten, "Mythical Self, Mythical Soul: James Hillman's Depth Psychology," *The Magic Mirror: Myth's Abiding Power* (Albany, N.Y.: State Univ. of New York Press, 1996), pp. 141–162.

34. James Hillman, *A Blue Fire: Selected Writings*, ed. Thomas Moore (New York: HarperPerennial, 1989), p. 18.

35. Hillman, *Re-Visioning Psychology*, p. x.

36. James Hillman, "Silver and the White Earth (Part Two)," *Spring: An Annual of Archetypal Psychology and Jungian Thought* 1981, p. 49. Hillman's two-part meditation on silver is rife with suggestive points of comparison to Jarman's thought. Brooding over the associations of color, Hillman's essay looks toward Jarman's *Chroma*, and the focus on "silver" everywhere attaches itself to Jarman's cinematic concerns with mirroring, reflection, and transparency. Along the way, Hillman points out the interesting alchemical idea that "mirrors catch images because they are 'moist'" (p. 37).

37. Paul Schrader, *Transcendental Style in Film: Ozu, Bresson, Dreyer* (Berkeley, Calif.: Univ. of California Press, 1972).

38. Bruce Kawin, "The Mummy's Pool," in *Film Theory and Criticism*, ed. Leo Braudy and Marshall Cohen (Oxford: Oxford Univ. Press, 1999), p. 684.

39. Gilles Deleuze, *Cinema 2: The Time-Image*, trans. Hugh Tomlinson and Robert Galeta (Minneapolis: Univ. of Minnesota Press, 1989), pp. 70, 73. *Film Theory and Criticism* edited by Braudy and Cohen may be indicative of the acceptance or utility of Deleuze's work on film; there is only one small reference to Deleuze's work on film in the entire 850-page collection. Even though there are at least two book-length studies devoted to explaining Deleuze's *Cinema* (David Rodowick, *Gilles Deleuze's Time Machine* [Durham, N.C.: Duke Univ. Press, 1997] and Gregory Flaxman, ed., *The Brain Is the Screen: Deleuze and the Philosophy of Cinema* [Minneapolis: Univ. of Minnesota Press, 2000]), his work is often taken to be merely a curious excursion by an interesting writer, but with no particular consequences to be drawn for further research and interpretation. Perhaps the most successful critical

use of Deleuze to date is Steven Shaviro, *The Cinematic Body* (Minneapolis: Univ. of Minnesota Press, 1993), which includes readings of both Fassbinder's *Querelle* and the films of Warhol and repeatedly contrasts the "accretions" and "accumulations" of Deleuze with the blunt, Manichean conceptions of Freudian theorizers.

40. Deleuze, *Cinema 2*, p. 75.

41. The "apparatus" of cinema receives its most powerful and singular description in Jean-Luis Baudry, "The Apparatus: Metapsychological Approaches to the Impression of Reality in Cinema," in *Film Theory and Criticism*, ed. Braudy and Cohen, pp. 760–778. This important essay appeared in 1975, and the many attacks that have been made on it since then show how difficult it is to generalize about the basic elements of film.

42. Cocteau, *The Testament of Orpheus*, in *Two Screenplays*, trans. Carol Martin-Sperry (New York: Orion Press, 1968), p. 83.

43. Ibid.

44. Ibid., p. 99.

45. Ibid., p. 141.

46. From the English subtitles to the videotape version of *Orpheus* released by Home Vision Entertainment in January 2000.

47. On the several versions of *The Bees of Infinity*, which have more to do with Artaud than Cocteau, see Peake, *Derek Jarman*, pp. 255, 286.

48. Ibid., p. 290.

49. Jarman, *Kicking the Pricks*, pp. 196–197.

50. Cocteau, *Two Screenplays*, p. 120.

51. Ibid., p. 124.

52. Ibid., p. 104.

53. Ibid., p. 114.

54. Ibid., p. 95.

CHAPTER THREE

1. Dyer, *Now You See It*, p. 168.

2. Derek Jarman, *At Your Own Risk: A Saint's Testament*, ed. Michael Christie (Woodstock, N.Y.: The Overlook Press, 1993), p. 83.

3. Jarman, *At Your Own Risk*, p. 83.

4. Michael O'Pray, *Derek Jarman: Dreams of England* (London: British Film Institute, 1996), p. 88. Another critic who touches on the thematics of mirroring in Jarman's films is Tracy Biga: "For Jarman, undifferentiation [that is, men who appear similarly] is almost always shown to be an unequivocal good, as well as a political position; he consistently asserts the radical nature of the same ('Homo means same means equal')" ("The Principle of Non-Narration in the Films of Derek Jarman," in Lippard, *By Angels Driven*, p. 20).

5. Jarman, *Dancing Ledge* (Woodstock, N.Y.: The Overlook Press, 1993), p. 142.

6. Another artist who brought Latin dialogue into a contemporary artwork was Stravinsky, in his version of *Oedipus Rex*. First Cocteau wrote dialogue in French, and that was then translated into Latin. Latin, said Stravinsky, "had the great advantage of giving me a medium not dead but turned to stone and so monumentalized as to have become immune from any risk of vulgarisation." Stephen Walsh, *Stravinsky: Oedipus Rex* (Cambridge: Cambridge Univ. Press, 1993), p. x. Clearly Jarman's use of Latin dialogue does not aim for the monumental or attempt to avoid the vulgar. And the example of Stravinsky helps us recall how truly unprecedented Jarman's choice of language is; at least in music we are used to hearing Latin sung, in Bach or in Britten, but we have probably never heard a Latin movie before, nor will we again.

7. Peter Wollen, "The Last New Wave: Modernism in the British Films of the Thatcher Era," in *Fires Were Started: British Cinema and Thatcherism*, ed. Lester Friedman (Minneapolis: Univ. of Minnesota Press, 1993), p. 44.

8. "The film, as everyone knows by now, is done entirely in Latin. This has been interpreted in many ways—as an attempt to mask the inanity of the script, as a gesture toward historical authenticity, as an appeal toward the liturgical inclinations of the presumed audience, and as a clever gimmick. It is successful only as the last of these." Thomas Waugh, *The Fruit Machine: Twenty Years of Writing on Queer Cinema* (Durham, N.C.: Duke Univ. Press, 2000), pp. 70–71.

9. Dyer, *Now You See It*, p. 169.

10. Ibid.

11. Jarman, *Dancing Ledge*, p. 154.

12. Peake, *Derek Jarman*, p. 217.

13. Martin A. Berger, *Man Made: Thomas Eakins and the Construction of Gilded Age Manhood* (Berkeley, Calif.: Univ. of California Press, 2000).

14. Paul Melia, "Showers, Pools, and Power," in *David Hockney*, ed. Paul Melia, Critical Introductions to Art (Manchester, England: Manchester Univ. Press, 1995), p. 52.

15. Jarman, *At Your Own Risk*, p. 131.

16. Ibid., p. 134.

17. Scripts for *Akenaten*, *Jubilee*, and *Neutron* are quoted from Derek Jarman, *Up in the Air: Collected Film Scripts* (New York: Vintage, 1996). Quotes from these scripts will be cited parenthetically and abbreviated *A*, *J*, and *N*, respectively.

18. O'Pray, *Dreams of England*, p. 94.

19. "Punk doesn't lend itself easily to the medium of film. Films are rarely impetuous. They take too long to watch and longer to make . . . Of course there are exceptions. Several feature films to emerge on the back of punk rock may be classed as genuine examples of Punk cinema—the aforementioned *D.O.A* [dir. Lech Kowalski, 1981], Derek Jarman's *Jubilee* (1978), and Jack Hazan and David Mingay's *Rude Boy* (1980), for example." David Kerekes, "Tinseltown Rebellion: Punk, Transgression, and a Conversation with Richard Baylor," in *Punk Rock: So What? The Cultural Legacy of Punk*, ed. Roger Sabin (London: Routledge, 1999), p. 69.

20. Greil Marcus, *Lipstick Traces: A Secret History of the Twentieth Century* (Cambridge, Mass.: Harvard Univ. Press, 1989), p. 8. Blake is also a constant reference for rock and roll, and even punk; the name for Jim Morrison's group, *The Doors*, of course, comes from Blake's *The Marriage of Heaven and Hell*, and, just to take one example, former punk rocker Jah Wobble has released an album on which he reads poems by Blake.

21. Peake, *Derek Jarman*, p. 246.

22. O'Pray, *Dreams of England*, p. 12.

23. Edward Ahearn, *Visionary Fictions: Apocalyptic Writing from Blake to the Modern Age* (New Haven, Conn.: Yale Univ. Press, 1996).

24. Ibid., p. 117.

25. Ibid., p. 126.

26. Ibid., p. 166. For a reading of Blake from the perspective of sexual identity, see Christopher Z. Hobson, *Blake and Homosexuality* (New York: Palgrave, 2000).

27. On this tradition, see Tony Trigilio, *"Strange Prophecies Anew": Rereading Apocalypse in Blake, H. D., and Ginsberg* (Madison, N.J.: Fairleigh Dickinson Univ. Press, 2000).

28. Jarman, *Dancing Ledge*, p. 172.

29. Frances A. Yates, *Theatre of the World* (Chicago: Univ. of Chicago Press, 1969), p. 3. The first two chapters of this book focus on John Dee: "John Dee and the Elizabethan Age," pp. 1–19, and "John Dee and Vitruvius," pp. 20–41.

30. Yates, *Theatre of the World*, p. 11.

31. Ibid., p. 5.

32. Peake, *Derek Jarman*, p. 250.

33. The definitive introduction to the history of performance art is RoseLee Goldberg, *Performance Art: From Futurism to the Present*, rev. and enl. ed. (New York: Abrams, 1988).

34. Peake notes Jarman's formative studies of buildings, especially under the tutelage of Nikolaus Pevsner (*Derek Jarman*, pp. 71, 75).

35. Jarman, *Dancing Ledge*, p. 100.

36. Ken Russell, *The Lion Roars: Ken Russell on Film* (London: Faber and Faber, 1993), p. 27.

37. Jarman, *Dancing Ledge*, p. 100.

38. Peake details Jarman's work, based on the entries in *Dancing Ledge*, in *Derek Jarman*, pp. 173–176.

39. See Russell Jackson, ed., *The Cambridge Companion to Shakespeare on Film* (Cambridge: Cambridge Univ. Press, 2000), pp. 323–324.

40. Jarman, *Dancing Ledge*, p. 194.

41. Frances A. Yates, "Magic in the Last Plays: *The Tempest*," in *Shakespeare's Last Plays: A New Approach* (London: Routledge and Kegan Paul, 1975), p. 94.

42. Ibid., p. 104.

43. Colin MacCabe, *The Eloquence of the Vulgar: Language, Cinema, and the Politics of Culture* (London: British Film Institute, 1999), p. 110.

44. Peake, *Derek Jarman*, p. 266.

45. W.H. Auden, *The Dyer's Hand and Other Essays* (New York: Random House, 1962), p. 130.

46. MacCabe, *Eloquence of the Vulgar*, p. 110.

47. Stanley Cavell, *The World Viewed: Reflections on the Ontology of Film* (New York: The Viking Press, 1971), pp. 40–41. Cavell also concludes this fascinating text with a description of what it would mean for films to find poetry again.

CHAPTER FOUR

1. O'Pray, *Dreams of England*, pp. 132, 135.

2. Ibid., p. 132.

3. Jarman, *Modern Nature*, p. 231.

4. Jarman, *Kicking the Pricks*, p. 142.

5. Simon Field and Michael O'Pray, "On Imaging October, Dr Dee and Other Matters: Derek Jarman in Interview," *Afterimage* 12 (1985), p. 52. Quoted in O'Pray, *Dreams of England*, p. 132.

6. Jarman, *Kicking the Pricks*, p. 145.

7. Ibid., p. 15.

8. Jarman, *Modern Nature*, p. 199.

9. Jarman, *Kicking the Pricks*, p. 133.

10. Christina Rossetti subtitled her fourteen-poem sonnet sequence *Monna Innominata* a "sonnet of sonnets."

11. Sitney, *Visionary Film*, p. 18.

12. Jarman, *War Requiem*, p. 10. In what follows, this text will be abbreviated "WR" and cited parenthetically by page.

13. Jim Ellis, "Strange Meeting, Wilfred Owen, Benjamin Britten, Derek Jarman, and the *War Requiem*," in *The Work of Opera: Genre, Nationhood, and Sexual Difference*, ed. Richard Dellamore and Daniel Fischlin (New York: Columbia Univ. Press, 1997).

14. Nigella Lawson, quoted in Mervyn Cooke, *Britten: War Requiem* (Cambridge: Cambridge Univ. Press, 1996), p. 90.

15. Wilfred Owen, *The Collected Poems of Wilfred Owen* (New York: New Directions, 1964), p. 31.

16. Derek Jarman, *Queer Edward II* (London: British Film Institute, 1991), preface.

17. Cooke, *War Requiem*, p. 90.

18. On male tenderness, see Ellis, "Strange Meeting," p. 289.

19. David Lee, "Jagger's Edge," *Arts Review* 45 (1993), p. 55.

20. Ibid.

21. Boyd is making a point made by Jarman in the body of the text: "The poems provide no role for a woman, except, perhaps, the Earth in 'The End.'" (*WR*, p. 1).

22. Ellis, "Strange Meeting," p. 290.

23. Michael Wood, "Séverine and the Wheelchair," in *Belle de Jour* (London: British Film Institute, 2000), pp. 59–69.

24. Quoted in Wood, *Belle de Jour*, p. 69

25. The accidental meeting between enemy soldiers can be compared to a similar scene in *All Quiet on the Western Front* (Lewis Milestone, 1930), where a German soldier jumps into a foxhole with an American and the American is forced to stab him with a mortal wound. Pinned down by artillery fire, the American soldier is obliged to stay next to the dying German, and he comes to realize that his enemy is just another man like himself. There are many more words in this sequence from *All Quiet on the Western Front*, as the American laments to the dying German, but there is also a surreal, interior quality, the men trapped together in a place beyond time.

CHAPTER FIVE

1. Derek Jarman, *Derek Jarman's* Caravaggio: *The Complete Film Script and Commentaries* (London: Thames and Hudson, 1986) p. 133. References to this text will be cited parenthetically with the abbreviation, C.

2. See Kaja Silverman, "The Author as Receiver," *October* 96 (2001), pp. 17–34.

3. Jarman, *Dancing Ledge*, p. 18.

4. Vladimir Mayakovsky, "Past One O'Clock . . ." in *The Bedbug and Selected Poetry*, ed. Patricia Blake, trans. Max Hayward and George Reavey (Bloomington, Ind., and London: Indiana Univ. Press, 1975), p. 237.

5. Peake, *Derek Jarman*, p. 188. Peake continues: "In the pantheon of European film-makers revered by Jarman, Pasolini ranked an undisputed first, not least because it fascinated his disciple how closely the Italian's Marxist concern for the proletariat was linked to his sexual interest in working-class youth" (p. 188).

6. Jarman, *Dancing Ledge*, p. 9.

7. Ibid., p. 10.

8. Ibid., p. 22.

9. Bersani and Dutoit, *Caravaggio*, p. 19.

10. Pasolini is a main character in David Gardner, "Perverse Law: Jarman as Gay Criminal Hero," in Lippard, *By Angels Driven*, pp. 31–64.

11. "The Cinema of Poetry," in Pier Paolo Pasolini, *Heretical Empiricism*, ed. Louise K. Barnett, trans. Ben Lawton and Louise K. Barnett (Bloomington and Indianapolis: Indiana Univ. Press, 1988), p. 172. For a full-scale discussion of poetry in Pasolini, see Sam Rohdie, *The Passion of Pier Paolo Pasolini* (London: British Film Institute, 1995).

12. See "Comments on Free Indirect Discourse" in Pasolini, *Heretical Empiricism*, pp. 79–101.

13. On the "cinema of poetry" see Viano, *A Certain Realism*, pp. 93–98.

251

14. Dalle Vacche, *Cinema and Painting*, p. 157.

15. Ibid., p. 146.

16. Le Fanu, *Cinema of Tarkovsky*, p. 49.

17. Laurence Olivier reads a poem at the beginning of *War Requiem*, but Jarman's films are otherwise notably without stars.

18. Pasolini, *Heretical Empiricism*, pp. 179–80.

19. Bersani and Dutoit, *Caravaggio*, p. 75.

20. Ibid.

21. Ibid., p. 78

22. Of late-twentieth-century painting, Jarman writes, "Content erased, painting became a dollar bill drowned in a sea of gold—buzz saw echoes in the Garden of Eden" (C, p. 42).

23. "Cover-boy martyrs," Bersani and Dutoit, *Caravaggio*, p. 81.

24. Very good on the many-sidedness of glamour in Warhol is Richard Martin, "Pre-Pop and Post-Pop: Andy Warhol's Fashion Magazines," in *Who Is Andy Warhol?*, ed. Colin MacCabe, with Mark Francis and Peter Wollen (London: British Film Institute, 1997), pp. 41–48.

25. This is detailed under the heading "Lux Aeterna" (C, p. 22).

26. "Chiaroscuro, light and dark, the living in the throes of death, violent subjects painted with classical restraint, sinners as saints, always, the contrast, painting on the run." (C, p. 7).

27. Jarman, *Dancing Ledge*, p. 13.

28. Ibid., p. 25.

29. Ibid., p. 14.

30. Bérénice Reynaud, "Tarkovsky: Seeing Is Believing," interview with Olivier Assayas, *Sight and Sound* 7 (Jan. 1997), p. 25.

31. Frederic Jameson, *The Geopolitical Aesthetic: Cinema and Space in the World System* (London: British Film Institute, 1992), pp. 12, 100.

32. Frederic Jameson, *The Political Unconscious: Narrative as a Socially Symbolic Act* (Ithaca, N.Y.: Cornell Univ. Press, 1981).

33. Jameson, *Geopolitical Aesthetic*, p. 92.

34. Ibid., p. 100.

35. Ibid., p. 111.

36. Stephen Kern, "Time and Art in Twentieth-Century Culture," in *Tempus Fugit: Time Flies*, ed. Jan Schall (Seattle, Wash.: Univ. of Washington Press, 2000), p. 23.

37. Rosalind E. Krauss, *The Optical Unconscious* (Cambridge, Mass.: MIT Press, 1993), p. 214.

38. Krauss, *Optical Unconscious*, p. 216.

39. Not in script; tedium on pp. 38–39.

40. On boredom and cinematic emptiness, see Leo Charney, *Empty Moments: Cinema, Modernity, and Drift* (Durham, N.C.: Duke Univ. Press, 1998); Patrice Petro, "After Shock/Between Boredom and History," in *Fugitive Images: From Pho-*

tography to Video, ed. Patrice Petro (Bloomington, Ind.: Indiana Univ. Press, 1995), pp. 265–284.

41. Deleuze, *Cinema 2*, p. 17.

42. Oscar Wilde, *The Picture of Dorian Gray*, ed. Isobel Murray (Oxford: Oxford Univ. Press, 1981), p. 224.

CHAPTER SIX

1. Jarman, *Kicking the Pricks*, pp. 185, 187.

2. Ibid., p. 188.

3. Ibid., p. 166.

4. Ibid., p. 170.

5. Justin Wyatt, "Autobiography, Home Movies, and Derek Jarman's History Lesson," in *Between the Sheets, in the Streets: Queer, Lesbian, and Gay Documentary*, ed. Chris Holmlund and Cynthia Fuchs (Minneapolis: Univ. of Minnesota Press, 1997), p. 161.

6. Ibid., p. 161.

7. Ibid., p. 171.

8. O'Pray, *Dreams of England*, p. 159.

9. John Hill, *British Cinema in the 1980s: Issues and Themes* (Oxford: Clarendon Press, 1999), p. 157. For an excellent collection of Jennings's writings, including selections from his poetry, see *The Humphrey Jennings Film Reader*, ed. Kevin Jackson (Manchester, England: Carcanet, 1993).

10. Annette Kuhn, *Family Secrets: Acts of Memory and Imagination* (London: Verso, 1995), pp. 109–113.

11. Kuhn, *Family Secrets*, p. 113.

12. "4 AM" appears in Jarman, *Kicking the Pricks*, p. 167; "Imperial Embers" appears on p. 189.

13. Goldberg, *Performance Art*, p. 101.

14. Jarman, *Kicking the Pricks*, p. 196.

15. Ibid.

16. Ibid., pp. 159–160.

17. Ibid., p. 179.

18. Hill, *British Cinema*, p. 157.

19. O'Pray, *Dreams of England*, p. 160.

20. Jarman, *Kicking the Pricks*, p. 182.

21. Ibid., p. 211.

22. Kuhn, *Family Secrets*, p. 112.

23. Janet Maslin, "Glimpses of a Depressing Future," *New York Times*, 28 Sept. 1988, sec. C.

24. Jarman, *Kicking the Pricks*, p. 104.

25. *La Ricotta* is the third film of *Rogopag*, a collection of short films by Rossellini, Godard, Pasolini, and Ugo Gregoretti.

26. The turn toward the poetic can be seen in the earlier films, in Accattone's extended dream at the end of that film, and in the point-of-view shot in *Mamma Roma*, as argued convincingly in Viano, *A Certain Realism*, pp. 93–98.

27. Janet Maslin, "Derek Jarman's 'Garden' Offers Visions of Decay," *New York Times*, 17 Jan. 1991, sec. C.

28. Ibid.

29. Bersani and Dutoit, *Caravaggio*, pp. 80–81.

30. Despite the appearance of "an apparently directionless succession of images," Bersani and Dutoit note the "escalation of violence" in *Sebastiane, Jubilee,* and *The Garden* (*Caravaggio*, p. 49).

31. Jarman, *Modern Nature*, pp. 69–70.

32. Daniel O'Quinn, "Gardening, History, and the Escape from Time: Derek Jarman's *Modern Nature*," *October* 89 (1999), p. 119.

33. Ibid.

34. "Scarlet Poppies" is printed in Jarman, *Modern Nature*, pp. 8–9.

CHAPTER SEVEN

1. In this chapter the following abbreviations will be used for Jarman's works: "*Q*" for *Queer Edward II*; "*CH*" for *Chroma: A Book of Color* (Woodstock, New York: The Overlook Press, 1995); "*W*" for *Wittgenstein: The Terry Eagleton Script; The Derek Jarman Film* (London: British Film Institute, 1993); "*B*" for *Blue: Text of a Film* (Woodstock, New York: The Overlook Press, 1994).

2. See, for example, Lawrence Normand, "*Edward II*, Derek Jarman, and the State of England," in *Constructing Christopher Marlowe*, ed. J. A. Downie and J. T. Parnell (Cambridge: Cambridge Univ. Press, 2000), pp. 177–193, which sorts through Renaissance notions of same-sex sexuality vis-à-vis contemporary notions; see also Thomas Cartelli, "*Queer Edward II*: Postmodern Sexualities and the Early Modern Subject," in *Marlowe, History, and Sexuality: New Critical Essays on Christopher Marlowe*, ed. Paul Whitfield White (New York: AMS Press, 1998), pp. 213–224. David Hawkes's essay, "'The Shadow of This Time': The Renaissance Cinema of Derek Jarman" (in Lippard, *By Angels Driven*, pp. 103–116), is weighted more heavily toward structure. Hawkes suggests that Jarman was interested in Renaissance theater (*The Tempest* and *Edward II*) for two reasons: the "early modern period" was fundamental to the development of modern identity and sexuality, and the period was at the threshold of what we take to be narrative ("we can discern the emergence of the mode of storytelling known as 'narrative realism'" [p. 103]). The disruptions of narrative and heterosexism are therefore joined.

3. Bersani and Dutoit, *Caravaggio*, p. 18.

4. Quoted in Susan Bennett, *Performing Nostalgia: Shifting Shakespeare and the Contemporary Past* (London: Routledge, 1996), p. 113.

5. MacCabe, *Eloquence of the Vulgar*, p. 111.

6. Gilles Deleuze, *Cinema 1: The Movement-Image*, trans. Hugh Tomlinson and Barbara Habberjam (Minneapolis: Univ. of Minnesota Press, 1986), pp. 111–112.

7. Peake, *Derek Jarman*, p. 352.

8. On the "abattoir" in art, see Yve-Alain Bois and Rosalind E. Krauss, *Formless: A User's Guide* (New York: Zone Books, 1997), pp. 43–51.

9. Quoted in *Francis Bacon: A Retrospective*, ed. Dennis Farr (New York: Harry N. Abrams, 1999), p. 17.

10. Ludwig Wittgenstein, *Remarks on Frazer's* Golden Bough, ed. Rush Rhees, trans. A. C. Miles (Atlantic Highlands, New Jersey: Brynmill Press, 1979), p. vi.

11. Marjorie Perloff, *Wittgenstein's Ladder: Poetic Language and the Strangeness of the Ordinary* (Chicago: Chicago Univ. Press, 1996).

12. Ray Monk, *Ludwig Wittgenstein: The Duty of Genius* (New York: Free Press, 1990), p. 33. In his life of Jarman, Peake points out that Jarman carefully studied Monk's *Wittgenstein* (p. 502).

13. Ludwig Wittgenstein, *Remarks on Colour*, ed. G. E. M. Anscombe, trans. Linda L. McAlister and Margarete Schättle (Oxford: Basil Blackwell, 1977), p. 6e.

14. Monk, *Ludwig Wittgenstein*, p. 308.

15. Ibid., p. 311.

16. For a brief treatment of *Blue* as radio play, see Tim Crook, *Radio Drama: Theory and Practice* (London: Routledge, 1999).

17. On spoken-word poetry and Holman's poetry video, see the discussions in Christopher Beach, *Poetic Culture: Contemporary American Poetry between Community and Institution* (Evanston, Ill.: Northwestern Univ. Press, 1999).

18. See Michael Rush, "Exploring the Lyrical," *New Media in Late 20th-Century Art* (London: Thames and Hudson, 1999), pp. 138–148.

19. These videos are available on Bill Viola's *Selected Works*, distributed by AGF Media Services. For his ideas expressed in prose, see Bill Viola, *Reasons for Knocking at an Empty House: Writings, 1973–1994*, ed. Robert Violette (Cambridge, Mass.: MIT Press, 1995).

20. Peake, *Derek Jarman*, p. 473.

21. Ibid., p. 474.

22. Quoted from Nicolas Charlet, *Yves Klein*, trans. Michael Taylor (Paris: Vilo/Adam Biro, 2000), p. 100.

23. Ibid.

24. Ibid., p. 128.

25. The text for *Blue* is identical to that found in *Chroma* and republished in Jarman, *Blue*.

255

Bibliography

Abel, Richard. *French Cinema: The First Wave, 1915–1929*. Princeton, N.J.: Princeton Univ. Press, 1984.

———. *French Film Theory and Criticism: A History/Anthology, 1907–1939*. 2 vols. Princeton, N.J.: Princeton Univ. Press, 1988.

Agee, James. *Agee on Film*. Boston: Beacon Press, 1958.

Ahearn, Edward. *Visionary Fictions: Apocalyptic Writing from Blake to the Modern Age*. New Haven, Conn.: Yale Univ. Press, 1996.

Amengual, Barthélemy. *Alexandre Dovjenko*. Paris: Éditions Seghers, 1970.

Andrew, Geoff. *The "Three Colours" Trilogy*. London: British Film Institute, 1998.

Anger, Kenneth. "Modesty and the Art of Film." *Cahiers du Cinéma* 5, Sept. 1951.

Auden, W. H. *The Dyer's Hand and Other Essays*. New York: Random House, 1962.

Baecque, Antoine de. *Andrei Tarkovsky*. Paris: Éditions de l'Étoile (Cahiers du Cinéma), 1989.

Baeten, Elizabeth M. *The Magic Mirror: Myth's Abiding Power*. Albany, N.Y.: State Univ. of New York Press, 1996.

Banks, Russell. *The Sweet Hereafter*. New York: HarperCollins, 1991.

Barr, Burlin. "Lyrical Contact Zones: Representation and the Transformation of the Exotic." Ph.D. diss., Cornell Univ., 1999.

Baudry, Jean-Louis. "The Apparatus: Metapsychological Approaches to the Impression of Reality in Cinema." In *Film Theory and Criticism*, edited by Leo Braudy and Marshall Cohen. Oxford: Oxford Univ. Press, 1999.

Beach, Christopher. *Poetic Culture: Contemporary American Poetry between Community and Institution*. Evanston, Ill.: Northwestern Univ. Press, 1999.

Bennett, Susan. *Performing Nostalgia: Shifting Shakespeare and the Contemporary Past*. London: Routledge, 1996.

Berger, Martin A. *Man Made: Thomas Eakins and the Construction of Gilded Age Manhood*. Berkeley, Calif.: Univ. of California Press, 2000.

Bergstrom, Janet, ed. *Endless Night: Film and Psychoanalysis, Parallel Histories*. Berkeley, Calif.: Univ. of California Press, 1999.

Bersani, Leo. *Homos*. Cambridge, Mass.: Harvard Univ. Press, 1995.

Bersani, Leo and Ulysse Dutoit. *Caravaggio*. London: British Film Institute, 1999.

Biga, Tracy. "The Principle of Non-Narration in the Films of Derek Jarman." In *By Angels Driven: The Films of Derek Jarman*, edited by Chris Lippard, pp. 12–30. Westport, Conn.: Praeger, 1996.

Bois, Yve-Alain, and Rosalind E. Krauss. *Formless: A User's Guide*. New York: Zone Books, 1997.

Bongie, Chris. *Exotic Memories: Literature, Colonialism, and the Fin de Siècle*. Stanford, Calif.: Stanford Univ. Press, 1991.

Bordwell, David. *Narration in the Fiction Film*. Madison, Wisc.: Univ. of Wisconsin Press, 1985.

Bordwell, David, Janet Staiger, and Kristin Thompson. *The Classical Hollywood Cinema: Film Style and the Mode of Production to 1960*. New York: Columbia Univ. Press, 1985.

Brakhage, Stan. *The Brakhage Lectures: Georges Méliès, David Wark Griffith, Carl Theodore Dreyer, Sergei Eisenstein*. Chicago: The GoodLion, 1972.

Braudy, Leo, and Marshall Cohen, eds. *Film Theory and Criticism*. Oxford: Oxford Univ. Press, 1999.

Bruhm, Steven. *Reflecting Narcissus: A Queer Aesthetic*. Minneapolis: Univ. of Minnesota Press, 2001.

Burke, Thomas. "The Chink and the Child." In *Limehouse Nights*. New York: McBride and Company, 1917.

Butler, Judith. *Gender Trouble: Feminism and the Subversion of Identity*. New York: Routledge, 1990.

Cartelli, Thomas. "Queer Edward II: Postmodern Sexualities and the Early Modern Subject." In *Marlowe, History, and Sexuality: New Critical Essays on Christopher Marlowe*, edited by Paul Whitfield White. AMS Studies in the Renaissance, no. 35. New York: AMS Press, 1998.

Cavell, Stanley. *The World Viewed: Reflections on the Ontology of Film*. New York: Viking Press, 1971.

Cazals, Patrick. *Serguei Paradjanov*. Paris: Éditions de l'Étoile (Cahiers du Cinéma), 1993.

Charlet, Nicolas. *Yves Klein*. Translated by Michael Taylor. Paris: Vilo/Adam Biro, 2000.

Charney, Leo. *Empty Moments: Cinema, Modernity, and Drift*. Durham, N.C.: Duke Univ. Press, 1998.

Clark, VeVe, Millicent Hodson, and Catrina Neiman. *The Legend of Maya Deren: A Documentary Biography and Collected Works*. Vol. 1, part 1, *Signatures, 1917–1941*. New York: Anthology Film Archives/Film Culture, 1984.

Cocteau, Jean. *The Art of Cinema*. Edited by André Bernard and Claude Gauteur; translated by Robin Buss. New York: Marion Boyars, 1992.

———. *Two Screenplays: The Blood of a Poet; The Testament of Orpheus*. Translated by Carol Martin-Sperry. New York: Orion Press, 1968.

Cooke, Mervyn. *Britten: War Requiem*. Cambridge: Cambridge Univ. Press, 1996.

Crook, Tim. *Radio Drama: Theory and Practice*. London: Routledge, 1999.

Dalle Vache, Angela. *Cinema and Painting: How Art Is Used in Film*. Austin, Tex.: Univ. of Texas Press, 1996.

Deleuze, Gilles. *Cinema 1: The Movement-Image*. Translated by Hugh Tomlinson and Barbara Habberjam. Minneapolis: Univ. of Minnesota Press, 1986.

———. *Cinema 2: The Time-Image*. Translated by Hugh Tomlinson and Robert Galeta. Minneapolis: Univ. of Minnesota Press, 1989.

Doty, Mark. *My Alexandria: Poems*. Urbana, Ill.: Univ. of Illinois Press, 1993.

Dovzhenko, Alexander. *The Poet as Filmmaker: Selected Writings.* Edited and translated by Marco Carynnyk. Cambridge, Mass.: MIT Press, 1973.

Downie, J. A., and J. T. Parnell, eds. *Constructing Christopher Marlowe.* Cambridge: Cambridge Univ. Press, 2000.

Driscoll, Lawrence. "'The Rose Revived': Derek Jarman and the British Tradition." In *By Angels Driven: The Films of Derek Jarman,* edited by Chris Lippard. Westport, Conn.: Praeger, 1996.

Dyer, Richard. *Now You See It: Studies on Lesbian and Gay Film.* New York: Routledge, 1990.

Eberwein, Robert T. *Film and the Dream Screen: A Sleep and a Forgetting.* Princeton, N.J.: Princeton Univ. Press, 1984.

Egoyan, Atom. "Recovery." *Sight and Sound* 7 (Oct. 1997): p. 21.

Eisner, Lotte. *The Haunted Screen: Expressionism in the German Cinema and the Influence of Max Reinhardt.* Translated by Roger Greaves. Berkeley, Calif.: Univ. of California Press, 1969.

Ellis, Jim. "Strange Meeting: Wilfred Owen, Benjamin Britten, Derek Jarman, and the *War Requiem.*" In *The Work of Opera: Genre, Nationhood, and Sexual Difference,* edited by Richard Dellamore and Daniel Fischlin. New York: Columbia Univ. Press, 1997.

Farr, Dennis, ed. *Francis Bacon: A Retrospective.* New York: Harry N. Abrams, 1999.

Field, Simon, and Michael O'Pray. "On Imagining October, Dr. Dee and Other Matters: Derek Jarman in Interview." *Afterimage* 12 (1985).

Flaxman, Gregory, ed. *The Brain Is the Screen: Deleuze and the Philosophy of Cinema.* Minneapolis: Univ. of Minnesota Press, 2000.

Friedman, Lester, ed. *Fires Were Started: British Cinema and Thatcherism.* Minneapolis: Univ. of Minnesota Press, 1993.

Gardner, David. "Perverse Law: Jarman as Gay Criminal Hero." In *By Angels Driven: The Films of Derek Jarman,* edited by Chris Lippard. Westport, Conn.: Praeger, 1996.

Genet, Jean. *The Selected Writings of Jean Genet.* Edited by Edmund White. Hopewell, N.J.: Ecco Press, 1993.

Giles, Jane. *The Cinema of Jean Genet: Un Chant d'amour.* London: British Film Institute, 1991.

Godard, Jean-Luc. *Godard on Godard: Critical Writings by Jean-Luc Godard.* Edited by Jean Narboni and Tom Milne; translated by Tom Milne. New York: Da Capo, 1986.

Goldberg, RoseLee. *Performance Art: From Futurism to the Present.* Revised and enlarged edition. New York: Abrams, 1988.

Gunning, Tom. *D. W. Griffith and the Origins of American Narrative Film: The Early Years at Biograph.* Urbana and Chicago: Univ. of Illinois Press, 1991.

———. *The Films of Fritz Lang: Allegories of Vision and Modernity.* London: British Film Institute, 2000.

Hansen, Miriam. *Babel and Babylon: Spectatorship in American Silent Film.* Cambridge, Mass.: Harvard Univ. Press, 1991.

Hawkes, David. "'The Shadow of This Time': The Renaissance Cinema of Derek Jarman." In *By Angels Driven: The Films of Derek Jarman,* edited by Chris Lippard. Westport, Conn.: Praeger, 1996.

Hill, John. *British Cinema in the 1980s: Issues and Themes.* Oxford: Clarendon Press, 1999.

Hillman, James. *A Blue Fire: Selected Writings.* Edited by Thomas Moore. New York: HarperPerennial, 1989.

———. *Re-Visioning Psychology.* New York: Harper and Row, 1975.

———. "Silver and the White Earth (Part Two)." In *Spring: An Annual of Archetypal Psychology and Jungian Thought,* 1981.

Hobson, Christopher Z. *Blake and Homosexuality.* New York: Palgrave, 2000.

Holmlund, Chris, and Cynthia Fuchs, eds. *Between the Sheets, in the Streets: Queer, Lesbian, and Gay Documentary.* Minneapolis: Univ. of Minnesota Press, 1997.

Irigaray, Luce. *Marine Lover of Friedrich Nietzsche.* Translated by Gillian C. Gill. New York: Columbia Univ. Press, 1991.

———. *Speculum of the Other Woman.* Translated by Gillian C. Gill. Ithaca, N.Y.: Cornell Univ. Press, 1985.

Jackson, Jr., Earl. *Strategies of Deviance: Studies in Gay Male Representation.* Bloomington and Indianapolis: Univ. of Indiana Press, 1995.

Jackson, Russell, ed. *The Cambridge Companion to Shakespeare on Film.* Cambridge: Cambridge Univ. Press, 2000.

Jagose, Annamarie. *Queer Theory: An Introduction.* New York: New York Univ. Press, 1996.

Jameson, Frederic. *The Geopolitical Aesthetic: Cinema and Space in the World System.* London: British Film Institute, 1992.

———. *The Political Unconscious: Narrative as a Socially Symbolic Act.* Ithaca, N.Y.: Cornell Univ. Press, 1981.

Jarman, Derek. *At Your Own Risk: A Saint's Testament.* Woodstock, N.Y.: The Overlook Press, 1993.

———. *Blue: Text of a Film.* Woodstock, N.Y.: The Overlook Press, 1994.

———. *Chroma: A Book of Color.* Woodstock, N.Y.: The Overlook Press, 1995.

———. *Dancing Ledge.* Woodstock, N.Y.: The Overlook Press, 1993.

———. *Derek Jarman's* Caravaggio: *The Complete Film Script and Commentaries.* London: Thames and Hudson, 1986.

———. *A Finger in the Fishes Mouth.* Bettiscombe, England: Bettiscombe Press, 1972.

———. *Kicking the Pricks.* Woodstock, N.Y.: The Overlook Press, 1997 (reprint of *The Last of England,* London: Constable Robinson, 1987).

———. *Modern Nature.* Woodstock, N.Y.: The Overlook Press, 1991, 1994.

———. *Queer Edward II.* London: British Film Institute, 1991.

Derek Jarman and Lyric Film

———. *Up in the Air: Collected Film Scripts*. New York: Vintage, 1996.

———. *War Requiem*. Boston: Faber and Faber, 1989.

———. *Wittgenstein: The Terry Eagleton Script; The Derek Jarman Film*. London: British Film Institute, 1993.

Jennings, Humphrey. *The Humphrey Jennings Film Reader*. Edited by Kevin Jackson. Manchester, England: Carcanet, 1993.

Johnson, Vida T., and Graham Petrie. *The Films of Andrei Tarkovsky: A Visual Fugue*. Bloomington, Ind.: Indiana Univ. Press, 1994.

Jung. C. G. *Alchemical Studies*. Edited by Gerhard Adler; translated by R. F. C. Hull. Collected Works of C. G. Jung, vol. 13. Princeton, N.J.: Princeton Univ. Press, 1968.

———. *The Gnostic Jung: Selections from the Writings of C. G. Jung and His Critics*. Edited by Robert A. Segal. Princeton, N.J.: Princeton Univ. Press, 1992.

———. *Memories, Dreams, Reflections*. Compiled and edited by Aniela Jaffé; translated by Richard and Clara Winston. New York: Vintage, 1965.

Kawin, Bruce. "The Mummy's Pool." In *Film Theory and Criticism*, edited by Leo Braudy and Marshall Cohen. Oxford: Oxford Univ. Press, 1999.

Kepley, Vance. *In the Service of the State: The Cinema of Alexander Dovzhenko*. Madison, Wisc.: Univ. of Wisconsin Press, 1986.

Kerekes, David. "Tinseltown Rebellion: Punk, Transgression, and a Conversation with Richard Baylor." In *Punk Rock: So What? The Cultural Legacy of Punk*, edited by Roger Sabin. London: Routledge, 1999.

Kern, Stephen. "Time and Art in Twentieth-Century Culture." In *Tempus Fugit: Time Flies*, edited by Jan Schall. Seattle, Wash.: Univ. of Washington Press, 2000.

Kline, T. Jefferson. *Bertolucci's Dream Loom: A Psychoanalytic Study of Cinema*. Amherst, Mass.: Univ. of Massachusetts Press, 1987.

Kracauer, Siegfried. *From Caligari to Hitler: A Psychological History of the German Film*. Princeton, N.J.: Princeton Univ. Press, 1947.

Krauss, Rosalind E. *The Optical Unconscious*. Cambridge, Mass.: MIT Press, 1993.

Kuhn, Annette. *Family Secrets: Acts of Memory and Imagination*. London: Verso, 1995.

Lee, David. "Jagger's Edge." *Arts Review* 45 (1993).

Le Fanu, Mark. *The Cinema of Andrei Tarkovsky*. London: British Film Institute, 1987.

Lewis, Brian. *Jean Mitry and the Aesthetics of the Cinema*. Ann Arbor, Mich.: UMI Research Press, 1984.

Leyda, Jay. *Kino: A History of Russian and Soviet Film*. 3rd edition. Princeton, N.J.: Princeton Univ. Press, 1983.

Lindsay, Vachel. *The Art of the Moving Picture*. 1915; revised 1922. Reprint, New York: Liveright, 1970.

Lippard, Chris, ed. *By Angels Driven: The Films of Derek Jarman*. Westport, Conn.: Praeger, 1996.

Lorraine, Tamsin. *Irigaray and Deleuze: Experiments in Visceral Philosophy.* Ithaca, N.Y.: Cornell Univ. Press, 1999.

Luckyj, George S. N. *Literary Politics in the Soviet Ukraine, 1907–1934.* Revised ed. Durham, N.C., and London: Duke Univ. Press, 1990.

MacCabe, Colin. *The Eloquence of the Vulgar: Language, Cinema, and the Politics of Culture.* London: British Film Institute, 1999.

————, ed., with Mark Francis and Peter Wollen. *Who Is Andy Warhol?* London: British Film Institute, 1997.

Marchetti, Gina. *Romance and the "Yellow Peril": Race, Sex, and Discursive Strategies in Hollywood Fiction.* Berkeley, Calif.: Univ. of California Press, 1993.

Marcus, Greil. *Lipstick Traces: A Secret History of the Twentieth Century.* Cambridge, Mass.: Harvard Univ. Press, 1989.

Martin, Richard. "Pre-Pop and Post-Pop: Andy Warhol's Fashion Magazines." In *Who Is Andy Warhol?*, edited by Colin MacCabe, with Mark Francis and Peter Wollen. London: British Film Institute, 1997.

Maslin, Janet. "Derek Jarman's 'Garden' Offers Visions of Decay." *New York Times,* 17 Jan. 1991, sec. C.

————. "Glimpses of a Depressing Future." *New York Times,* 28 Sept. 1988, sec. C.

Mayakovsky, Vladimir. *The Bedbug and Selected Poetry.* Edited by Patricia Blake; translated by Max Hayward and George Reavey. Bloomington, Ind., and London: Indiana Univ. Press, 1975.

Melia, Paul, ed. *David Hockney.* Critical Introductions to Art. Manchester, England: Manchester Univ. Press, 1995.

Metz, Christian. *Film Language: A Semiotics of the Cinema.* Translated by Michael Taylor. Chicago: Univ. of Chicago Press, 1991.

Mitry, Jean. *Semiotics and the Analysis of Film.* Translated by Christopher King. Bloomington and Indianapolis: Univ. of Indiana Press, 2000.

Monk, Ray. *Ludwig Wittgenstein: The Duty of Genius.* New York: Free Press, 1990.

Morrison, Blake, and Andrew Motion, eds. *The Penguin Book of Contemporary British Poetry.* New York: Penguin, 1982.

Munsterberg, Hugo. *Hugo Munsterberg on Film: The Photoplay: A Psychological Study and Other Writings.* Edited by Allan Langdale. New York: Routledge, 2002.

Normand, Lawrence. "*Edward II*, Derek Jarman, and the State of England." In *Constructing Christopher Marlowe*, edited by J. A. Downie and J. T. Parnell. Cambridge: Cambridge Univ. Press, 2000.

Oms, Marcel. *Alexandre Dovjenko.* Lyon: Société d'études, recherches et documentation cinématographiques, 1968.

O'Pray, Michael. *Derek Jarman: Dreams of England.* London: British Film Institute, 1996.

O'Quinn, Daniel. "Gardening, History, and the Escape from Time: Derek Jarman's *Modern Nature.*" *October* 89 (1999).

O'Toole, Lawrence Michael, and Ann Shukman, eds. *Film Theory and General Semiotics*. Russian Poetics in Translation, vol. 8. Oxford: Russian Poetics in Translation (distributed by Holdan Books), 1981.

Owen, Wilfred. *The Collected Poems of Wilfred Owen*. New York: New Directions, 1964.

Pasolini, Pier Paolo. *Heretical Empiricism*. Edited by Louise K. Barnett. Translated by Ben Lawton and Louise K. Barnett. Bloomington and Indianapolis: Indiana Univ. Press, 1988.

Peake, Tony. *Derek Jarman: A Biography*. Woodstock, N.Y.: The Overlook Press, 2000.

Perloff, Marjorie. *Wittgenstein's Ladder: Poetic Language and the Strangeness of the Ordinary*. Chicago: Univ. of Chicago Press, 1996.

Petro, Patrice. "After Shock/Between Boredom and History." In *Fugitive Images: From Photography to Video*, edited by Patrice Petro. Bloomington, Ind.: Indiana Univ. Press, 1995.

Rayns, Tony. Review of *The Sweet Hereafter*. *Sight and Sound* 7 (Oct. 1997).

Rees, A. L. *A History of Experimental Film and Video*. London: British Film Institute, 1999.

Reynaud, Bérénice. "Tarkovsky: Seeing Is Believing." Interview with Olivier Assayas. *Sight and Sound* 7 (Jan. 1997).

Rodowick, David. *Gilles Deleuze's Time Machine*. Durham, N.C.: Duke Univ. Press, 1997.

Rohdie, Sam. *The Passion of Pier Paolo Pasolini*. London: British Film Institute, 1995.

Rush, Michael. *New Media in Late Twentieth-Century Art*. London: Thames and Hudson, 1999.

Russell, Ken. *The Lion Roars: Ken Russell on Film*. London: Faber and Faber, 1993.

Sabin, Roger, ed. *Punk Rock: So What? The Cultural Legacy of Punk*. London: Routledge, 1999.

Schall, Jan, ed. *Tempus Fugit: Time Flies*. Seattle, Wash.: Univ. of Washington Press, 2000.

Schickel, Richard. *D. W. Griffith: An American Life*. New York: Simon and Schuster, 1983.

Schneemann, Carolee. "Kenneth Anger's 'Scorpio Rising.'" In *Film Culture Reader*, edited by P. Adams Sitney. New York: Praeger, 1970. Reprint, New York: Cooper Square Press, 2000.

Schrader, Paul. *Transcendental Style in Film: Ozu, Bresson, Dreyer*. Berkeley, Calif.: Univ. of California Press, 1972.

Shaviro, Steven. *The Cinematic Body*. Minneapolis: Univ. of Minnesota Press, 1993.

Silverman, Kaja. "The Author as Receiver." *October* 96 (2001).

Simic, Charles. *Dime-Store Alchemy: The Art of Joseph Cornell*. Hopewell, N.J.: Ecco Press, 1992.

Simmon, Scott. *The Films of D. W. Griffith*. New York: Cambridge Univ. Press, 1993.

Sitney, P. Adams, ed. *Film Culture Reader*. New York: Praeger, 1970. Reprint, New York: Cooper Square Press, 2000.

———. *Visionary Film: The American Avant-Garde, 1943–1978*. 2nd Edition. New York: Oxford Univ. Press, 1979.

Stam, Robert. *Film Theory: An Introduction*. Malden, Mass.: Blackwell, 2000.

Tarkovsky, Andrey. *Sculpting in Time: Reflections on the Cinema*. Translated by Kitty Hunter-Blair. Austin, Tex.: Univ. of Texas Press, 1989.

Thompson, Kristin. *Storytelling in the New Hollywood: Understanding Classical Narrative Technique*. Cambridge, Mass.: Harvard Univ. Press, 1999.

Trigilio, Tony. *"Strange Prophecies Anew": Rereading Apocalypse in Blake, H. D., and Ginsberg*. Madison, N.J.: Fairleigh Dickinson Univ. Press, 2000.

Turovskaya, Maya. *Tarkovsky: Cinema as Poetry*. Translated by Natasha Wood; edited by Ian Christie. Boston and London: Faber and Faber, 1990.

Uricchio, William, and Roberta E. Pearson. *Reframing Culture: The Case of the Vitagraph Quality Films*. Princeton, N.J.: Princeton Univ. Press, 1993.

Viano, Maurizio. *A Certain Realism: Making Use of Pasolini's Film Theory and Practice*. Berkeley, Calif.: Univ. of California Press, 1993.

Viola, Bill. *Reasons for Knocking at an Empty House: Writings, 1973–1994*. Edited by Robert Violette. Cambridge, Mass.: MIT Press, 1995.

Walsh, Stephen. *Stravinsky: Oedipus Rex*. Cambridge: Cambridge Univ. Press, 1993.

Waugh, Thomas. *The Fruit Machine: Twenty Years of Writings on Queer Cinema*. Durham, N.C.: Duke Univ. Press, 2000.

White, Paul Whitfield, ed. *Marlowe, History, and Sexuality: New Critical Essays on Christopher Marlowe*. AMS Studies in the Renaissance, no. 35. New York: AMS Press, 1998.

Wilde, Oscar. *The Picture of Dorian Gray*. Edited by Isobel Murray. Oxford: Oxford Univ. Press, 1981.

Williams, Martin. *Griffith: First Artist of the Movies*. New York: Oxford Univ. Press, 1980.

Wollen, Peter. "The Last New Wave: Modernism in the British Films of the Thatcher Era." In *Fires Were Started: British Cinema and Thatcherism*, edited by Lester Friedman. Minneapolis: Univ. of Minnesota Press, 1993.

Wittgenstein, Ludwig. *Remarks on Colour*. Edited by G. E. M. Anscombe; translated by Linda L. McAlister and Margarete Schättle. Oxford: Basil Blackwell, 1977.

———. *Remarks on Frazer's* Golden Bough. Edited by Rush Rhees, translated by A. C. Miles. Atlantic Highlands, New Jersey: Brynmill Press, 1979.

Wood, Christoper. *Victorian Painting*. Boston and New York: Little, Brown and Co., 1999.

Wood, Michael. *Belle de Jour*. London: British Film Institute, 2000.

Wyatt, Justin. "Autobiography, Home Movies, and Derek Jarman's History Lesson." In *Between the Sheets, in the Streets: Queer, Lesbian, and Gay Documentary*, edited by Chris Holmlund and Cynthia Fuchs. Minneapolis: Univ. of Minnesota Press, 1997.

Yates, Frances A. *Shakespeare's Last Plays: A New Approach*. London: Routledge and Kegan Paul, 1975.

———. *Theatre of the World*. Chicago: Univ. of Chicago Press, 1969.

Yingling, Thomas E. *Hart Crane and the Homosexual Text: New Thresholds, New Anatomies*. Chicago and London: Univ. of Chicago Press, 1990.

Young-Eisendrath, Polly, and Terence Dawson, eds. *The Cambridge Companion to Jung*. Cambridge: Cambridge Univ. Press, 1997.

Zarkhi, Natan Abramovich, trans. Mother, *a Film by V. I. Pudovkin;* Earth, *a Film by Alexander Dovzhenko*. New York: Simon and Schuster, 1973.

Index

268

270

271

www.ingramcontent.com/pod-product-compliance
Ingram Content Group UK Ltd.
Pitfield, Milton Keynes, MK11 3LW, UK
UKHW022039060225
454777UK00010B/894